**DO NOT REMOVE
CARDS FROM POCKET**

Contemporary issues in health, medicine, and

social policy · *General Editor: John B. McKinlay*

Issues in the political economy of health care

Edited by John B. McKinlay

Issues in the political economy of health care

Tavistock Publications · New York · London

First published in 1984 by
Tavistock Publications
in association with Methuen, Inc.
733 Third Avenue, New York,
NY 10017

First published in the UK in 1985 by
Tavistock Publications Ltd
11 New Fetter Lane,
London EC4P 4EE

© 1984 Tavistock Publications Ltd

Printed in the United States of
America

*Library of Congress Cataloging in
Publication Data*
Main entry under title:
Issues in the political economy of
health care.
(Contemporary issues in health,
medicine, and social policy)
Bibliography: P.
Includes index.
1. Medical economics – addresses,
essays, lectures.
2. Social medicine – addresses,
essays, lectures.
3. Medical policy – addresses,
essays, lectures.
I. McKinlay, John B.   II. Series.
RA410.188   1984   362.1'042
84–16212

ISBN 0–422–78040–5
ISBN 0–422–78050–2 (pbk)

*British Library Cataloguing in
Publication Data*
Issues in the political economy of
health care. – (Contemporary issues
in health, medicine, and social
policy)
1. Medical economics
2. Medicine – Political aspects
I. McKinlay, John B.   II. Series
338.4'73621   RA410

ISBN 0–422–78040–5
ISBN 0–422–78050–2 Pbk

Contents

7080492

Part Three   Selected issues

**Part Four   The penetration of the developing world
by the transnational medical industrial complex**

List of contributors

Editor

John B. McKinlay PhD is a Professor of Sociology and Research Professor of Medicine at Boston University. He holds appointments in the Departments of Medicine at the Beth Israel Hospital and the Massachusetts General Hospital (Harvard Medical School). He is currently Director of Research at the Cambridge Research Center of the American Institutes for Research (a nationwide, nonprofit research organization), and has written extensively on health services research. He is presently involved in several research projects concerning the epidemiology of health and effective functioning of men and women during the middle and later years.

Contributors

Debabar Banerji MBBS, MA, is a Professor at the Centre of Social Medicine and Community Health of Jawaharlal Nehru

University, New Delhi. He has been engaged in the study of the relationship between health technology and people and in developing people-oriented health technologies and programmes for India. He has conducted a study on this relationship in nineteen villages from different parts of India for a period of nine years. His book, *Poverty, Class and Health Culture in India*, 1982 (Prachi, New Delhi) contains a part of the report on this study. He has completed an extensive report entitled: *The Making of the Health Services in India*, which is to be published shortly. He has written extensively on various aspects of the political economy of health services in India. His fields of interest include primary health care, population control, communicable diseases, nutrition, health manpower development, health education, and social sciences.

Thomas S. Bodenheimer MD, MPH, is a practicing physician in internal medicine and a research associate at the Institute for the Study of Labor and Economic Crisis in San Francisco. He is also Assistant Clinical Professor at the University of California at San Francisco School of Medicine. He has written extensively on issues such as the need for a national health service in the United States, the relation of taxation to health services, and the effects of American militarism on health services in the US and Central America. He is currently involved in the development of the Center for the Study of American Militarism at the Institute for the Study of Labor and Economic Crisis.

Robert Crawford PhD is currently on the faculty of the University of Chicago. He has written on ideologies of health promotion and is currently writing a book on the meaning of health in contemporary American culture.

Charles Derber PhD is Associate Professor of Sociology teaching in the Social Economy and Social Policy Program of the Sociology Department at Boston College. He is Principal Investigator of a three-year study funded by NIMH called ''Professionals as Workers,'' which explores the work and class position of physicians, attorneys, scientists, and engineers. Derber is also Project Director of a new three-year project funded by the US Department of Education called ''Worker Education in the 1980s,'' a joint project with the Massachusetts AFL-CIO to explore innovative approaches for labor to help revitalize declining industries.

Joseph Eyer PhD is a biologist by training, presently teaching preventive medicine in the Biology Department, University of Pennsylvania. He has specialized in the social and psychological origins of disease, focusing particularly on coronary heart disease and hypertension. He has recently examined the relationship of the death rate to the business cycle. His current work focuses on interpersonal healing.

Vicente Navarro MD, DMSA, DrPH is Professor of Health Policy at The Johns Hopkins University. He is an advisor to several governments and international agencies as well as to labor organizations in many countries. Founder and President of the International Association of Health Policy and founder and Editor-in-Chief of the *International Journal of Health Services*, he has written extensively on sociology, political sociology, and the political economy of medical and social services.

J. Warren Salmon PhD is a Professor in the School of Urban Policy and Planning at the University of Illinois at Chicago and Coordinator of the Health Specialization. He has held faculty appointments in the Department of Community Medicine and Environmental Health at Hahnemann University and in the College of Allied Health Sciences at Thomas Jefferson University, both in Philadelphia. His doctorate in Medical Care Organization and Administration is from Cornell University. He has held several administrative, planning, and consulting positions in the health field and written extensively on health policy, corporate involvement in medical care, and the self-care and holistic health movements. He is editor of *Alternative Medicines: Popular and Policy Perspectives* in this Contemporary Issues in Health, Medicine, and Social Policy series.

Introduction

John B. McKinlay

People commenting on the health care scene seem always to bemoan the fact that they cannot understand the chaos which is the worldwide medical industrial complex. They complain that medical care arrangements are "inexplicable" and depict them as "unmanageable," as a "non-system," or in a "state of crisis." These complaints result, in large part, from the type of health services research that, unfortunately, now dominates the health field around the world. Such research suffers from at least the following limitations: much of it is atheoretical, frequently ahistorical, usually apolitical, defensive of the status quo and dominated by managerialism. There have indeed been few broad-ranging structural analyses of the overall health care sector and of the political and economic forces that influence its shape and content, both in the western world and in developing countries. This book goes some way towards filling this gap.

Most of the work to date tacitly accepts the prevailing ideology of the medical industrial complex as espoused by its own protagonists and embarks on the futile task of understanding that "system" in terms of its own *internal* logic. At the same time, it generally ignores the possibility of competing *external* logics and the potentialities for explanation offered by their use. Clearly, we must distinguish between organizations which are merely chaotic and activities and institutions which are patently illogical. It is not that what is going on in the health care field is illogical but rather that a chaotic system is being viewed in terms of an inappropriate logic.

Much of what is presently inexplicable and seemingly illogical would be rendered explicable if the worldwide medical industrial complex and the ideologies and activities that support it were considered in terms of the *logic of capitalist expansion* with which its ideologies, activities, and institutions are consistent.

The phenomenal and uncontrolled expansion of the medical industrial complex over the last fifty years has paralleled the now uncontrollable requirements of advanced capitalism. Up to recently we have had few accounts of how emerging developments in health care are both reflective of some fundamental structural constraints of capitalism and consistent with events in related sectors of the economy – where the ramifications of these constraints have already been manifested or are now manifesting themselves. In order to explain why the ideologies and institutions comprising the health care complex have developed as they have we require first, some understanding of the logic, pressures, and contradictions with which capitalism is beset; and second, an awareness of the reasons why predatory corporations have penetrated and now dominate health-related activities around the world.

The term "predatory" is employed here to characterize the rapinous activities of large-scale capitalist institutions (mainly banks, insurance companies, and industrial corporations): the act of invading, exploiting, and ultimately despoiling a field of endeavor – with no necessary humane commitment to it – in order to seize and carry away an acceptable level of profit. To account more meaningfully for the expansion of the health care complex initially, perhaps, we should not look at health care at all, but rather at the underlying structural constraints imposed on all social institutions (one of them being health care) by the apparently uncontrollable requirements of capitalism.

We begin, then, with a series of interrelated questions: what is the basic or underlying logic of advanced capitalism? What pressures are thought to derive from this logic? What contradictions and consequences result from these pressures? Following on from these, how and why have predatory capitalist institutions captured the worldwide health care complex and what ramifications are beginning to ensue?

The logic of expansion under capitalism

The most fundamental prerequisite and defining characteristic of capitalism is held to be *the inexorable requirement of profitability*. In societies dominated by a capitalist mode of production, all institutions and every activity are thought to be derivative of and subsumed by this fundamental requirement. All endeavors are organized, controlled, and driven by this system-produced, never-ending, increasingly intensified pressure to realize (if not maximize) a profit. For our purposes the logic of capitalism can be summarized as follows:

(a)   some form of competition *forces* capitalists to expand productive output and sales irrespective of questions concerning the use value of the commodities produced;

(b)   such output and sales *result* in expanded profits and the accumulation of capital;

(c)   the presence of this accumulated capital *necessitates* its reinvestment in even more enterprises or in the development of more technologically efficient enterprises;

(d)   since profits must also be realized on these new investments, and a falling rate of profit avoided, even greater productive output and sales are *required*;

(e)   the resulting *pressure* to find new buyers leads to increased penetration of the domestic market and ultimately, through deceptive advertising, the creation of a commodity fetishist culture;

(f)   when the domestic market is eventually saturated, attention is directed toward susceptible foreign markets, either through expropriation of resources in less developed countries to reduce costs and risks (economic imperialism), or through the capture of foreign markets through direct investment (multinational expansion);

(g)   finally, the resulting capital from the profits of this

expanded output and sales *must*, once again, be reinvested
and the whole cycle is repeated – albeit on a more escalated
scale.

The key decision-making under advanced capitalism concerning initiatives such as where to invest, the types of
activities to be penetrated, where emerging technology should
be applied, the various types of manpower to be trained, etc. is
seldom influenced by an awareness of collective needs or of the
social costs likely to be entailed. Such decisions are always
dictated by criteria of profitability in accordance with the logic
of capitalist expansion outlined above. Accordingly, those
activities whose product or result is either clearly unprofitable
or unable to be measured according to profitability criteria,
including frequently the most socially needed activities, cannot under capitalism be given priority and hence may never be
produced. Given this disjunction between, say, social needs on
the one hand and the profitability constraints imposed on all
capitalist initiatives on the other, one can understand quite
easily the contradiction of gigantic waste co-existing with
unsatisfied urgent human needs, increasing poverty and famine
in times of overproduction, and an absolute increase in illness
and disability when medical technology, health services, and
health manpower have never been in such abundance. To date,
few researchers have investigated the underlying structural
constraints that advanced capitalism imposes on the medical
industrial complex. While sometimes considering how similar
constraints manifest themselves in such related areas as the
family, workplace, and the school, researchers generally have
overlooked what they may portend for medical and health care.
We should begin to inquire of the ways in which the medical
industrial complex – in addition to sometimes providing services to people with needs – fosters and reinforces the broader
interests of capitalism.

The magnitude of the forces shaping health care systems

Only a few of the major political and economic influences now
shaping health care systems worldwide can be discussed:

1 For a variety of reasons, *the business of medicine and health care has been rendered a highly desirable arena for the presence of capitalist institutions.* The features that make it so attractive for such institutions are sometimes shared with all other sectors of the economy, with some other sectors, and with no other sector; but it is in the area of medicine that these features cluster as a unique constellation that is conducive to reducing uncertainty in the marketplace and to maximizing the probability of stabilizing at some acceptable level of profit. In addition, then, to the well-established fact that medicine is immensely profitable, some reasons for it being so are: (a) there exists *a large and often captive market;* (b) *demand by the public for medicine is often given primacy* over other commodity consumption and appears to be insatiable; (c) the association with *medicine facilitates a strategic control over a near total consuming public;* (d) it makes possible *strategic control over valued technology* in a particular area which eventually suffuses to other parts of a corporation thereby *enhancing competitive position;* (e) it is an arena where *the state acts as a guarantor of profit;* and (f) it enables exploitive institutions to project a false image of *conspicuous benevolence.* There is little doubt that some of these economically attractive features have been associated with medicine for a long time, while the presence of others, particularly the partisan involvement of the state, has been fostered by those interests and institutions most likely to benefit from their presence.

2 Given such attractive features, but also because of internal pressures in other sectors of the economy, it is not surprising that *predatory organizations have invaded and now dominate the business of medicine.* Some institutions have been in the medical business for a long time and, almost without exception, have experienced phenomenal success. Over the last few years especially, many multinational corporations with highly diverse operations have become variously involved in the medical business.

Such conglomerates as General Electric and AT&T now have large medical enterprises within their corporate families. In the United States, for example, aerospace companies are involved in everything from computerized

medical information systems (Lockheed) to life-support
systems (United Aircraft). Even tobacco companies (Philip
Morris manufactures surgical supplies) and transportation
enterprises (Greyhound manufactures drugs) have invaded
the medical care arena. In addition to industrial or manufacturing capital, there are many even larger financial capital
institutions (in the form of commercial banks, life insurance companies, mutual and pension funds, diversified
financial organizations, foundations, and so forth) that are
also stepping up their incursions into the house of medicine
and experiencing phenomenal success.

3   The presence of large-scale financial and industrial capital
in the medical arena has *dramatically transformed what formerly resembled a cottage industry into a multi-billion dollar industry.* Medical care is now one of the largest
industries in most countries and is often the fastest growing.
In the United States, for example, it now consumes about 10
per cent of the gross national product (GNP). In terms of
expenditures, there are only seven countries with a total
GNP as large as the many billions that are spent annually in
the United States on the medical business. The magnitude
of the resources diverted to medical care around the world
and the rate at which they increase is a subject of serious
concern in just about every country. It has been estimated
that world spending on medical/health care rose from $396
billion in 1976 to $550 billion in 1983 – a 40 per cent
increase – and will jump an additional 38 per cent to $786
billion by about 1990. Some years ago, Brian Able-Smith
(1967) analyzed health expenditure in twenty-nine widely
scattered countries and concluded that there was no limit to
personal health expenditures. He found that developed
countries transferred an additional 1 to 2 per cent of GNP to
health services every ten years and that total expenditure
bore little relation to health needs. The proportion of the
GNP spent on health in his study varied from 2.5 per cent to
6.3 per cent, but there was no correlation between investment and need for service, even among countries at a similar
stage of development. Furthermore, the distribution of
resources between the various components of health services appeared to be inversely related to their effectiveness.

If present trends continue, quite a few countries will be devoting around a tenth of their resources to health services before the turn of the century. Australia has been projected to reach 12 per cent of GNP within twenty-five years and France between 11 and 13 per cent of GNP by 1985. One wag in New Zealand predicted that in the first quarter of the next century, that country will devote its entire GNP to health care! Now such investments may be justified if they can be shown to return the outcome for which they are intended. Unfortunately, it is now well known that they do not do so. Such knowledge, in the context of the fiscal crisis besetting many governments, is now being seized upon by conservatives seeking substantial and seemingly arbitrary cutbacks in human services expenditures.

To account for the changing shape of the house of medicine in the United States and elsewhere, and its consequences for all levels of workers within it, one must first understand the nature and magnitude of the political and economic developments described above and the logic they impose on all medical care activities.

4 *There is only a "coincidental relationship" between the production of goods and services in accordance with the logic of capitalism and any resulting improvements in the health and general welfare of mankind.* Key decision-making under advanced capitalism (concerning where to invest, the spheres to be penetrated, which technology should be applied and where, and so forth) is seldom influenced by an awareness of collective needs or the social costs likely to be involved. Such decisions are always dictated by criteria of profitability in accordance with the logic of capitalism outlined above. Accordingly, those activities whose product or result is either unprofitable or unable to be measured according to profitability criteria (including, frequently, the most socially needed activities), cannot, under capitalism, be given priority and hence may never be produced. Since there is no logical connection between the dictates of profitability and the fulfillment of collective needs, one cannot assume, as many do, that these two will naturally and inevitably be joined. Both are premised on distinct and often conflicting ideologies. Consequently, medicine

under capitalism will never contribute to improvements in health unless such improvements facilitate an acceptable level of profit.

Now, there are occasions when the fulfillment of collective needs does happen to coincide with the initiatives of capitalist institutions, but these rare occasions, which we are seldom permitted to overlook, do not represent an abandonment or any weakening of the logic of capitalism. Rather, they constitute either a profit motivated investment in some form of social welfare (for example, public transportation, pollution control, or medical care) or, as Andre Gorz puts it, "the pursuit of optimum human and economic goals and the pursuit of maximum profit from invested capital *coincide only by accident*" (1967: xx). What are termed here "coincidental benefits" are all that one could ever expect to derive from any institution dominated, as medical care now clearly is, by the logic of capitalism. Understanding the magnitude of the forces behind and now in the house of medicine around the world, the logic that they impose on this economic sector, and the resulting disjunction between production for profit and the fulfillment of the collective needs of the public, provides I believe, *the* analytic key for understanding the worldwide medical complex.

Levels of analysis and the scope of health services research

Elsewhere, I have found it useful to distinguish between four separate levels of analysis, each of which affords quite different ideological views of the changing nature of the medical business (McKinlay 1977). These four levels of analysis can be distinguished, in the order of their determining influence, as follows:

1 *The level of financial and industrial capital* Here I refer to the activity of vast multinational capitalist institutions – both financial and industrial corporations and the individuals and interests controlling them – and how their presence in and around the medical business is profoundly changing all spheres of medical care and especially the nature of medical work.

2 *The activities of the capitalist state* At this level we are

concerned with how the vast resources of the state, subordinated as now they clearly are to the institutions and interests identified with the first level, are employed to: (a) protect and brokerage the prerogatives of these institutions; (b) ensure that medical care, as an area of investment, remains conducive to the realization of profit; and (c) shape, through partisan legislative action, the scope and content of medical work and the consumptive behavior of the public with respect to medical care.

3 *The level of medicine itself* At this level we are interested in how – within the constraining context of the partisan activities of the capitalist state on behalf of the prerogatives of financial and industrial interests – medical activity is actually conducted. This most common level of analysis includes, for example, research on the training and content of medical labor, managerial studies of medical organizations, positivistic accounts of the efficiency of medical practice, and epidemiological rationalizations for the existence of medicine. And it is at this, and the following fourth level, that most conservative medical sociology continues to be conducted.

4 *The level of the public* Here we are concerned with the vast number of people who are the potential users of, and increasingly the subjects for, medicine; a category loosely termed "the public", which may actually be incidental to medical activity itself (it could conceivably proceed without their involvement) and is presently the most vulnerable of all to the activities of those at the three other levels already distinguished.

By way of analogy therefore, one can conceive of medical care-related activities as *the game* among a group of highly trained players, carefully selected for the affinity of their interests with the requirements of capitalist institutions, that is watched by a vast number of *spectators* (involving all of the people some of the time and, increasingly, some of the people all of the time). And surrounding this game, with its interested public, is the *capitalist state* (setting the rules by which the game ought to be played before the public), the presence of which ensures the legitimacy of the game and guarantees, through resources derived from spectators, that the prerogatives and interests of the owners of the park *(financial and industrial capital)* are always protected and advanced.

In the context of this analogy, it becomes clear where most of the research and teaching effort in health care, among several other fields, is now being focused. When supposedly independent medical care researchers are not caught up in observing the game of medicine itself (and I admit that it is sometimes very difficult not to), they are usually to be found observing the observers of the game (the public). And, given recent developments, some health researchers are even becoming involved in the observation of those observing the observers of the game! Once one becomes fully aware of the magnitude of the structural changes now being forced upon the business of medicine, then the very issues selected for investigation and the levels of analysis and concepts adopted to explain them are profoundly influenced. Health services research, as it is generally practiced, overlooks the political and economic setting within which the medical game is currently played and, consequently, remains preoccupied with issues of relative unimportance. I am of the opinion that there is very little in the existing common fund of knowledge of health services research that will enable us to get a handle on what is now going on in and around the business of medicine. Most current research and teaching is likely to yield little that will enable us to understand the changing nature of the medical game and the position of participants within it (both medical care workers and a consuming public) which could result in political action, effective social policy, and change aimed at fulfilling collective needs.

This book organizes contributions by a distinguished group of writers into four distinct sections. The first section is generally concerned with "the social production of health and illness." *Joseph Eyer*, a biologist by training, with interests in the political economy of illness and health care, provides an excellent background to some of the issues that are returned to in greater detail in later chapters of the book. He argues that capitalism is unique in human health history. The emergence of capitalism and an accompanying revolution in agriculture brought about vastly increased agricultural output, which was the cause of the major health gains under capitalism. Unfortunately, the very same changes that increased agricultural productivity are also the fundamental causes of the health risks that have increased with capitalism – especially the uprooting of people from stable communities and the subjugation of all areas of life to constantly changing demands of the market for labor. Attendant upon the so-called achievements of capitalism then were considerable negative costs and the rise of many modern diseases. These have, unfortunately, fallen disproportionately upon certain social groups, particularly ethnic minorities and men. With respect to the excess in male mortality for example, Eyer rejects the thesis that this is a "natural condition" whereby females have benefited more than men from the health advances associated with capitalism while men have suffered from the rise of stress-induced and other risk factors. He argues that we now know enough about what is happening to men to conclude that what is emerging among women – a new generation of denying, competitive, drug-addicted, risk-taking, individualist wage workers in the current labor market – is absolutely the wrong way to go. Eyer draws material from different national settings and historical periods and from many different disciplines such as epidemiology, economics, psychology, history, demography, nutrition, and the natural sciences. By looking at emerging trends in health and illness from the vantage point of the logic of capitalist expansion, a semblance of order emerges from an empirical chaos. Eyer suggests several alternative scenarios. He rather pessimistically concludes that the forces of capitalism have enough power at the present time to destroy some of the more hopeful possibilities.

Robert Crawford, a political scientist from the University of Illinois at Chicago Circle, presents a very thoughtful discussion of the cultural meaning of health in capitalist society. His more ethnographic approach contrasts with and complements Eyer's sociohistorical account of the relationship of capitalism to health and emerging patterns of illness. Crawford reports some of the results of his own intensive field work with sixty adults in the Chicago metropolitan area and gets behind what many people superficially report in social survey-type studies. Capitalism's appropriation of health and health services appears to represent the seizure of an important part – perhaps the very essence – of our culture. Aspects of our "healthist" culture are described; health behavior is viewed as a moral duty and illness a moral failing. Relative obesity is considered as a specific example: thinness is rewarded as evidence of discipline, self-control, mastery, and will power (all important personal attributes for economic productivity under capitalism) and fatness is a confirmation of loss of control, moral failure, impulsiveness, self-indulgence, and sloth. Women in particular are subject to or are the objects of a manufactured "tyranny of slenderness."

The chapter by Crawford represents an important extension of his earlier work where he argued that the effect and frequently the ideological motivation of the prevailing health promotion model, which emphasizes lifestyle change and individual responsibility, has been to blame the victim (of capitalism, largely). He argues that the emerging emphasis of personal responsibility for health mystifies the social production of disease and undermines demands for rights and entitlements for health care. Beneath the rhetoric about the cost of medical care and the obligation of the individual to remain healthy lies a political program to shift the burden of costs back to labor and consumers and to paralyze regulatory efforts undertaken to control environmental and occupational hazards.

The second major section, "Capital interests and the role of the state," contains *Vicente Navarro*'s important contribution on "The crisis of the international capitalist order and its implications on the welfare state". This expanded version of an earlier article offers a refreshing alternative to those increasingly disenchanted with conservative and liberal positions. Despite the unpopularity of Navarro's position in some quarters, he has remained a consistent and resolute observer of the health care scene. He openly admits that his stark Marxist analysis of current realities is often dismissed as "crude, rhetorical, dated, etc." by the "asphyxiating orthodoxy" that exists in the United States and elsewhere.

Still, Navarro continues to provide one of the best general descriptions of the current international crisis. There is a compelling logic to his argument as he traces out the origins of the crisis and its implications for health care. Building on what was suggested earlier, he eschews the system's own rationalization and renders the chaotic explicable in terms of the logic of capital accumulation. While primarily illustrating his argument with data from the United States, he shows how similar phenomena, driven by the same general logic, are occurring in other countries as well.

Despite the claims of some observers that the welfare state is being dismantled, Navarro argues that it is, rather, being restructured by capitalist interests so as to reduce the level of collective consumption, to disempower workers, render ideological alternatives unthinkable, and restore a situation more conducive to capital accumulation. The utility of the appeal to the logic of capital accumulation and expansion is well illustrated with respect to the emergence of self-care, which Navarro views as part of a movement to lower expectations that, regrettably for the capitalist class, rose during the 1960s with the emergence of the welfare state. Holistic medicine, for example, while presented as an avant-garde movement, generated from cultures of protest, is seen to steer people from the development of political consciousness and is part of the restructuring of bourgeois ideology that is needed to retain dominance. Aspects of this theme are developed in greater detail in the earlier contribution by Robert Crawford. What is particularly valuable and timely about Navarro's contribution is the ability to locate the dismantling of health and welfare programs in the context of the necessity for an international capitalist order, confronted with a crisis almost entirely of its own making, to return once again to an accumulationist mode.

The third general section of the book deals with three selected issues: changes in the organization of medical care for profit, the growth and activities of the transnational pharmaceutical industry, and changes in the nature of medical work. *Jack Salmon*, a sociologist who has extensively researched the recent emergence of alternative medicine – especially holistic health care – in the context of broader structural developments in the political economy, here traces some of the causes and consequences of the corporate invasion of health care. Ever larger, for-profit companies are penetrating the health arena, driving out smaller-scale operators and independent entrepreneurs (for example, solo practitioners), and commercializing health and illness. Nearly every facet of health care is affected – proprietary hospitals, nursing homes, hospital management companies, mental health facilities, dialysis centers, home health care agencies, among others. Even Arnold Relman, editor of the *New England Journal of Medicine*, has alerted a wide readership to some of the consequences of the emergence of the "*new* medical industrial complex."

Salmon views the subjugation of health care to the logic of capitalism as supporting the emergence of a new organizational form, which is conducive to profit accumulation and to an escalation of the concentration process in the delivery of services. Investor-owned health care corporations are becoming transnational in scope (see, for example, the following chapter by Bodenheimer, which discusses the pharmaceutical industry) and their ever closer association with and dependence upon financial capital (for example, banking institutions and insurance companies) will place them in a dominant position with respect to health care policy over the next decade. Competition in the health care marketplace is already emerging as a dominant ideology. Other movements such as cost containment, rationing, the rise of alternative health practices, and managerialism, among others, are reinforcing the trends described by Salmon. Furthermore, demographic changes – especially the well-documented aging of the population of most western countries – coincide with and support these movements, creating an especially lucrative market for proprietary health firms.

Particularly worrisome is the way in which smaller-scale institutions faced with fierce competition from multinational giants and inadequate government support are bing forced out of business, thereby rendering large social segments of the population, particularly the poor, the elderly, and minorities, without adequate health care. The so-called "inverse care law" (that the availability of good medical care tends to vary inversely with the need for it in the population served) not only persists, but given the developments described by Salmon, among others, is likely to increase in application. Salmon discusses the nationwide closings of US hospitals – 26 county hospitals in California, 25 in New York City, and so forth. Over the six years up to 1980, the American Hospital Association (AHA) showed a net loss of 186 hospitals and this was even before the Reagan administration began health budget cutbacks. The AHA reported a continuing decline in the total number of hospitals in 1981 to 6933 and approximately 1.3 million beds – a further decline of 33 hospitals and more than 3000 beds less than 1980. According to one report, by 1990 the so called "money crunch" will force about 1000 hospitals to shut their doors forever. A recent report from the US Congressional Budget Office reveals that President Reagan's proposed budget for the fiscal year 1985 shows that the increase in interest payments on the federal debt since he took office exceeds all the savings his administration has achieved in health education, welfare, and social service programs. The increase in interest payments is almost entirely a result of the growth of the budget deficit. If government revenue falls short of spending in any given year, it creates a budget deficit and the government must borrow more money from the public. Major cutbacks in domestic human service spending were at the heart of Reagan's program for US economic recovery. He initially maintained that such cutbacks would permit him to balance the budget, while increasing military spending and cutting tax rates. For the four-year period from 1982 through 1985, the Congressional Budget Office estimated the cumulative total of all savings in human service programs at $110 billion. That is less than the $124 billion increase in spending on interest payments required over the same four-year period. Thus, savings in domestic programs have been swallowed up by higher interest costs.

Lest these developments be considered exclusively American, Salmon also discusses the health care situation in Great Britain under Prime Minister Margaret Thatcher. He describes the draconian reductions in social welfare spending in Britain – hospital closings, research funding cutbacks, restrictions on medical education, and so forth. Proposals are being discussed to switch health care financing from general taxation revenues to an insurance system with high patient co-payments in order to shunt one third of all cases to private medicine. The British government has actively assisted the growth of the proprietary medical sector (20 per cent of the British population is expected to have private health insurance by 1985). American multinational hospital companies have staked out Britain as an especially "bright opportunity." The developments that Bodenheimer discusses next in relation to the transnational pharmaceutical industry are well outlined here by Salmon in relation to hospitals, health care management, and health insurance, both in the United States and in Great Britain.

The chapter by *Thomas Bodenheimer*, a staff member of the Institute for the Study of Labor and Economic Crisis and a practicing physician in San Francisco, is an important contribution to the burgeoning literature on the transnational pharmaceutical industry. Consistent with the general thrust of this book, it illustrates how what has been described in various places as occurring in different parts of the world is part of a consistent explicable phenomenon (namely, the accumulation of massive wealth through the misappropriation by a few of the scientific advances which most properly are needed by and belong to the world). Through a description of the pharmaceutical industry as a transnational enterprise, he shows how the important actors on the world stage are transnational corporations, not national states. The pharmaceutical industry uses patent protected innovations to survive the economic crisis, the origins and characteristics of which already have been well described by Navarro. In contrast to nearly every other activity, the pharmaceutical industry has emerged from the recent economic crisis relatively unscathed. Through technological innovation and monopoly patterns, it has rendered itself almost crisis proof.

Bodenheimer discusses the commercialization of research and the questionable value of much of the work done by researchers employed by drug companies. Although primarily concerned here with the United States, other researchers have uncovered pretty much the same phenomenon in the Scandinavian countries. The increasing corruption of science receives structural support from Reagan and Thatcher cutbacks in government research support which force otherwise well-intentioned but grantless scientists to turn to the private sector, where the product of their labor becomes the sole property of the employing company. Physicians are bribed from the very day they are admitted to medical school ($5000 per year per doctor cost of drug company promotion). The invasion of the pharmaceutical arena by capital has turned it into at best, a mixed, at worst, a negative factor for the people of the world. An estimated 130,000 people in the United States die every year from adverse reactions to medications, with as many as 60 per cent of these being entirely unnecessary. About 1 million children die each year from malnutrition and infection caused by bottle-feeding by commercial infant formulas. Unsafe drugs that are banned or limited in the United States and Britain are sold indiscriminately in the developing world. The contribution of the pharmaceutical industry to the worldwide epidemic of iatrogenesis is now well documented. Particularly vulnerable groups discussed by Bodenheimer are women and people of color; on to existing cases of exploitation has been added the burden of pharmaceutical exploitation. Several specific proposals for reform are suggested. While logical and reasonable, the likelihood of their passage remains slim. Multinational capitalism is not about to be easily budged from so lucrative an arena as pharmaceuticals.

Charles Derber, a sociologist with interests in labor studies at Boston College, looks at the profound consequences for physicians and other health workers of the phenomenon discussed in the previous chapters, especially by Jack Salmon. So far, the book has discussed the corporatization, commercialization, and fetishization of illness and health care and how large multinational corporations have been invading the health arena and profoundly altered its overall shape and content. What do these changes and the subordination to profitability constraints do for one uniquely situated occupational category – physicians? How do they impinge on their autonomy and decision-making? Derber introduces the concept of "sponsorship" to identify any relation between producers and providers of capital, upon which the providers are dependent for capitalization of production and/or mediation of the market. He argues that while the functions of production, capitalization, and market mediation have been joined in the capitalist employer, in the area of medicine they can be separated in two senses. Producers who lose control over one function do not necessarily surrender control of the other. Thus, physicians who by the 1890s lost the capacity to capitalize a significant part of their own work, none the less maintained a direct relation to the market until the post-war period and continue in some respects to do so today. Capitalization and market mediation can also be separated in the sense that even when they are lost by the producer, they are not necessarily joined in a single outside agent. In the case of medicine, the two functions are not typically united in a single employer but reside separately in what Derber calls proprietary sponsors (normally hospitals) and market sponsors (typically insurance companies and other third party reimbursers). Recognizing that a new political economy of medicine is arising, Derber sees powerful class forces developing a new and direct interest in control of medical costs. This, he believes, will profoundly affect all sectors of medicine including physicians. The new political economy will lead to major changes in the prevailing pattern of sponsorship. Sponsorship systems with a greater capacity to control costs and physician behavior are already in the process of development. Should these fail, a system of political control is likely to emerge with direct regulation of prices and costs by the state. New sponsorship arrangements arising from fundamental change in the organization of the medical market are emerging. He believes it is becoming a predominantly institutional market, in which individual patient demand is channeled through two central consumers: corporations and the state. For Derber, this has three major consequences which will profoundly affect sponsorship relations. First, powerful class actors now have a direct interest in limiting medical costs, the "pass through" of costs by the traditional third party reimbursers that creates direct new costs for corporations and the state, putting pressure on their budgets rather than on those of thousands of individuals. Second, the capacity of corporations and the state to absorb these pass-through costs has disappeared because of major changes in the national and international economy. He does not feel that corporations or the state can continue to absorb increased medical costs by increasing debt because of the already high level of indebtedness and crisis. Third, corporations and the state not only have an interest now in controlling medical costs, but the resources and the capacity to exercise such control. As the most powerful institutional forces in society, they fundamentally shift the balance of market power in medicine. Derber is understandably unclear as to the exact shape of the future relation between hospitals and physicians, but suggests that physicians will almost certainly be subject to ever greater control. Not only will both nonprofits and for-profits have economic incentives to control physician behavior, but they will also have a greater structural capacity to do so because of the slowly dwindling role of the physician as the principal market sponsor of the hospital. Derber also sees the current oversupply of physicians as an additional factor weakening their position in the health care system.

The final general section of the book concerns "the penetration of the developing world by the transnational medical industrial complex." *Debabar Banerji*, a physician with broad experience working at the Jawaharlal Nehru University in New

Delhi, India, applies a political economy approach to the problem of health and the strengthening of health services in the developing world. He suggests that the most distinctive feature of the growth of health services in Third World countries is that these services have been profoundly influenced by affluent countries and this influence has severely inhibited the growth of health services in Third World countries as organic components of their respective social structure. The introduction of western medicine in Third World countries sets very complex interactions in motion within the country, particularly with the pre-existing health culture of the population. An historical approach is adopted as Banerji discusses the ways in which colonialism promoted dependence on western powers for health manpower, drugs, medical equipment, and research, among other things. Attempts to change this dependency and the distortions which western medicine brings to the health systems of developing countries have not yielded much success. He believes prevailing political systems and social structures in many Third World countries have ensconced political leaderships incapable of severing links with the western conceptualization, development, and delivery of health services systems. Banerji concludes with a set of suggestions for immediate social action.

References

Able-Smith, B. (1967) An International Study of Health Expenditure and Its Relevance for Health Planning. *Public Health Papers* No. 32. Geneva: WHO.

Gorz, A. (1967) *Strategy for Labor*. Boston: Beacon Press.

McKinlay, J.B. (1977) The Business of Good Doctoring, or Doctoring as Good Business: Reflections on Freidson's View of the Medical Game. *International Journal of Health Services* 7:459–88.

Part One

The social production
of health and illness

One

Capitalism, health, and illness

Joe Eyer

Capitalism is a kind of class society that came into being some-time in the late Middle Ages of Europe, and has extended to dominate the whole world today. Since the nineteenth century, capitalist ways of organizing labor and extracting economic surplus have had ever greater consequences for the patterns of human health and disease. These impacts have been so great that it is fair to say that capitalism is unique in human health history. The watershed of changes in health and disease with capitalism is larger and more fundamental than even those associated with the origins of agriculture and class society itself, seven to ten thousand years ago.

At the core of the capitalist social process is the transforma-tion of people from rural agricultural villagers living in kinship-based, settled, traditional communities into migratory, largely urban wage workers without fundamental community ties. This deprivation of social support systems and exposure to new hazards and stresses are important in the rise of peculiarly capitalist modern diseases. The transformation of peasants into wage workers critically depends on vastly increasing agricultural output, and thus food surplus, to feed a productive urban working class. The greatly expanded supply of food through a revolution in agriculture is the cause of the major health gains under capitalism. With an economic surplus from both agriculture and industry several orders of magnitude larger than that at the disposal of any previous human society, capitalism has been able to grow at the expense of these other social forms to dominate the people and resources of the world today.

This process of transformation, growth, and expansion causes the specific health changes highly characteristic of capitalism. In this chapter we will review these changes: the great lengthening of life expectancy from birth; the rise of new diseases in adulthood, especially for males; the redrawing of the whole picture of health by class through the creation of the working class and especially a large, highly disrupted lowest social class; the dramatic creation of surplus population; and the emergence of a new pattern of short-term death rate fluctuation synchronized with business cycles. So characteristic are these changes that one can almost diagnose "capitalism" once they are all in evidence.

Health achievements of capitalism

Looked at in the broadest possible way, capitalism has had two historically unprecedented major health achievements. First, the world population alive today is much larger than any previous form of society could support. Second, this manifold expansion of population has been achieved by improvement in health and decline in death rates to levels lower than those enjoyed even by the elites of the past.

Late ice-age hunter-gatherers had an average life expectancy from birth of about thirty-eight years. With the rise of agriculture-based class society, life expectancy probably declined to thirty to thirty-five years, with a great expansion of population. In cities of slave civilizations life expectancies as short as twenty or twenty-five years were common. After six thousand years of agricultural class societies, world population had grown to about 500 million by the end of the European Middle Ages. In Europe at that time, rural life expectancy was again about thirty-five, with that in cities lower (Glass and Eversley

1965; Acsadi and Nemeskeri 1970; Angel 1975).

Under capitalism the human population has expanded almost tenfold since the sixteenth century, to 4.7 billion today. Most of this expansion has occurred since the nineteenth century and is associated with the extension of average life expectancy at birth to over seventy years in advanced countries and to forty, fifty, or sixty even in the poorest areas of the periphery, in Africa and.South Asia (Waldron and Ricklefs 1973; United Nations Dept of International Economic and Social Affairs 1982).

Nutritional improvement has been fundamental to this death rate decline, especially in advanced countries. In experimental field trials, it is clear that improved nutrition, particularly for protein, has a much larger impact on sickness and mortality than other public health or medical measures (Scrimshaw, Guzman, and Gordon 1967; Scrimshaw *et al.* 1968; Scrimshaw, Taylor, and Gordon 1968; Scrimshaw *et al.* 1969). Historically, the major infectious diseases declined long before specific medical countermeasures became available (McKeown and Record 1962, 1975; McKeown, Brown, and Record 1972; McKeown 1976a, 1976b, 1978; McKinlay and McKinlay 1977). Beyond better nutrition, many other factors have been significant in the decline of the death rate (World Health Organisation 1974; Powles 1976). Basic literacy is necessary to the functioning of an industrial society. Scientific methods of birth limitation are key for the decline of female adult mortality. Mass public health and sanitation measures have restricted or eliminated disease vectors and improved food storage and handling. Immunization has been developed against many infectious organisms, and antibiotics for treatment and prophylaxis.

A highly developed, expensive, labor and capital intensive medical care system is not, however, necessary to the great reduction in death rates. Now most countries experience most of the possible death rate decline before they develop a large medical system, and many very poor countries have achieved almost the whole of this decline simply by better distribution of existing food, mass public health campaigns, and immunization, without even mass use of antibiotics. In international cross-sections, the addition of hospital beds per capita or doctors per capita beyond this very basal level results in little change in gross health statistics (Waldron and Ricklefs 1973).

Parts of highly developed medicine may indeed increase the death rate. For example, when doctors went on strike in Los Angeles County in 1976, limiting elective surgery for the most part, the death rate fell by about 15 per cent and rose well above its previous level when the doctors resumed practice, before returning to normal. This means at least one out of every six deaths in Los Angeles is due to the overdevelopment of medicine (Roemer and Schwartz 1979; James 1979).

Corresponding to the dramatic decline in infectious diseases due to all these measures, infant and child mortality have been dramatically reduced, people grow up to a foot taller, mature sexually earlier, and in adulthood no longer suffer from the chronic impairment of parasitic or recurrent infectious disease. As a result, humans now have demonstrably greater mental and physical potential (Waldron and Ricklefs 1973).

But the full extent of this potential has not been realized under capitalism (Waitzkin 1981). To appreciate this, we can contrast two widespread patterns of mortality by age in the recent death rate decline. If improvement in nutrition and public health measures occurs without much urbanization – as in Sweden from the eighteenth through the mid-nineteenth centuries, Ceylon after World War II, and China 1950–65 – death rates are reduced all across the ages from infancy through at least age eighty years by roughly the same proportions (Preston 1970, 1976). The fact that death rates in older ages decline with equal rapidity as those in younger ages is important. It means it is possible to reduce selection pressure on the population in infancy – from 20 per cent losses in the first year to less than 5 per cent losses – without a proliferation of "genetic defectives" into the adult population, who previously would have died in infancy but now suffer elevated death risk in adulthood. Contrary to the still usual medical assumption, the reduction of death rates in infancy and childhood is not accompanied by a necessary tendency for people to die sooner in adulthood and old age (Eyer and Sterling 1977).

The second major pattern of death rate decline occurs in countries which undergo large-scale capitalist social transformation and health improvement in parallel. This pattern shows great reductions in death rates for children, then in infancy and childbearing ages for females, but much slower declines, if at all, for adult males and older people generally. For males over fifty in most developed countries, there has been no increase in life expectancy despite the allocation of the majority of highly developed health care resources to this age group. Especially for men, death rates may even rise at labor market entry ages (fifteen to thirty) compared to precapitalist levels, and there is a very marked tendency for such a rise to move through the age pattern of death rates as the first group showing it ages, as if it were exposed to a health risk in young adulthood which continues to develop and increase in effect with age in those still alive. As a result, male death rates at ages fifty to seventy in most advanced capitalist countries are notably higher than comparable death rates for less transformed countries where nutrition, immunization, and basic public health measures have been applied (Eyer and Sterling 1977).

The improvement of nutrition, immunization, and mass public health measures make possible a deep reduction of infectious and parasitic diseases from the beginning to the end of the lifespan, with corresponding death rate reductions even to the oldest ages. This potential has only been partly realized in the advanced capitalist countries because noninfectious diseases have risen in adult ages with capitalist social transformation. These diseases include cardiovascular diseases, cancers, cirrhosis of the liver, diabetes, obstructive lung disease, automobile and industrial accidents, suicide, ulcers, and many smaller causes of death. Behind the rise of these diseases stands the rise of their major risk factors: hypertension, smoking, type A behavior, obesity, elevated blood fats and cholesterol, excess alcohol consumption. These risk factors in turn are directly linked to the stressful nature of the capitalist social process. Important contributions to the rise of modern diseases also come from occupational and environmental hazards characteristic of capitalism (Eyer 1980; Sterling and Eyer 1981). Were these diseases to be eliminated, average life expectancy from birth could be extended into the nineties.

Capitalism causes the rise of modern diseases

The basic social process of capitalism is itself the source of increased stress. The very same social changes which increased agricultural productivity and made possible a large nonagricultural labor force are also the fundamental causes of the health risks that increase with capitalism. These changes can be summarized as the uprooting of people from stable communities and the subjection of life to the constantly changing demands of the market for labor.

There is approximately a twofold increase in death risk associated with each of these: long distance emigration from a settled traditional rural area, family breakdown, long-term unemployment, and long hours at demanding jobs over which the worker has little control. All of these sources of stress rise dramatically as capitalist social transformation gets under way and continue at high levels with further capitalist development. In addition, they show the same age pattern as the health risks that rise with capitalism: rising dramatically in young adulthood (the maximal age of migration and family breakdown) and continuing at high levels through middle age (high pressure, alienated work, and long-term unemployment) (Eyer and Sterling 1977; Eyer 1977b).

These stressful social changes, and many others, lie behind the rise of risk factors for modern diseases. Cardiovascular diseases dominate modern excess mortality, and the most common and powerful risk factor for cardiovascular disease in Framingham and other large prospective studies is elevated blood pressure. Hypertension is involved in over 80 per cent of all cardiovascular deaths in the Framingham study, and is at least twice as strong a predictor of death as smoking or blood cholesterol levels (Kannel and Sorlie 1975).

Waldron and her coworkers have compiled and analyzed all of the international cross-cultural studies of blood pressure. Cross-cultural sampling of blood pressure in different kinds of societies shows that undisrupted hunter-gatherers, pastoralists, or subsistence agriculturists have average population blood pressures at low levels – 110/60 mm Hg. – from childhood through old age. The critical point for blood pressure increase comes between traditional subsistence agriculturists who do not market their goods, and farmers who may have small plots and not use machinery but market more than a quarter of their produce. Beyond this point, whether the sample is from mechanized family agriculture, plantation workers, large industrial firms, or any other setting involving the market, blood pressures start at about 110/60 in childhood but rise

sharply with age from young adulthood onward, reaching population average pressures about 150/95 by age sixty. Since cardiovascular death risk rises in an accelerating fashion with
blood pressures above about 120/70, this means that over a
third of modern populations are at increased risk from hypertension, compared to a tiny fraction among precapitalist groups
(Eyer 1975; Waldron *et al.* 1982).

When the cross-cultural samples were evaluated for social
characteristics, based on anthropological studies of the same
groups, by raters who had no knowledge of the blood pressure
data, blood pressures were higher and the slopes of blood pressure increase with age were greater in groups that had greater
involvement in the money economy, more economic competition, more contact with people of different culture or beliefs,
and in which the predominant family type was nuclear or
father-absent, as opposed to an extended family. Detailed study
clearly implicates the stressful effects of disruption of co-operative relationships and traditional culture, which occurs during
economic modernization, in the rise of blood pressure (Sterling
and Eyer 1981; Waldron *et al.* 1982).

Elevated blood fats and cholesterol levels are risk factors for
cardiovascular disease. Cross-cultural comparisons of blood
cholesterol and fat levels show the same pattern with economic
type as that found for blood pressure, with a sharp increase with
transformation of life into market activity (Waldron 1979).
This is probably a combined result of obesity, elevation of
dietary intake of fats, and the mobilization of these substances
in the body which occurs under stress. The interaction between
diet and stress further increases the risk associated with a given
dietary intake (Eyer 1979; Kaplan *et al.* 1983).

Beyond the elevation of blood pressure, fats and cholesterol,
capitalism is marked by increased drug consumption. The mass
drugs fall into two categories: pain killers (alcohol and opiates)
and stimulants (coffee, tobacco, amphetamines, etc.). People
do not have an innate urge to consume these drugs, nor do
animals. Naive animals will not choose the drug over water or
food unless reinforced for consumption. The most effective
reinforcement for alcohol is simply randomly shocking the
animal. Per capita alcohol consumption rises early in the
modernization process, as the village community is broken
up and rural–urban migration begins. Alcohol consumption

subsequently is highest for the lowest urban class, which has the highest rates of unemployment, family breakup, and migration. High alcohol consumption might be thought of as a response to the stresses of massive social disruption (Eyer 1977a; Egger 1980).

After the initial market transformation, alcohol consumption is maintained at high levels in a whole group of countries where worker productivity tends to be lower and a characteristic alcohol pattern of diseases emerges alongside the elevated blood pressure pattern of cardiovascular diseases in modern excess mortality. Continental Europe is the center of this area, and here stroke is the major expression of elevated blood pressure and accidents, suicide, cirrhosis of the liver, tuberculosis, pancreatic and liver cancer stand out as the characteristic alcohol pattern (Eyer 1977a).

In contrast, stimulant consumption rises somewhat later in capitalist transformation and is highly associated with the rise of mass production industry in the twentieth century. Today smoking is heaviest among industrial workers, and this potentiates the risks associated with many other occupational hazards, such as asbestos. Tobacco consumption per capita increased over tenfold in the United States from 1900–29, and coffee consumption doubled. England, Canada, Australia, and to some extent Scandinavia all show a large rise of stimulants in this period, combined with a temporary cutback in alcohol consumption. As American industrial organization has been imitated in Europe, Japan, the Soviet Union or Eastern Europe since World War II, cigarette consumption has also risen. We are in the midst of a worldwide increase in smoking (Eyer 1980).

Along with elevated blood pressure, smoking is the second most important factor in excess cardiovascular disease, particularly ischemic or coronary heart disease. Smoking also causes lung cancer, bronchitis, emphysema, and ulcers, all of which are important in the excess mortality of high-smoking modern countries (US Dept of Health, Education and Welfare 1979).

In animal experiments, it is impossible to get rats or monkeys to self-administer nicotine spontaneously; as with alcohol, reinforcement is necessary to initiate consumption. The most effective reinforcement paradigm involves subjecting the animals to precise, high intensity work to avoid punishment. In the laboratory world, this is the analogue of industrial labor after Ford.

This kind of labor, and behavior patterns that result from it, independently increases risk for cardiovascular death. Robert Karasek has analyzed data from large Swedish and American longitudinal surveys of job characteristics and health. Two factors associated with a job strongly predict prospectively not only coronary heart disease and hypertension mortality, but death rates for many other causes as well. Job demand, including both intensity and novelty is one dimension; the other is degree of control or decision-making power the worker exercises over the work process and its demands. Jobs at opposite extremes of risk on these two factors (high demand, low control versus low demand, high control) show a threefold difference in coronary heart disease. Modern jobs, such as production line worker, keypunch operator, secretary, tend to be in the high-risk quadrant, while traditional jobs, such as blacksmith, woodcutter, gardener, tend to be in the low-risk quadrant (Karasek *et al.* 1981).

Perhaps because of the rise of high-demand, low-control types of labor in modern industrial organizations (Braverman 1974) or from deeper roots in the Protestant Ethic (Weber 1957; Friedman and Rosenman 1974), type A behavior pattern has become common in advanced capitalist countries. This is a behavior pattern characterized by "extremes of competitiveness, striving for achievement, aggressiveness (sometimes stringently repressed), haste, impatience, restlessness, hyperalertness, explosiveness of speech, tenseness of facial musculature and feelings of being under the pressure of time and the challenge of responsibility." Compared with its polar opposite behavior pattern, the relaxed, easy-going, slower-paced type B, type As show a fivefold increase in coronary heart disease death risk under age sixty-five (Rosenman *et al.* 1970, 1975).

Part of this increased risk is because type A "gathers" the other risk factors: smokers tend to be type A, and type As smoke heavily; blood pressure and cholesterol are both elevated in type As. This association provides evidence for the linkages suggested above between work demands, behavior, drug consumption, and physiological changes. Independent of the effect of the other risk factors, type A alone is prospectively associated with a twofold elevation of coronary heart disease risk (Jenkins 1971, 1976, 1983; Jenkins and Zyzsanski 1980).

The development of new products, processes, and raw materials in industrial work since the late nineteenth century has imposed new, and largely unevaluated, occupational and environmental hazards. These risks greatly increase the frequencies of certain diseases, as for example asbestos with lung cancer, polychlorinated biphenyls for liver cancer, radiation for leukemia (Selikoff, Hammond, and Curg 1968). These risks have developed at an accelerating pace, especially since World War II, and are just now beginning to have significant impacts on older age death rates. These risks are clearly caused by the capitalist social process, since profit is the prime criterion for new product development, knowledge of toxic effects is often well known by the manufacturer early in the development process but is deliberately suppressed, and wastes are freely dumped into the environment, often illegally and without regard for ultimate social cost in health or remedial action (Stellman and Daum 1973).

The emergence of male excess mortality

One can view the rise of modern diseases from another perspective, in its differing impact on the two sexes. Before capitalism, male and female death rates through the lifespan were at roughly comparable levels (Retherford 1975; Preston 1976). It was quite common then for female death rates somewhat to exceed male in childbearing ages. In societies with a very pronounced preference for sons, as in the rural elites of northern India to this day, female infant and child mortality exceeds male, due to poorer feeding and more neglect of daughters. In these cases female life expectancy from birth is as much as three years shorter than male, but in general, average life expectancy of males and females in precapitalist societies differs by only a year or so (Waldron 1982a, 1982b).

With modern capitalist development the gap between male and female life expectancy widens progressively, with males dying now about eight years sooner on the average than females. So common and pervasive is the large male excess mortality today that many have taken it to be a natural condition, referring it to a universal biological weakness of the male of all species. This is clearly a wrong generalization about nature, since there are many species in which females have higher death rates, and in any case there is no evidence of this wide gap in human populations before the twentieth century (Waldron 1976).

The key to understanding modern male excess mortality is to see that females have benefited much more than men from the health advance possible with capitalism, while men have suffered more from the rise of stress-induced and other risk factors. Part of this very different impact pattern is due to biologically influenced, culturally determined sex roles, some to genetic–environment interactions, and some to purely social causes (Waldron 1983b).

When infant and child mortality were high and no social security system existed to provide for old age beyond the extended family, more births were needed to ensure surviving adults when the parents became old. Combined with the effects of higher levels of infectious disease in producing miscarriages, and the fact that the majority of women were married, and without effective birth control methods, women spent a considerable part of adulthood pregnant and/or nursing. Along with poorer nutrition, physically taxing farm work, and lack of knowledge of asepsis in delivery, all these factors together contributed to the adult female excess of deaths over males through childbearing ages, largely from maternal mortality and tuberculosis. This excess reached its peak in many developing capitalist countries during the early period of rapid urbanization, as more and more single young women went to work in the factories under exceptionally exploitative conditions, and early scientific medicine increased childbirth risks by concentrating births in hospitals before antisepsis.

The improvement of nutrition, spread of contraception and family planning, and decline in the number of births per woman all made for a more dramatic decline of infectious disease among women than men. This difference is clearly biologically determined, since men do not bear children, but would have been impossible without modern environmental changes. Part of the reason for the decline in infant and maternal mortality is the increased use of medical facilities by women – for gynecological and prenatal care, delivery and pediatric care – since the technical effects of these facilities have become health promoting through antisepsis, antibiotics, immunization, and the appreciation of the role of nutrition. Men by and large do not use the medical system for these reasons, and this difference is largely responsible for the sizable female excess in doctor and hospital visits in advanced countries. It would be a mistake to interpret this excess as evidence for higher female sickness, as many have done. For cardiovascular diseases and cancer, which dominate modern excess mortality, it is plain that the male–female difference in death rates beyond about age forty is not due to different effects of medical treatment on the two sexes, since prognosis for men and women with similarly developed chronic disease is similar. It is the degree of exposure to risk factors before a person ever comes to medical attention that is responsible for most of the modern male death rate excess (Waldron 1983b).

Men and women alike suffered the rise of stress characteristic of capitalist transformation, as evident in the rise of blood pressure trends or blood cholesterol patterns by age to similar levels for both (Waldron 1982a). However, they diverged dramatically in drug use, with men drinking and smoking and using illegal drugs more; while women increasingly depended on medically prescribed drugs and over-the-counter remedies. In addition, type A behavior pattern has developed more among men and many more men than women went into hazardous occupations. Together these differences account for most of the rise of male excess mortality with capitalism (Waldron 1976, 1983b).

Overall, these changes make sense as capitalism's impact on people emerging from the patriarchal class societies that preceded capitalism. The long male tradition of denial of pain, taking risks, and competing for power is developed into the self-administration of risky drugs to assuage fear and stimulate performance, resolute one-dimensional positive thinking, relentless internal pressure to produce and succeed in competition, and willing exposure to incalculable occupational and environmental hazards in order to be a good provider. The widespread cultural linkage of female childbearing to female childcare is continued in capitalism despite rising female labor force participation and results in a whole different set of attitudes, with more emphasis on communication, caring, the fact of developing ambiguity, less individualism and risk taking, and more reliance on medical authority.

Many genetic differences influence male–female differences in death rates and health, but for the most part these differences result in compensating shifts in overall health with the environment change characteristic of capitalism. Thus, males appear to have inherently lower resistance to infectious disease than females, due to x-linked immunoregulatory genes. However, as we have pointed out, females often had higher infectious mortality before the death rate watershed due to excessive childbearing, poor nutrition and medical care. Since infectious disease has been dramatically reduced, a male excess of infectious disease has indeed emerged, but it is a very small part of total male excess mortality (Waldron 1983a).

Inherent sex differences in reproductive physiology and anatomy contribute to higher female mortality for breast and uterine cancer than for corresponding male sexual cancers, and only women suffer maternal mortality. On the other hand, female sex hormones may exert some protective effect against coronary heart disease, though this point is still not definitively established, and the effect is probably smaller than the cultural effects mentioned previously; for example, women equally as type A and smokers as men in a California sample show nearly equal risks of developing coronary heart disease over time (Waldron 1976).

The most important biological contributions to the male–female difference in death rates and health come from the culturally-developed behaviors that go with linking female childbearing to female childcare. This is clearly not an inherent genetic necessity. Changing the increased health risks for males that come from the modern form of the old male traditions will probably require equal male participation in the nurturance and development of children as part of the reconstruction of co-operative community forms. This in turn will require relief from the pressures of competition.

That it is males who suffer most from the modern form of male domination should make it clear that the other possibility – turning women into equally denying, competitive, drug-addicted, risk-taking individualist wage workers in the pyramidal labor market – is not the direction to take. Unfortunately, this seems to be happening in the United States and other countries, as women's alcohol and tobacco consumption have started to rise rapidly in parallel to their influx into the labor market (US DHEW 1979).

Surplus population

Capitalism has always produced surplus population, principally by two means: the dispossession of the peasantry, driving them into the labor market; and the excess of births over deaths produced by reductions in the death rate. Surplus population created in either of these ways may in turn become wage workers integrated by rapidly expanding capital, or become unemployed or underemployed surplus population if capital is not expanding rapidly enough (Marx 1971). In the now-developed nations, dispossession of the peasantry or farmers was the primary driving force and the emigrants from the land became productive urban workers (Glass and Eversley 1965).

Since World War II, the relation of the two sources of surplus population has changed. The dispossession of rural populations in Africa, Asia, and Latin America continues apace via legal changes, the pressure of the world agricultural market, and wars, generating surplus population in greater numbers than at any previous period in capitalist history (Amin 1977; Frank 1978). But added to this is a much larger surplus population emergent from the extraordinary lowering of the death rates in these regions after the World War II. At the same time, the market demand growth for this surplus population has slowed and recently disappeared completely. The result is evident in the massive growth of shantytowns and favelas around all Third World cities, rural overpopulation of peasant villages from Brazil to China, and enormous growth of rural migrant labor forces engaged in temporary or seasonal work. Now numbering almost a billion people, this surplus population is the most rapidly growing world social stratum and could easily comprise half the world's people by the year 2000 if present trends continue (Center for International Studies 1978; Griffith 1976).

Two fundamental developments have produced this situation: the invention of means to sustain a large marginal population cheaply; and the massive and growing waste of world economic surplus, particularly in military spending (Baran and Sweezy 1966; Melman 1981).

While nutritional improvement was clearly the primary factor in the historical death rate reduction for advanced capitalist societies, since World War II there has been a drastic inner transformation in the means by which low death rates can be achieved. Nutritional improvements play a lesser role, often simply in the better distribution of existing food to prevent local famine, and mass immunization, public health campaigns and mass use of antibiotics have come to the fore (WHO 1974; Evans, Hall and Warford 1981). This shift makes possible such paradoxes as the death rate reductions from 30–40/1000 to about 15/1000 in much of Africa and South Asia from 1935 to 1970, while caloric and protein intake, already at a low level, declined (Haub 1962–82).

Clearly it has become possible cheaply to sustain large and rapidly growing populations without the consistent advance in food production per capita. This cannot continue indefinitely: there are limits to how many diseases one can immunize against or eliminate from the environment; infectious organisms resistant to antibiotics are emerging at an accelerating rate; and a certain minimum of calories are necessary even if humans engage in little physical labor. Indeed, since 1970, further death rate decline has stopped in much of the Third World, and in many places important death rate increases have occurred, as in the Sahel, the Horn of Africa, Bangladesh, Southeast Asia, and Brazil. Throughout Africa and South Asia, life expectancy from birth has levelled off at between forty-five and fifty-five (UN Dept of International Economic and Social Affairs 1982). In these areas, infant and child mortality are exceptionally high compared to death rates at other ages, reflecting the growing presence of malnutrition, now estimated to affect at least 500 million people (UNRISD 1976; George 1977; Brown 1982). Lacking education and sufficient nutrition, the productivity of this population should it be employed would be very low. By undermining labor power, capitalism is also undermining future economic surplus.

In addition, there has been a rising tide of wars fought to keep control in the periphery. This trend begins with the Southeast Asia War and extends through wars against the liberation of central and southern Africa, the wars in the Horn of Africa, Bangladesh, and Afghanistan, to the Central American and Middle Eastern wars today. These wars have destroyed agriculture and natural resources and made millions refugees. They have also supplied the main focus for the development of new diseases or resistant strains of old ones, threatening the health advances of the metropoles as well. Besides overt war, many resources have gone into the development of repressive political regimes capable of forcing real wage levels downward, as in much of South America during the 1970s. These developments strikingly illustrate the connection between waste of world economic surplus for military purposes and the creation of marginal population.

The growth of this giant surplus population has led world elites to mobilize mass campaigns to restrict birth rates at a social stage much earlier than economic development would normally produce this result. However, population will continue to grow and probably reach between 8 and 10 billion by the middle of the next century, before even the most rapid birth rate declines result in no further population growth. Clearly a major reorganization of world capital will be necessary merely to sustain the growing surplus population, much less employ it productively (Lappe and Collins 1978).

This reorganization is all the more necessary because of a fundamental change in the nature of the agricultural base. The countries now developed achieved great food expansion by developing industrial agriculture over large fertile areas of the globe not previously used for agriculture at all. Not only are there no remaining unused high fertility areas, but everywhere soil degradation and erosion is decreasing the natural basis of agriculture, necessitating higher fertilizer, pesticide, and mechanical compensations. The development of new strains and farming methods in the Green Revolution has pushed back production limits and genetic engineering may enable further progress, but there is no question that world agriculture must become the focus of large new capital investments not now forthcoming (Barr 1981).

The transformation of health by class

In precapitalist Europe, the two main classes were the aristocracy, who stood a foot taller than the peasants and lived twenty years longer if they did not kill themselves in hand-to-hand combat, and the great mass of the peasantry, who were shorter and had higher infant and childhood mortality due to poorer nutrition. Cities were a tiny fraction of the population, death rates there were two to three times higher across the ages than in the surrounding countryside, and did not vary much by class among traders or craftsmen (Glass and Eversley 1965).

In the early capitalist period to about the end of the eighteenth century, the health conditions of the aristocracy and peasantry remained much the same, but the cities started to grow because of the rise of two new classes to urban dominance, the wage working class and the surplus population or lumpenproletariat. During this period, hours of work were lengthened, per capita nutrition in the cities declined, and much surplus population was forced off the land to become the lowest social class of the cities without any obvious means of making a living. As a result, city death rates rose further, particularly infant mortality for the lowest urban class. Cities grew only because of massive immigration, since death rates exceeded birth rates. At this time, class differentials of the death rate reached their widest, with average life expectancies at birth of ten or fifteen years in the lumpenproletariat of the largest cities, twenty-five to thirty among workers, forty to forty-five among urban bourgeoisie or rural farmers, and sixty or more among the rural landowners (Glass and Eversley 1965; Acsadi and Nemeskeri 1970).

With the great decline in the death rate, class differences in death rates in advanced capitalist countries have greatly narrowed. Now the lowest urban class has life expectancies of about sixty years, the mass of workers about seventy-two, and seventy-five to eighty among the elite or well-off farmers. Among urban classes, the sharpest difference in health still comes between the lowest urban class – which experiences concentrated unemployment, social disruption, crime, drug use, poor nutrition and housing – and all higher social groups (Syme and Berkman 1976; Leclerc *et al.* 1979). Mental illness also shows this sharp divergence between the lowest urban class and all other groups. Since the vast majority of developed country populations now live in cities, the poor health conditions of the modern lumpenproletariat play a large role in determining the country's average health statistics (Antonovsky 1972; Kitagawa and Hauser 1973).

While this convergence developed in the advanced countries, the rest of the world was swept up into the capitalist process, so the really large divergences in capitalism now are between countries and even continents characterized by a different mix of classes. The lumpenproletariat (or surplus population), though very significant in developed countries is much larger and poorer in the rest of the world. Living on the margin in the villages, roving the countryside in search of temporary work, or crowding into the shantytowns of Third World cities, life expectancy of this group ranges between thirty and forty. As it moves out of the village, the lumpenproletariat is experiencing a very large increase in social stress, accompanied by increased alcohol, tobacco, and other drug use. Especially in the cities, this group suffers the combined ills of malnutrition, unsanitary environments, and stress-related diseases. Numbering now nearly a billion people worldwide, this class is now larger than the whole world population of the eighteenth century.

In stark contrast to this group is the remaining relatively untransformed communal village peasantry which has benefited from modern public health, immunization, antibiotics, and food redistribution and improvement. China now has most of this population, which in the world as a whole, also numbers perhaps as many as 1 billion. These groups have life expectancies as high as sixty-five, with moderately low infant mortality and adult mortalities lower than even the elities of developed countries (Saleff 1973; Banister and Preston 1981; Rui Zhu 1981; Banister 1983).

Overall, capitalism has replaced the contrast of a tiny healthy elite whose males had a penchant for personal violence, amidst a large peasant population in moderately poor health due to marginal nutrition, with the picture of a fairly healthy world elite, amidst a moderately unhealthy working class suffering modern diseases, flanked by a very large surplus population suffering both malnutrition and stress, and a shrinking communal peasant population, much of which is in even better health as adults than the world elites.

Business cycles and death rate fluctuations

The death rate has always fluctuated up and down within a particular range, with epidemics of infectious disease at the peaks. Capitalism is set off from previous social forms both by a different pattern of death rate peaks and a different underlying set of social causes.

In precapitalist Europe, peaks in the death rate occurred at erratic intervals and were strongly associated with either widespread crop failure and resulting famine or the disruptions and deprivations of large-scale war (Glass and Eversley 1965). In Europe this pattern reached its ultimate expression in the Irish famines of the 1840s, but it persists in Africa and South Asia today.

From the middle of the nineteenth century onward, these patterns shifted to a new one, with epidemic peaks occurring more regularly and coincident with the *boom* phase of the business cycle in developing capitalism (Thomas 1927). This shift is probably due to two phenomena: the improvement of nutrition and in particular the progressive limitation of crop failure-induced famines through better long distance transportation; and the vast increase in cyclic migration which marks the creation of urban industrial capitalism.

From stable settled rural communities with a few small urban centers, one goes to a world in which as many as a fifth of the total population migrates long distances each year. This enormous migration flux becomes important on a world scale by the late nineteenth century between Europe and America. Migration peaks very markedly with the boom of the business cycle, and reaches its low during the depression phase. Simply put, once a new disease strain arises, it is much more likely to become epidemic during the boom through rapid spread to populations lacking immunity from prior exposure to similar agents (Eyer 1977a, 1977b).

The rise of migration is also fundamental to the increased social stress of capitalism. The breakup of settled-kin community occurs through migration, and breakup of the nuclear family in the city is often followed by migration. Both migration and family breakup peak with the boom of the business cycle, as do long hours of work. These three important social sources of stress produce a decline in population immunity, which also contributes to the genesis of epidemics during the boom (Eyer 1977b).

Unemployment is also an important social source of stress, which peaks during the depression phase of the business cycle. The suicide rate and mental hospital admissions rate rise and

fall with unemployment, as does the percentage of the population in prison and a component of homicide (Bonger 1916;
Durkheim 1951; Henry and Short 1954; MacMahon, Johnson,
and Pugh 1963; Brenner 1973a; Eyer 1976).

Which phase of the business cycle has more health risks associated with it? Alcohol consumption and smoking rise and peak
with the boom and reach their low in depressions, perhaps
because the stresses that peak with the boom somewhat outweigh those that peak with the depression, or because people
have more money to spend during booms (Ledermann 1964;
Brenner 1975). Transport and work accident death rates peak
with the boom because transportation intensifies and overtime
hours increase (Eyer 1977b). More pollution is produced during
booms. On the other side of the equation, housing, nutrition,
and medical care improve during booms and deteriorate during
depressions (Eyer 1977b).

In terms of the overall impact on the death rate, it is clear that
the health risks of the boom strongly outweigh those of the
depression in nineteenth-century capitalist countries. Since
then, the death rate has declined, infectious disease plays a
much smaller role in the level and variation of the death rate,
and as a result, the overall variation is much smaller. The
factors that produced the mass epidemics during booms when
nutrition, medical care, and housing were insufficient are now
buffered during booms by these health-protective influences.
For infant mortality, this shift has gone so far that there is now a
notable tendency for this death rate to rise during depressions
(Brenner 1973b).

Nevertheless, at all other ages and for all the leading causes of
death – cardiovascular disease, stroke, cancer, liver cirrhosis,
bronchitis, emphysema, and asthma – the death rates peak
with the boom still. The variation of cardiovascular-respiratory
disease is over 90 per cent of the business cycle variation of the
death rate, far outweighing the variation of suicide. The peaks
in accidents clearly parallel the intensity of use of industrial
and transport facilities and car driving, but all the other major
causes of death show peaks that parallel the influenza epidemics. This could be because people debilitated by chronic
noninfectious disease are at greater risk of dying from a serious
case of the flu, or because the stresses and other risks that
potentiate the epidemic also independently cause heart attacks

and strokes (Brenner 1971, 1976, 1979a; Eyer 1977a, 1977b; Bunn 1979).

There are major unresolved issues in interpreting the business cycle variation of the death rate and ill health (Brenner 1977, 1979b; Kasl 1979; Lew 1979; Gravelle, Hutchinson, and Stein 1981; Catalano and Dooley 1983). It is fairly certain that unemployment experience during the depression cannot directly produce both the concurrent rise in suicide and the subsequent much larger rise of flu-associated deaths during the boom about three years later. This is because unemployment for short durations has little health effect, and stress impacts on ill health have short time delays in existing prospective studies (Eyer 1977b). However, it is possible that persons suffering long-term unemployment during the recession may be much more likely to become divorced, migrate, or take work with extra long hours or higher risk exposure during the subsequent boom, as well as consume more alcohol or smoke more at this time as well. This would link unemployment experience with the much larger peak in stress-induced health risk that occurs during the boom. So far no prospective study has followed individual long-term unemployed people for the periods of time necessary to demonstrate this possible linkage. Short of this evidence, the increased migration, community fragmentation, and long hours of work, with the concomitant increase in smoking and alcohol consumption that occur during the boom, provide a first level of explanation for the fact that the death rate as a whole peaks with the boom.

Before World War I, booms in America tended to coincide with European depressions and vice versa, and the rapidly developing Japan–East Asia area had a distinct cycle pattern. Death rates in each area peaked with the local boom, and the epidemic diseases were bacterial, with eliminable reservoirs in the environment, such as cholera and yellow fever. World War I synchronized world epidemic patterns, especially with the influenza epidemic of 1918; thereafter, more and more of a common pattern has grown up. Since World War II, the business cycle from Singapore to West Germany has synchronized, as have death rate cycles around influenza epidemic patterns.

The same general pattern of flu peaks is also found in the socialist sphere, though modified in a way we will point out in the next section. Since the socialist countries do not show the same economic fluctuation patterns as the west, and lack cyclical unemployment, this overlap points to both the centrality of influenza in death rate variations, and the fundamental role played by the western economy in generating and spreading new strains. As we have pointed out, these strains tend to arise in areas combining initial poverty, rapid growth, and prolonged war. Southeast Asia was the main such area from the late 1950s, when immunological typing of new strains became current on a worldwide basis, until the late 1970s; so most new strains in the last thirty years have been first identified in Hong Kong or Australia (Eyer 1977a).

Socialism or capitalism?

It was characteristic of socialist countries after World War II to put an emphasis early in development on education and mass improvement in health conditions. At a time when the great reduction of infectious disease became possible relatively cheaply – without great increases in agricultural production – death rates were dramatically reduced from Eastern Europe to China, and Cuba in the 1960s. China pressed this health advance furthest, with infant mortalities comparable to western developed countries by the late 1970s and adult death rates half those of the United States, largely due to very low rates of modern diseases in the overwhelmingly rural village population (Durand 1960; Quinn 1974; Rui Zhu 1981). In East Germany, Czechoslovakia, or Hungary these diseases were already at high levels before the Red Army marched through, and remained at levels comparable to West Germany or Austria throughout the recent period (UN Dept of International Economic and Social Affairs 1982).

By the mid-1950s, the Soviet data showed moderately low infant mortality. It also had adult death rates below levels in the United States or other developed countries, particularly for males. This pattern was even more pronounced in Bulgaria and Rumania, which then had among the lowest adult male death rates, in older ages, in the world. In young adulthood, however, these countries all showed very large excess mortality, particularly for males, so that death rates from fifteen to thirty were well above western levels (Cooper 1981; Cooper and Schatzkin 1982; Eyer 1982).

The general death rate decline halted in the Soviet Union and Eastern Europe by the early 1960s, and since then death rates have risen, particularly for males over age thirty-five. By the late 1970s, death rates for older males in Poland, the Soviet Union, Bulgaria, and Rumania have risen to the highest levels among developed countries. Cardiovascular diseases accounted for most of this rise and more than doubled over this fifteen-year period, the most rapid increase seen in any historical data (Davis and Feshbach 1980; Feshbach 1982).

Looking at underlying mediating factors, Soviet adult blood pressure samples were below other developed countries in the 1950s but are now at slightly higher levels; smoking has increased, but is still less than half United States' levels; dietary fat has increased, but only to one third the cholesterol or saturated fat per capita consumed in the United States; and alcohol consumption has also increased, to levels comparable to the United States. Though the data is fragmentary, it seems plain that the rise of blood pressure has played the fundamental role in the increase of Soviet adult male death rates (Cooper, 1981; Cooper and Shatzkin 1982; Eyer 1982).

Poland, Russia, Bulgaria, and Rumania may have had the female excess death rate pattern in the spotty data from the late nineteenth and early twentieth century. By the mid-1950s, the male excess had clearly emerged. Since female adult death rates changed little in this area after the mid-1960s, while male death rates rose dramatically, the characteristic modern capitalist male excess mortality has emerged very strongly in this region. The Soviet male–female life expectancy difference at birth may stand at ten years, which would place it highest in the world.

During the Southeast Asia War period and the big military buildup of the mid-1970s, Soviet Central Asia experienced a regression in basic health statistics similar to that which occurred in the western sphere in Brazil, South Asia, and parts of Africa. Either infant mortality from Central Asia was previously greatly underreported, or it rose well above developed countries' levels by the late 1970s (Davis and Feshbach 1980). In Southeast Asia, western capitalism unleashed war and destruction of agriculture, and socialism presided over the following mass famines, with millions dead all told.

In the socialist sphere, as in the west, enormous problems of surplus populations have arisen with the combined effects of dramatic increases in survival through infancy and childhood and inadequacy of investment capital to productively employ this population. These problems became most critical in China, with its heavy burden of military spending and social disorder from the mid-1960s onward, and led to the most effective and far-reaching birth control program in the world. As in many parts of rural Asia with crash birth control programs backed up by punitive government policies, infant mortality from female infanticide has risen in China. Unlike peripheral countries in the western sphere, so far China has deliberately restricted its underemployed population to the rural villages, preventing the rise of a rural and urban lumpenproletariat. This may change in the future with the introduction of sweeping private incentive systems in agricultural production and marketing (Tien 1983).

The major outlines of the health statistics in the socialist third of the world show trends and levels very much parallel to the characteristic patterns and changes of capitalist development in the nonsocialist world. As we have argued above, this is not evidence for basic biological universals or technical effects of industrialism narrowly understood, but is best seen as a product of the shared capitalist *social* process essential to all of these societies. The basic social process of capitalism turns peasants living in settled rural communities into urban wage workers living a rootless, fragmented, and overworked life assuaged by consumption of higher levels of both health-promoting and health-detracting consumer goods. This process is much the same in east and west.

For example, the great excess mortality in young adulthood evident in the mid-1950s Soviet data clearly corresponds to the major period of urbanization in Soviet society, when the Soviet population was transformed into a working class three times more rapidly than in any previous process of capitalist development. From 1945 to 1960, the Soviet Union went from being less than 25 per cent urban to over 60 per cent, migration rates were at very high levels, marriage was delayed and transformed to the nuclear unit, divorce and separation rates began their accelerating uptrend, and birth rates fell to very low levels. The dramatically stressful changes of this decade and a half generated the very large excess mortality of young males, which then moved through the ages cohort-fashion as this highly stressed group got older, and was followed by successive waves living with high migration, community breakdown, and modern labor.

In a different social sphere, the military have come to play a leading, even dominant, economic, social, and political role in both east and west, as the center of the state organization of capital and as a basic source of elite legitimacy. It is from the military demands that much else in financial organization or social stratification follow. The military waste of surplus is a model for symbolic surplus waste elsewhere by the elite, and the precondition for both the rise of stress, which produces much excess mortality, and the authority to enforce this stress on the newly created working class (Eyer 1982).

What makes the Soviet statistics so dramatic is the achievement of practically the whole technically possible death rate reduction early in this social transformation process. Rather than simply declining much more slowly than death rates at other ages, as in the history of developed capitalist countries where health advance had paralleled capitalist social transformation, Soviet adult male death rates first decline rapidly to low levels in older ages, and then turn around and go up again. The rise of modern diseases is already beginning in China and will clearly be all the more dramatic, since adult male death rates have been at very low levels for a long period of time (Rui Zhu 1981).

There are clear differences between the socialist form of organization and the western capitalist form. Perhaps the most important is the organization of the elite into a Party which develops capital in almost all areas through the state, rather than a class which privately owns capital and also dominates the state. Socialist capitalism also has a modified form of the labor market, with no unemployment but thoroughgoing state control. This means there is no real lumpenproletariat with its concentrated health risks, as in the west, but problems of disruption, alienation, and arbitrary and destructive authority are then diffused more widely, with little net difference in the overall data, as the basic transformation from peasants to workers proceeds.

Finally, the direct creation of state-owned industrial farms has not as effectively advanced the generation of agricultural surplus as allowance of some degree of private property to farmers in an agricultural market. Nutritional advance has therefore been slower, but this makes little difference since healthy and productive workers do not need as much nutrition as they did prior to immunization and antibiotics, mass public health campaigns, and mechanical mobilization of nonhuman energy sources in production. China has clearly done the best job distributing food evenly, but inequality of distribution may lie behind the rise of infant mortality in Soviet Central Asia. Paradoxically, the restriction of surplus generation in agriculture may have some health-protective effects, since its makes it very difficult to feed half of all grain crops to cattle to generate beef, as in the United States.

The organization of the elite and its relationship to agriculture and the working class make for a different pattern of economic fluctuations as well. Early development is marked by attempts to rapidly transform the countryside, extract surplus and build an urban working class, which end up in reversals with large death rate increases from famine, as in the Soviet 1930s or China, 1957–62. As agriculture develops, this danger disappears and longer waves of growth followed by stagnation and leadership reorganization follow. This leadership reorganization characteristic of the stagnant periods accomplishes many of the same functions that economic depressions used to achieve in a western capitalist economy. In the west this power reorganization is mediated by property claims, while in the east, the power contest between organizational leaderships occurs directly. Stagnations have occurred about every fifteen years in the Soviet sphere so far (growth, 1945–60 and 1965–78) and are erratic in China, and it is probably too soon even to say the Soviet periods are characteristic. These periods are generally longer than the western business cycle at about 4.5 years' average length, but bear some comparison with the long cycles between major depressions in western capitalism before World War I.

Except for the famines, influenza epidemics with western peak timing have created the basic year-to-year death rate fluctuation pattern in the socialist capitalist sphere, but these epidemics are more severe during the rapid growth periods and milder during stagnations (UN 1946–82). As both Eastern

Europe and China become more integrated through debt and trade into western capitalism, one might expect synchronization of economic fluctuations as well.

While there are many differences, the broad similarities in both social organization and health data make it plain that what exists in the world are a variety of forms of capitalism. The centers are contesting for dominance or against being made subordinate sources of surplus, and capitalism as a whole social process is still spreading and intensifying. Less than 2 per cent of the world's people worked for wages in the seventeenth century, and today still less than half do. With the prospect of doubling the world population in the next seventy-five years, the major part of the historical-social role of capitalism is still in the future.

Future prospects

The productivity of labor has increased at an accelerating rate with capitalist development in advanced countries. This is due primarily to increased health, education, and discipline of the labor force, and the development of capital and energy intensive, highly sophisticated production and transportation methods. If advanced labor were productively employed – producing for human needs or the capital equipment necessary for this production – advanced industrial labor would produce a truly enormous surplus (Baran and Sweezy 1966). If this surplus, in turn, were used to develop the less developed countries, there would be no problem feeding or absorbing into gainful employment the emergent surplus population either now, or the increase likely to occur in the next century (Waldron and Ricklefs 1973).

As so many times before in the history of capitalism, the needed surplus is now increasingly wasted and not even produced, as the world economy bumps downward toward a major depression. Because of this waste and nonutilization of potential, the possibility of an overflowing excess of real capital – food, materials, equipment – appears now as a scarcity, increasingly choked off by precisely those efforts to stave off depression. Nowhere is this more evident than in the accelerating expansion of debt at rising interest rates, taking

Keynesian measures to the extreme to finance an escalating military budget, and the conspicuous consumption of the subelites in Third World countries subjected by debt-led growth.

It may be possible to prevent a deep collapse, but only by imposing a long period of stagnation. Even then, one must realize that capitalism has only recovered from such situations in the twentieth century through the fundamental readjustment of power, property, and class relations that comes with a world war. World wars have created the economic conditions for recovery from the most serious depressions by controlling the working class, reorganizing property claims, destroying competitor capital centers, and/or enabling the victor to subordinate these centers financially. It may be possible to resubordinate the working class in the west through a long period of moderately high unemployment combined with the growth of a patriotic police state, and to continue the use of direct military suppression and state controls in the east, especially in the context of a renewed arms race. But it is doubtful that nuclear intimidation will suffice to keep Japanese or West German capital from challenging American financial primacy in the west, and the unified coordination of western and Soviet capital cannot by any stretch of the imagination be achieved by a suitable combination of Citibank lending, with nuclear shadow boxing and conventional wars against the Third World. Meanwhile, vast amounts of capital are being wasted in the pretense that some form of world war-readjustment process might be possible.

Under these conditions, the death rate in developed countries will marginally decline, reflecting the normal decline in the epidemic death rate during slow growth. In the long run, death rates in older ages from chronic disease may rise once again, as the present younger cohorts subjected to vastly increased status anxiety and competition age, particularly if social security systems have been substantially cut back by then. More immediately, suicide and mental illness will continue to rise rapidly, accelerating the uptrend that began in the 1960s; infant mortality will level off or rise due to increases in malnutrition and drug use among the urban lumpenproletariat; and surplus population in the rest of the world will continue to grow rapidly and suffer more frequent famines, as the extension of credit and arms sales to the Third World turn back on themselves in accelerating interest payments for rescheduled loans at high interest rates, without much expansion of basic production.

Nuclear holocaust and environmental disaster are possible down this road, but barring these catastrophes, world surplus population very marginally maintained will come to dominate world population, and the militarization of the developed world will find its relentless use in political control of this uprooted, malnourished majority. Though even more sophisticated ways of keeping people alive without food, housing, or education undoubtedly will be invented in this empire of poverty, terror, and splendor, it would not be surprising if world health conditions regressed fundamentally in this future.

Alternatively, capitalism may discover some historically unprecedented means to regenerate itself and put its potentially enormous economic surplus to productive use. The basic components of this reorganization are technically clearcut, and have even been worked out in detail in many cases. What is lacking is the political will among the elite to go ahead and alter property and power relationships that stand in the way. In the past capitalists have preferred to destroy each other's societies rather than face these necessities, but nuclear weapons and germ warfare have made the historical and traditional option totally unworkable.

What is needed is some form of top level coordination of world investable economic surplus, which would allow the socialist capitalist elite to compete side by side with western capitalists, and allow both to purge the wasteful users of surplus from their own ranks. This would make possible a great reduction in military waste to levels necessary for political stability, the abolition of many other forms of waste, and the heightening of the political effectiveness of the forms of waste that remain. Whole strata of the elite would be dispossessed in this process, which is clearly impossible without very strong elite leadership and mass popular backing.

World food production could then be greatly expanded and transformed. A decent standard of living could be possible for all the world's people, with life expectancies in the seventies for 10 billion people by mid-next century. Down this road, though, the rise of modern diseases will dominate world adult health trends, as three times as many peasants are turned into workers as exist as workers today. Also a practical certainty, are escalated rape and poisoning of the environment, depletion of nonrenewable resources, and the enormous gamble of nuclear power. Depending on the social policies enacted by this rebirth of capitalism, a massive upsurge in internal and international migration and community destruction could raise the epidemic death rate as well.

Finally, it is possible to imagine a world without modern excess mortality or starvation. Such a world is not possible without the abolition of all those unproductive uses of economic surplus that hold together class hierarchy itself. It is plain that this would yield a potentially useful economic surplus several times larger than in our second scenario. With this much surplus, it becomes possible to develop the rest of the world without massive community disruption and overwork, and to re-establish cooperative community and reasonable forms of work in the developed countries. Then modern excess mortality need not arise worldwide, and could be healed and prevented in the metropoles. Self-renewing sources of energy and materials are also possible in this scenario, as are rebuilding the world's soil so that agriculture might be sustainable for centuries to come (Eyer 1977a; Eyer and Sterling 1977).

Though attractive and technically possible, this third scenario is obviously unlikely. The ruling classes of the world are having a great deal of difficulty getting creatively beyond their habits of seven thousand years of class society. It will be a miracle indeed if they lead us into the second scenario without a catastrophe unparalleled in all human experience, and meantime, they have enough power to destroy more hopeful possibilities.

References

Acsadi, G.Y. and Nemeskeri, J. (1970) *History of Human Life Span and Mortality*. Budapest: Akademiai Kiado.

Amin, S. (1977) *Imperialism and Unequal Development*. New York: Monthly Review.

Angel, J.L. (1975) Paleoecology, Paleodemography and Health. In S. Polgar (ed.) *Population, Ecology and Social Evolution*. The Hague: Mouton.

Antonovsky, A. (1972) Social Class, Life Expectancy and Overall Mortality. In E. Gartly Jaco (ed.) *Physicians, Patients and Illness*. New York: Free Press.

Banister, J. (1983) *China's Changing Population*. Stanford, Calif.: Stanford University Press.

Banister, J. and Preston, S.H. (1981) Mortality in China. *Population and Development Review* 7(1): 98–110.

Baran, P. and Sweezy, P. (1966) *Monopoly Capital*. New York: Monthly Review.

Barr, T.N. (1981) The World Food Situation and Global Grain Prospects. *Science* 214: 1087–095.

Bonger, W. (1916) *Criminality and Economic Conditions* (tr. H.P. Horton). Boston, The Modern Criminal Science Series.

Braverman, H. (1974) *Labor and Monopoly Capital. The Degradation of Work in the Twentieth Century*. New York: Monthly Review.

Brenner, M.H. (1971) Economic Changes and Heart Disease Mortality. *American Journal of Public Health* 61: 606.

——(1973a) *Mental Illness and the Economy*. Cambridge, Mass.: Harvard University Press.

——(1973b) Fetal, Infant and Maternal Mortality During Periods of Economic Instability. *International Journal of Health Services* 3(2): 145–59.

——(1975) Trends in Alcohol Consumption and Associated Illnesses, Some Effects of Economic Changes. *American Journal of Public Health* 65(12): 1279–292.

——(1976) Estimating the Social Costs of National Economic Policy: Implications for Mental and Physical Health and Criminal Aggression. Joint Economic Committee of Congress Paper no. 5. Washington, DC: US Govt Printing Office.

——(1977) Health Costs and Benefits of Economic Policy. *International Journal of Health Services*

——(1979a) Mortality and the National Economy: A Review, and the Experience of England and Wales. *Lancet*, 15 September.

——(1979b) Unemployment, Economic Growth and Mortality. *Lancet*, 24 March.

Brown, L.R. (1982) *World Food Resources and Population: The Narrowing Margin*. Washington, DC: The Population Reference Bureau.

Bunn, A.R. (1979) Ischemic Heart Disease Mortality and the Business Cycle in Australia. *American Journal of Public Health* 69: 8.

Catalano, R. and Dooley, D. (1983) Health Effects of Economic Instability: A Test of Economic Stress Hypotheses. *Journal of Health and Social Behavior* 24: 46.

Center for International Studies (1978) *Landlessness and*

Near-landlessness in Developing Countries. Ithaca, NY: Cornell University Press.

Cooper, R. (1981) Rising Death Rates in the Soviet Union: The Impact of Coronary Heart Disease. *New England Journal of Medicine* 304: 1259-265.

Cooper, R. and Schatzkin, A. (1982) The Pattern of Mass Disease in the USSR: A Product of Socialist or Capitalist Development? *International Journal of Health Services* 12(3): 459-80.

Davis, C. and Feshbach, M. (1980) Rising Infant Mortality in the USSR in the 1970s. Foreign Demographic Analysis Division, Department of Commerce (Series p-95, no. 74). Washington DC: US Govt Printing Office.

Durand, J.D. (1960) The Population Statistics of China, AD 2-1953. *Population Studies* 13(3): 209-56.

Durkheim, E. (1951) *Suicide, a Study in Sociology*, eds J. Spaulding and G. Simpson, Glencoe, Illinois: The Free Press of Glencoe.

Egger, G. (1980) Psychosocial Aspects of Increasing Drug Abuse: A Postulated Economic Cause. *Social Science and Medicine* 14A: 163-70.

Evans, J.R., Hall, F.I., and Warford, J. (1981) Health Care in the Developing World: Problems of Scarcity and Choice. *New England Journal of Medicine* 305: 117-27.

Eyer, J. (1975) Hypertension as a Disease of Modern Society. *International Journal of Health Services* 5(4): 539-58.

——(1976) Capitalism and Mental Illness. *International Journal of Health Services* 6(1): 139-48, 157-68.

——(1977a) Prosperity as a Cause of Death. *International Journal of Health Services* 7(1): 125-50.

——(1977b) Does Unemployment Cause the Death-rate Peak in Each Business Cycle? A Multifactor Model of Death-rate Change. *International Journal of Health Services* 7(4): 625-62.

——(1979) A Diet-stress Hypothesis of Coronary Heart Disease Causation. *International Journal of Health Services* 9: 161-68.

——(1980) Social Causes of Coronary Heart Disease. *Psychotherapy and Psychosomatics* 34: 75-87.

——(1982) Changing Trends in Sischemic Heart Disease: Relations to Cohort Experience and Economic Trends in Industrial Countries. *Advances in Cardiology* 29: 50-5.

Eyer, J. and Sterling, P. (1977) Stress-related Mortality and Social Organization. *The Review of Radical Political Economics* 9(1): 1-44.

Feshbach, M. (1982) *The Soviet Union: Population Trends and Dilemmas*. Washington, DC: Population Reference Bureau.

Frank, A.G. (1978) *Dependent Accumulation and Underdevelopment.* New York: Monthly Review.

Friedman, M. and Rosenman, R. (1974) *Type A Behavior and Your Heart.* New York: Knopf.

George, S. (1977) *How The Other Half Dies: The Real Reasons for World Hunger.* Montclair, NJ: Allanheld, Osmun.

Glass, D.V. and Eversley, D.E.C. (1965) *Population in History.* London: Edward Arnold.

Gravelle, H., Hutchinson, S., and Stein, J. (1981) Mortality and Unemployment: A Critique of Brenner's Time Series Analysis. *Lancet 16.*

Griffith, K. (1976) *Land Concentration and Rural Poverty.* New York: Macmillan.

Haub, C. (1962–82) *World Population Data Sheet.* Washington, DC: Population Reference Bureau.

Henry, A.F. and Short, J.F. (1954) *Suicide and Homicide.* New York: The Free Press.

James, J. (1979) Impacts of the Medical Malpractice Slowdown in Los Angeles County: January 1976. *American Journal of Public Health* 69(5): 437–43.

Jenkins, C.D. (1971) Psychologic and Social Precursors of Coronary Disease. *New England Journal of Medicine* 284: 244–55, 307–17.

——(1976) Recent Evidence Supporting Psychologic and Social Risk Factors for Coronary Disease. *New England Journal of Medicine* 294: 987, 1033.

——(1983) Psychosocial Risk Factors for Coronary Heart Disease. *Acta Medica Scandinavica* (suppl.) 660: 123–36.

Jenkins, C.D. and Zyzsanski, S.J. (1980) Behavioral Risk Factors and Coronary Heart Disease. *Psychotherapy and Psychosomatics* 34: 149.

Kannel, W.B. and Sorlie, P. (1975) Hypertension in Framingham. In O. Paul (ed.) *Epidemiology and Control of Hypertension.* Miami: Symposium Specialists.

Kaplan, I., *et al.* (1983) Social Stress and Atherosclerosis in Normocholesterolemic Monkeys. *Science* 220(4598): 753–55.

Karasek, R., Baker, D., Marxer, F., Ahlbom, A., and Theorell, T. (1981) Job Decision Latitude, Job Demands and Cardiovascular Disease. A Prospective Study of Swedish Men. *American Journal of Public Health* 71: 694,

Kasl, S. (1979) Mortality and the Business Cycle: Some Questions about Research Strategies When Utilizing Macro-social and Ecological data. *American Journal of Public Health* 69: 782.

Kitagawa E.M. and Hauser, P.M. (1973) *Differential Mortality in the United States*. Cambridge, Mass.: Harvard University Press.

Lappe, F.M. and Collins, J. (1978) *Food First*. New York: Ballantine.

Leclerc, A., Aiach, P., Phillippe, A., Vennin, M., and Cebe, D. (1979) Morbidité, mortalité et classe sociale. Revue bibliographique portant sur divers aspects de la pathologie, et discussion. *Revue d'Epidemiologie et de Santé Publique* 27: 331–58.

Ledermann, S. (1964) *Alcool, Alcoolisme et Alcoolisation* (vols 1 and 2). Travaux et Documents Cahier no. 41. Paris: Presses Universitaires de France.

Lew, E. (1979) Mortality and the Business Cycle: How Far Can We Push an Association? *American Journal of Public Health* 69: 782.

MacMahon, B., Johnson, S., and Pugh, T.F. (1963) Relations of Suicide Rates to Social Conditions. *Public Health Reviews* 78(4): 285–93.

Marx, K. (1971) *Capital* (3 vols). Moscow: Progress Publishers.

McKeown, T. (1976a) *The Modern Rise of Population*. London: Edward Arnold.

——(1976b) *The Role of Medicine: Dream, Mirage or Nemesis*. London: Nuffield Provincial Hospitals Trust.

——(1978) Determinants of Health. *Human Nature* 1: 60–7.

McKeown, T., Brown, R.G., and Record, R.G. (1972) An Interpretation of the Modern Rise of Population in Europe. *Population Studies* 26: 345–82.

McKeown, T. and Record, R.G. (1962) Reasons for the Decline in Mortality in England and Wales during the Nineteenth Century. *Population Studies* 16: 94–122.

McKeown, T. and Record, R.G. (1975) An Interpretation of the Decline in Mortality in England and Wales during the Twentieth Century. *Population Studies* 29: 391–422.

McKinlay, J.B. and McKinlay, S.M. (1977) The Questionable Contribution of Medical Measures to the Decline of Mortality in the United States in the Twentieth Century. *Milbank Memorial Fund Quarterly/Health and Society* Summer: 405–28.

Melman, S. (1974) *The Permanent War Economy*. New York: Touchstone Books.

——(1981) Conversion from Military to Civilian Economy. *Ann. N.Y. Acad. Sci.* 368: 93.

Powles, J. (1976) Reasons for the Modern Decline in Mortality in the Third World. Paper delivered at the Australia and New Zealand Society of Epidemiology and Community Health Annual Conference, May. Mimeo.

Preston, S.H. (1970) Older Male Mortality and Cigarette Smoking. Institute of International Studies Population Monograph no. 7.

Berkeley, Calif.: University of California.

—(1976) *Mortality Patterns in National Populations.* New York: Academic Press.

Quinn, J. (ed.) (1974) *China Medicine as We Saw It.* Washington, DC: Fogarty International Center, US Dept of HEW, US Govt Printing Office.

Retherford, R.D. (1975) *The Changing Sex Differential in Mortality* Studies in Population and Urban Demography no. 1. Westport, Connecticut: The Greenwood Press.

Roemer, M.I. and Schwartz, J.L. (1979) Doctor Slowdown: Effects on the Population of Los Angeles County. *Social Science and Medicine* 130: 213–18.

Rosenman, R., Friedman, M., Strauss, R., Jenkins, C., Zyzsanski, S., and Wurm, M. (1970) Coronary Heart Disease in the Western Collaborative Group Study: A Followup Experience of $4\frac{1}{2}$ Years. *Journal of Chronic Diseases* 23: 173.

Rosenman, R., Brand, R., Jenkins, C., Friedman, M., Strauss, R., and Wurm, M. (1975) Coronary Heart Disease in the Western Collaborative Group Study: The Final Followup Experience of $8\frac{1}{2}$ Years. *Journal of the American Medical Association* 233: 872.

Saleff, J.W. (1973) Mortality Decline in the People's Republic of China and the US. *Population Studies* 27(3): 551–76.

Scrimshaw, N., Guzman, M., and Gordon, J. (1967) Nutrition and Infection Field Study in Guatemalan Villages, 1959–64. I. Study Plan and Experimental Design. *Archives of Environmental Health* 14: 657–62.

Scrimshaw, N., Guzman, M., Flores, M. *et al.* (1968) Nutrition and Infection Field Study in Guatemalan Villages, 1959–64. V. Disease Incidence Among Preschool Children under Natural Village Conditions, with Improved Diet and Medical and Public Health Services. *Archives of Environmental Health* 16: 223–25.

Scrimshaw, N., Taylor, C., and Gordon, J. (1968) Interactions of Nutrition and Infection. *WHO Monograph Series* 57: 3–329.

Scrimshaw, N., Behar, M., Guzman, M. *et al.* (1969) Nutrition and Infection Field Study in Guatemalan Villages, 1959–64. IX. An Evaluation of Medical, Social and Public Health Benefits, with Suggestions for Future Field Study. *Archives of Environmental Health* 18: 51–62.

Selikoff, I.J., Hammond, E.C. and Curg, J. (1968) Asbestos Exposure, Smoking and Neoplasia. *Journal of the American Medical Association* 204: 104.

Sivard, R.L. (1974–83) *World Military and Social Expenditures.* Washington DC: Council on World Priorities.

Stellman, J. and Daum, S. (1973) *Work is Dangerous to your Health.* New York: Vintage.

Sterling, P. and Eyer, J. (1981) Biological Basis of Stress-related Mortality *Social Science and Medicine* 15E: 3–42.

Stockholm International Peace Research Institute (1982) *SIPRI Yearbook: World Armaments and Disarmament*. New York: Taylor & Francis.

Syme, S.L. and Berkman, L.F. (1976) Social Class, Susceptibility and Sickness. *American Journal of Epidemiology* 104: 1–8.

Thomas, D.S. (1927) *Social Aspects of the Business Cycle*. New York: Knopf.

Tien, H.Y. (1983) *China: Demographic Billionaire*. Washington, DC: Population Reference Bureau.

United Nations (1946–82) *Demographic Yearbooks*. New York: United Nations.

United Nations Research Institute for Social Development (UNRISD) (1976) *Famine Risk and Famine Prevention in the Modern World*. New York: United Nations.

United Nations Dept of International Economic and Social Affairs (1982) *Levels and Trends of Mortality since 1950*. ST/ESA/SER A/74. New York: United Nations.

Waitzkin, H. (1981) The Social Origins of Illness: A Neglected History. *International Journal of Health Services* 11(1): 77–103.

Waldron, I. (1976) Why Do Women Live Longer than Men? *Social Science and Medicine* 10: 349–62.

——(1980) Sex Differences in Longevity. In Feinleib and Haynes (eds) *Proceedings of the 2nd Conference on the Epidemiology of Aging*. Washington, National Institute of Aging, US Dept. of HEW, US Govt Printing Office.

——(1982a) An Analysis of Causes of Sex Differences in Mortality and Morbidity. In W. Gove and G. Carpenter (eds) *The Fundamental Connection Between Nature and Nurture*. Lexington, Mass.: Lexington Books.

——(1982b) Gender, Psychophysiological Disorders, and Mortality. In I. Al-Issa (ed.) *Gender and Psychopathology*. New York: Academic Press.

——(1983a) Sex Differences in Human Mortality: The Role of Genetic Factors. *Social Science and Medicine* 17(6): 321–33.

——(1983b) Sex Differences in Illness Incidence, Prognosis and Mortality: Issues and Evidence. *Social Science and Medicine* 17(16): 1107–123.

Waldron, I. and Ricklefs, R.E. (1973) *Environment and Population: Problems and Solutions*. New York: Holt Rhinehart & Winston.

Waldron, I., Nowotarski, M., Freimer, M., Henry, J., Post, N., and Witten, C. (1982) Cross-cultural Variation in Blood Pressure: A Quantitative Analysis of the Relationships of Blood Pressure to Cultural Characteristics, Salt Consumption and Body Weight.

Social Science and Medicine 16: 419–30.

Weber, M. (1957) *The Protestant Ethic and the Rise of Capitalism.* New York: Scribner's.

World Health Organisation (1974) World Health Trends and Prospects. *World Health Statistics Report* 27(10): 1–43.

Two

A cultural account of "health": control, release, and the social body

Robert Crawford

The body is a cultural object. As our most immediate natural symbol it provides us with a powerful medium through which we interpret and give expression to our individual and social experience. "Human nature," the category of the inevitable (and often the desirable), finds its truth in the body. We live within a nature/culture opposition and the "natural body" confirms our place within a more "authentic" order. It is a vital foundation upon which behavior and values are predicated. Conversely, as a symbol of nature the body must be contained and transformed by culture. We invest the body with culture, thereby distinguishing ourselves from the rest of nature. Moreover, our biological being, always mediated by culture, delimits many of our most important social roles. It defines us in relation to others in kinship, sex, age groups, and larger social units such as race or caste. Bodily states are key markers in which are invested the social definitions of the self – not only regarding role, but normality and abnormality, inclusion and exclusion, domination and subordination. The body also supplies a universally experienced model of a living and dynamic unit, an organic whole, a prototype from which we can draw in our attempts to explain and give meaning to larger social units and experiences. It is our richest source for metonymy and metaphor.

Of course, our bodies do not come to us naturally, despite ideological notions to the contrary (Taussig 1980). The body is a culturally constructed body. The imposition of cultural categories makes it difficult to know where nature ends and culture begins. As Mary Douglas has stated in her well-known essay on "the two bodies,"

> The social body constrains the way the physical body is perceived. The physical experience of the body, always modified by the social categories through which it is known, sustains a particular view of society. There is a continual exchange of meanings between the two kinds of bodily experience so that each reinforces the categories of the other. As a result of this interaction the body itself is a highly restricted medium of expression.   (Douglas 1970: 65)

Anthropological studies of bodily experience attempt to uncover the semantic and social structures through which experience is organized in a culture. Beliefs and practices about birth, death, sex, affliction and healing, eating, bodily pollution, and body adornment reveal core assumptions and valuations derived from structured systems of meaning. As Turner (1980) argues with regard to body adornment, beliefs and practices concerning the body (those associated with the surface of the body for Turner) are particularly informative because they are located on the common frontier of society, the social self, and the psychobiological individual.

Another anthropologist, Jean Comaroff, has recently clarified why one particular bodily experience, serious illness or affliction, has come to occupy the center of so much attention among her colleagues. Affliction, Comaroff reasons (forthcoming), is a disordering event in that it implies a deviation from a common universe of experience and a disruption of existing personal relations, activities, and social roles. As a disorienting experience, it requires a cognitive reordering, a re-integration of the afflicted person into the shared meanings and social relations of the culture. All healing systems, reflecting underlying cultural paradigms, attempt to account for the apparent disorder and through such accounts – including disease categories, theories of causality, and prescriptions for recovery – reduce the dislocation occasioned by the affliction. By helping the afflicted person to answer the questions, Why me? and Why now? dominant values and categories for understanding reality (and the social arrangements they signify) are reaffirmed. Thus, the experience of illness and a culture's medical knowledge and practice reveal key aspects of the structuring of consciousness and objective social relations. Even outside the therapeutic encounter, there are few experiences of affliction and other forms of deviance untouched by a society's medical system and the collective meanings implicitly or explicitly expressed through it. The recent interest in the idea of the "medicalization" of society is testimony to the growing appreciation of this fact (Zola 1972; Illich 1975; Conrad and Schneider 1980).

While illness and its therapeutic management are crucial foci for informing our understanding of the cultural constitution of bodily experience and systems of meaning of a society, an equally vital direction of inquiry (at least for western cultures) has been neglected. The body is not only a cultural object in illness or affliction. Bodily experience is also structured through the symbolic category of *health*. Health, like illness, is a concept grounded in the experiences and concerns of everyday life. While there is not the same urgency to explain health as there is to account for serious illness, thoughts about health easily evoke reflections about the quality of physical, emotional, and social existence. Like illness, it is a category of experience that reveals tacit assumptions about individual and social reality. The very fact that people do not tend to question the terms of normal, everyday life means that notions of health will reflect ongoing, long-term concerns and conventional understandings; understandings, it should be added, that are replete with the very concepts and ambiguities that structure responses to illness. Talking about health is a way people give expression to our culture's notions of well-being or quality of life. Health is a "key word," a generative concept, a value attached to or suggestive of other cardinal values. "Health" provides a means for personal and social evaluation.

Health is a particularly important concept in the modern west. In disenchanted, secular, and materialist cultures, health acquires a greater symbolic importance. Health substitutes for salvation and becomes a salvation of its own.[1] In such cultures, "man becomes his own measure" (Comaroff, personal communication). The biomedical definition of the self is encoded as a cultural program with health as its personal, medical, and political objective.[2] There exists, then, in western societies, an elaborate health discourse – actually several discourses (professional–medical, political, literary, popular–reformist, everyday–personal). An anthropology of contemporary cultures would do well to examine closely all of these discourses.

The interviews

In the spring and summer of 1981, I interviewed sixty adults in the Chicago metropolitan area. Conversations averaged from one and a half to two hours and were tape recorded. I did not pre-define my interest in health as either physical or emotional, nor did I identify myself with a medical purpose or carry out the interviews in a professional setting. Interviews took place in the homes of those with whom I talked. I introduced myself as a person writing a book on how people think about health. My intention was to talk with people from a spectrum of American urban life. I did not control for specific demographic character-istics since I was not interested in one particular group or in comparing the views of two or more groups. I attempted, with only partial success, to achieve as much social class, race, sex, and age variance as possible. Initial contacts were made through references from friends and acquaintances and then each person interviewed was asked to recommend one or two other names. Several chains of subjects were developed simul-taneously and I followed up those chains that widened the demographics. By the end, however, almost two-thirds of those interviewed were white, middle class, under forty, and female. Large and important categories of people were obviously not included or were only minimally included.

The object of this kind of ethnographic research is to see things "from the native's point of view." The effort must rely upon interpretation. Interpretation is not an account from a privileged position of neutrality of how people "think" about health. It is an attempt to discern meaning from what people have chosen to tell this particular researcher in the context of an interview, with all its distinct properties as a special kind of social interaction. The study of meaning is riddled with problems of shared and opposed assumptions and categories as well as dangers of unconscious, personal projections. Several "readings" are possible. The identification of themes is derived from a systematic analysis of transcripts and tapes. Categories of interpretation involve an interplay of theory and data: listening to and reading the interviews, categorizing topics along several dimensions, searching for integrating concepts, and listening and reading once again. I did not come to these interviews with the idea of "testing" a particular theoretical proposition. I did not know what I would find. In the interviews I attempted to minimize my directiveness, to allow people to speak without interruption, and to remain open to unanticipated avenues of discussion. This approach, of course, needed to be balanced against the need to address a consistent set of concerns. I wanted to know how people describe their health; how they define the term and what concepts are employed (each interview began with the questions, Are you healthy? How do you know?). I also wanted people to talk about their explanations for their state of health: what they identify about themselves or their physical or social environments as important; what they perceive as a threat to their health; and what, if anything, they believe they can or should do to protect or enhance their health. I asked people to identify situations, people, or events that have been important for their health, or for how they think about health. I was also interested in people's notions about responsibility for health and their moral judgments of self and others connected with health.

Most people in these interviews start off by saying that they are healthy, reflecting in part a strong moral imperative attached to health and to the normality of health. (This response also reflects that by medical standards most of these people would be considered healthy.) Health clearly represents a status, socially recognized and admired and therefore important for our identities. Most often, however, people go on to describe their health as variable rather than fixed. Health, in other words, is a state of being that is understood to shift with experience. It is a matter of degree and it is dynamic. Nor is health viewed as simply a physical matter. While many people discuss health in the prevailing medical idiom, most use terms and notions that extend beyond the confines of definition and explanation offered by the bio-medical sciences. Perceptions and beliefs about the physical experiences suggested by the word health are frequently vehicles for explaining social and emotional experience, just as emotional and social life provide explanations for the life of the body. Emotional and social well-being, in other words, find their confirmation in the body, and bodily states "make sense" in terms of social and emotional occurrences. The two bodies – the physical and the social – are given varied and complex expression in these accounts.

Medical discourse in western societies, reflecting the differentiation and reification of modern bourgeois thought, rarely encourages the exploration of such concerns, connections, and ambiguities. The experiential meanings and the cultural capacities that enable us to understand and confront the social and emotional dimensions of our health and illness experiences are diminished in the medical encounter and by the dissemination of medical modes of thought (Illich 1975). The social relations embodied in those experiences become disguised as biological facts (Taussig 1980). Given the extent of medicalization in American society, it is remarkable that in an everyday context so varied a discourse persists. The tenacity of "metaphoric" thinking in illness noted by Sontag (1977) and Taussig (1980) – from opposing perspectives about its desirability – can also be found in our normal, everyday ways of talking about health. An adequate account of the meaning of health in our culture must attempt to discover the concrete social and material experiences for which the word health is regularly believed relevant and appropriate. It must also seek to uncover the symbolic categories that order such experiences. The conception of knowledge represented by medicine is crucial. It is the most powerful, institutional claimant to jurisdiction over matters of health. However, a broader symbolic order needs to be examined. We must begin with an identification and interpretation of the symbolic modalities through which "health" is given expressive form.

Health as self-control

> "To be healthy takes a little more discipline."

A consistent and unmistakable theme runs throughout the interviews. Health is discussed in terms of self-control and a set of related concepts that include self-discipline, self-denial, and will power. When people talk about threats to health, explanations for health, or prescriptions for maintaining and improving health, one or more of these related values frame the discussion and set the moral tone.

Since the mid-1970s in the United States, the boundaries of what is popularly considered essential health behavior, or minimally responsible health behavior, have been expanding. The new health consciousness has ushered in an era of rising expectations fixed on improving or protecting the body. Whether in the name of health, fitness, or weight loss – themes that become entangled – some disciplined activity is usually mandated. It is a cultural climate in which people express the desire to be doing more, or guilt about not doing what is now conventionally expected:

Q: Are you healthy?
A: I am generally healthy in that I don't have any problems that inhibit me from going to work or anything else. I guess where I feel that I am not particularly healthy, perhaps, is maybe just in the consciousness that everyone seems to be going through now about health – jogging, not smoking, and all this. I am not really doing any of that and so I am concerned. . . . The fact is that I'm taking such a passive view or a passive role in whether I am healthy now or stay healthy.

The changing standards about smoking, diet, and exercise make this person feel unhealthy by the mere violation of one or more of these new taboos or the failure to do something active for one's health. To be healthy is almost equivalent to pursuing health through adopting the appropriate disciplined activities or controls. The means to health acquire the quality of an end in themselves:

Q: How do you know you are healthy?
A: I guess I judge it by the standards that I would read about if people are healthy. I get exercise. I don't smoke. I don't eat a

lot of red meat. I don't have a lot of cholesterol. I take vitamins. I get a physical every year. I think I'm healthy. . . . I try to do all of those things, so I think I'm healthy.

Discussion about health as a matter requiring self-control, discipline, denial, and will power is most clearly associated with a conception of health as a distinct goal. In this formulation, health is made the object of intentional action. Health is not a given; nor is it simply a result of good luck or heredity, two alternatives frequently mentioned. Neither is it believed to be an outcome of normal life activities, such as one's work, upbringing or current lifestyle. Health must be achieved. It is dependent on health-promoting behaviors. As the goal of health acquires a new-found importance, priorities must be reordered, a commitment made. The goal of health competes with other goals and therefore requires an active choice:

I think generally we have to have a more healthy attitude. Health has to be a bigger part of our lives. . . . I have to go back and take a look and change my lifestyle. I have to find time for it. . . . I think I have to be more concerned or excited about being healthier. My attitude now is passive. I am thinking a lot about it but I'm not really doing anything. I think I have to have more perseverance with the problem, make it a goal. Just like I have this goal for work, I should have this goal for health.

For this woman the ethic of health must be like the ethic of work. The Protestant world view extends to the body; it invades the domain of leisure. To speak of health in this way is to speak of resolve. Health as a goal necessitates the adoption of a more determined regime of restraint and denial – more "perseverance." It involves an effort to impose what are often perceived to be difficult changes on personal behavior and lifestyle, an attempt to curb ingrained, unhealthy inclinations and dispositions.

When people talk about health in this way, they often express that they lack control over the conditions of life that would allow time and energy to be devoted to health-promoting activities. Since health does not flow from normal, everyday activities, it requires a commitment of time and energy. One

must do something differently, reallocate scarce time, eliminate something else. The torrent of health-hazard warnings,
the ever-growing list of do's and don'ts overruns the capacity to
keep pace. "You end up not really doing everything you say
you're going to do." Health as a goal must find a place among
other goals; and highly structured lives, saturated with other
commitments and desired activities leave little space for
pursuing health. The dilemma in which this busy, professional
woman finds herself illustrates the common refrain:

> I have a lot of thoughts about what to do about health. I have
> a view towards doing more things. But I don't do any of them
> at this point. I have to find time for it. I think for us [she and
> her husband] it would start by finding time to exercise, and
> then having time to do the things you need to do on a diet –
> which probably means going to the grocery store more often,
> getting fresh fruits and vegetables, cooking more, which is
> preparation time, and then eating and cleaning up. That's
> more a part of your evening.

> My husband and I have gone through and are still at the point
> where we're very involved in our careers and our relationship
> together. I think people go through their life of getting mar-
> ried, buying a house, these typical steps, and building a
> career, and these are the focal points of your life. I mean
> taking that extra half an hour every day to exercise gets shuf-
> fled somewhere else and you don't do it. I was single for a
> long time and that would have been the perfect time to keep
> up my health.

> We both belong to a private club that allows us to do more for
> our health as far as exercise is concerned. It's just fitting it
> into that bloody schedule. Right now it seems difficult. It's
> like saying I don't have time to be healthy. But I'm going to
> school at night now and I do hope that when I get out of
> school I'll have a lot more time for exercising and for putting
> more time into eating right and quitting smoking.

> Maybe I don't press myself enough. Maybe I should be press-
> ing myself to have less down time – just watching TV. But I
> guess I need to relax. Maybe, though, I don't need as much.
> (These paragraphs were drawn from different parts of the
> interview.)

"It's like saying I don't have time to be healthy." There was a
sense among several people that health is a goal that sometimes
must be, or is unavoidably sacrificed to other values and pursuits (see also Davis 1963: 170). Choosing health is an
unaffordable luxury. The demands of job and career, of becoming established, of supporting a family, mandate the sacrifice of
other, less tangible goals. Health defined as an absence (of disease) has a less legitimate space than more positively defined
goals. And yet the expanding belief that this absent state
requires very "present" efforts may leave one uneasy. Here
there is a sense that leisure or "down time" must be converted
to the "up time" of health promotion. The work of self-
improvement, so characteristic of the middle class, requires a
continuous striving. The demand on the self is for a disciplining
of the use of time, a stricter economy of energy.

There are several kinds of response to the overwhelming
number of declared threats, but a frequent one is a disappointment in oneself or harsh self-judgments about lack of control
and thus the inability to keep up with the current health norms.
Here are comments from two smokers:

> I'm disappointed that I don't have more control. . . . We all
> have different strengths for different things and we all have
> weaknesses and so this is a weakness of mine and I accept it
> in a negative sense, but I know this is a weakness.

> My children make me feel guilty because I smoke. They are
> getting worse and worse about it. And because it is some-
> thing that I have a difficult time trying to stop, it makes me
> feel that there is just not enough will power in me. That is
> something I generally tend to feel guilty about. I was brought
> up to believe you should have perfect control over every-
> thing – especially things like drinking and smoking.

If judgment is applied to oneself, it is readily directed toward
others as well. Here are just two examples:

> I think people that don't exercise and who drink and smoke,
> there's not much use in trying to study them at all – because
> they're a total loss. That's no way to live.

> Anybody that wanted to could be healthy. I'm not saying
> that about somebody that has been given six months to live
> because they have cancer; but if somebody is free of any

major illness, I don't think there's any reason why his life couldn't be healthy. It's totally up to yourself, except maybe for the people that lived at Love Canal. But the people I know and the people I'm friends with, I don't think there's any reason why anybody can't be healthy.

Judgment of others and self-blame are themes that can be found throughout these interviews,[3] reflecting a general moralization of health under the rubric of self-responsibility. In an increasingly "healthist" culture, healthy behavior has become a moral duty and illness an individual moral failing. (See my treatment of this theme as it appears in holistic health and self-care literature (Crawford 1980).) In these interviews moral attributions were most likely connected with the conception of health as self-control: "You have to be man enough, woman enough, you have to be adult enough to control your own life." "Unhealthiness for me has connotations of neglect." "If only I were more disciplined." "It's a matter of realizing that I can get back the strength of will that I had a few years ago." "People bring it on themselves." "Everybody knows I have no self-control." "I let myself go."

There seems to be an inevitable progression from seeing health as a goal requiring choice and active commitment, through seeing the "problem" of health as a matter of control, discipline, denial, and will power, to expressing a moral verdict for the inability of self or others to meet the rather extensive expectations for optimal health behavior being elaborated in the media and throughout largely middle-class social networks. As will be discussed below, this related set of beliefs is in part an internalization of the values of inner directedness and self-creation characteristic of the middle class in industrial, capitalist societies.

If health is a metaphor for self-control, body weight is the metaphor within the metaphor. When people talk about health as a goal they are often describing their desire to lose weight. To be healthy is to be thin, literally to be "in shape." As one man put it, "within a second you make a judgment saying this person is healthy or not." At the same time, thinness is believed to be an unmistakable sign of self-control, discipline, and will power. The thin person is an exemplar of mastery of mind over body and virtuous self-denial.

> I know some people that are real disciplined. I have a friend; I wish I had as much discipline as her. She goes to exercise class four days a week. She rides her bike at least three miles three times a week. She runs. She doesn't overeat. She doesn't have an ounce of fat on her body.

Conversely, fat is a confirmation of the loss of control, a moral failure, a sign of impulsiveness, self-indulgence, and sloth. "People who are overweight are slovenly. They are unhealthy on purpose." In our weight-obsessed culture, the addition of just a few pounds can arouse deep anxieties about loss of control. Condemnation of self and others can be relentless. These pressures are especially applied to women, and in the interviews it was consistently women who mentioned weight. One feminist author (Chernin 1981) claims that for women in our culture there is a "tyranny of slenderness." A woman I interviewed, who talked about what is now recognized to be an "epidemic" of self-starvation among women, put the control issue this way: "That's the high that I get from fasting – like I've got this incredible self-control, and I can do anything. Knock 'em dead!"

While the notion of health as self-control was primarily expressed by professional middle-class people, it was by no means confined to that group. Blue collar workers also spoke of health in terms of the virtues of discipline although there was not the same idea of pursuing health as an active goal.

> I always was competitive in life, more or less, and I've always tried to be up there competing, playing games and sports, and in my studies, and at work, and in order to do that you have to keep yourself in good health. You have to more or less train, discipline yourself, let's call it that. . . . The greatest hazard to your health, one of the greatest, is to be lazy. I think that's a detriment, just as much a detriment to man as smoking and drinking, because that just ruins a man. He can't do a thing when he becomes lazy. He's just no good. His body's no good. He can't perform. He's just no good.

And from a steel worker, here is a similar conception of body and health, even more clearly connected with the virtue of hard work:

> I believe in working. I believe in it. If I wasn't at a steel mill it

would be some place else. And I would probably work just as hard. Got to have it, man. It is another key to health.

Q: Why is that?
A: You got to work. You got to work at something, put a lot of energy into something. You have to. That is what your body was really designed for – to be functional.

In both of these examples the body is seen as the body of a worker. The orientation is *performative*. Health as discipline is *functional* for, or equivalent to, hard work. And unlike the middle-class woman who equated the goal of health with the goal of work, there is less here a notion of purposive self-creation. The value of discipline is the same as the value of work – they both bestow a sense of self-worth.

Health as self-control: an interpretation

How might one account for the prominence of the self-control theme in these interviews? The most straightforward explanation is that there are *practical reasons* why people associate health with self-control. The argument would run something like this: In contemporary American society, many of the most serious threats to health are associated with personal behaviors. Our lifestyle has become health-denying. We consume unhealthy products, live a sedentary life, become addicted to harmful substances, and pursue reckless, high-risk activities. If health does not flow from a way of life, then actions must be taken that require individual determination. The individual striving for health in an unhealthy society must refuse to give in to conventional lifestyles. In such a society, health maintenance is a matter of abstentions and renunciations. In other words, self-control, discipline, denial, and will power are precisely the qualities of character needed to combat "bad habits" and to negotiate the minefields of health hazards.

There is much to be said for such an explanation. Within this practical account, however, important questions remain unanswered. What, for example, is the implicit definition of health in the conception of health as self-control? The quotations I have drawn upon to illustrate the theme reveal that health is thought of in physical terms (although as I will discuss below, control figured in some psychosomatic conceptions as well) and most often as the absence of disease. The implied theory of disease causation and therefore disease prevention depends on an idea of the body as a biophysical entity that can be threatened and maintained by physical agents and processes.

But doesn't such a conception reflect an objective physical reality, the practical reasoner might ask? Hasn't the western enlightenment given us the tools for understanding the material origins of disease and the instrumental capacity to control (therapeutically and preventively) the physical conditions identified by medical science as threats or assets to bodily functioning? Doesn't scientific knowledge provide the means by which rational control over the body can be achieved?

Again, such an explanation is wanting, not because the contribution of western biomedicine to our ways of thinking about health is insignificant; just the opposite. It is wanting because of the assumption that a "practical logic" is an adequate explanation. The very significance of instrumental or practical activity, however, can only be understood in the context of culture (Sahlins 1976). The underlying assumption of medical thinking – the body as an object of rational control – is treated as unproblematic. The practical activity of health promotion, whereby health is viewed as a goal to be achieved through instrumental behaviors aimed at maintaining or enhancing biological functioning, is integral to an encompassing symbolic order. It is an order in which the individual body, separated from both mind and society, is "managed" according to criteria elaborated in the biomedical sciences. Medical knowledge, internalized and reproduced in our everyday discourse, represents a distinct, although by no means universal, way of experiencing our "selves," our bodies, and our world. As Comaroff writes (forthcoming), western medicine "imprints . . . the 'reality' of the person as biological individual, and of the world as the product of rational materialism." Medicine is itself a metaphor for an instrumental mode of symbolization:

> The apparently "instrumental" acts of modern medical practice have . . . become important symbolic foci of secular ritual for us, and its techniques and concepts serve as metaphors of our state of being as biophysical individuals, seeking to enlist "natural" science in our secular opposition to the

> forces of disease, decay and death. . . . Indeed, "science" has
> become our primary symbolic order, in which "instrumen-
> tal efficacy" serves as our ritual mode, and "rational prac-
> tice" our dominant ideology.   (Comaroff, forthcoming)

Thus, medicine (and the medical notions implicit in our popular concepts of health as self-control) reflects, even as it power-
fully reproduces, this larger cultural order. The master symbol
that links these systems of meaning together is control.

If a practical account of health as self-control is to be convincing, it requires still further cultural and historical con-
textualization. My interviews do not and cannot demonstrate
that health as self-control is more prominent now. It is clear to
even the casual observer, however, that health promotion has
in the last few years become a widely shared goal among the
middle class. The form this "new health consciousness" has
taken emphasizes the pursuit of individual lifestyle changes;
changes that for the most part demand self-control, self-
discipline, self-denial, and will power. I believe that the following social changes and events have contributed to this increased
concern with individual health promotion.

Americans have acquired a sense of somatic vulnerability.
First, there is a belated recognition that disease patterns have
changed from infectious to chronic diseases, especially cardiovascular disease and cancer, and that medicine is relatively
ineffective in terms of providing a cure for these dread maladies.
Second, throughout the 1970s, numerous health disasters, a
multitude of health warnings, and a marked politicization of
public health issues transformed our sense of safety. It became
impossible to ignore that our living environment had become
sickening. By the end of the decade an "everything causes
cancer" humor had become a cruel joke. The toxic society had
come of age.[4] When the macro-conditions that affect health
appear to be out of control, self-control over the considerable
range of personal behaviors that also affect health is an only
remaining option. Particularly in a conservative political climate, when both political and corporate leaders repeatedly
warn that our jobs are dependent on giving business a free hand;
when, in other words, the social conditions perceived to affect
health are too massive, too remote, too unchangeable, people
will normally opt for a course of action within the sphere of

personal control. As expressed by so many people with whom I talked, people who for the most part did not dwell on environmental hazards, "Why worry about something you can't do anything about?"

There has also been a multifaceted disillusionment with medicine, not only with regard to ineffectiveness, but with the high costs of medical services and insurance, its bureaucratic indifference, and its iatrogenic outcomes. The 1970s was a decade distinguished by media exposés of various medical abuses; a malpractice crisis; a feminist movement that targeted medicine as one of the major sources of oppression for women and that directed its efforts toward reclaiming bodily control; a massive self-help movement that identified dependence on medicine as an obstacle to the values of dignity, autonomy, and mutual aid; and myriad alternative, "natural" or "holistic" therapies that extended the anti-medical mood.[5] Along with our corporeal insecurity, the disillusionment with medicine (at best ambivalent) has again thrown open the age-old question of how best to protect our bodies. Medicine is no longer the automatic answer.

Americans have also been exposed to a virtual media and professional blitz for a particular model of health promotion; one that emphasizes lifestyle change and individual responsibility. I have previously argued (Crawford 1977) that the effect and frequently the ideological motivation of this prevention model has been to blame the victim. The emphasis on individual responsibility for health mystifies the social production of disease and undermines demands for rights and entitlements to medical care. Beneath the rhetoric about the costs of medical care and the obligation of the individual to remain healthy lies a political program to shift the burden of costs back to labor and consumers and to paralyze regulatory efforts undertaken to control environmental and occupational hazards. The message is clear: "living a long life is essentially a do-it-yourself proposition." Don't expect therapeutic or social solutions to the problem of health.

The abundance of news and commentary on lifestyle and health has, in fact, shaken our complacency with regard to our most popular addictions. By November, 1981, a *Time* cover story officially announced that health and fitness had themselves become lifestyle. Health promotion and fitness have now acquired the momentum of a fad. Bodies are in motion on the jogging paths and in health clubs, with Jane Fonda, Diana Nyad, and Richard Simmons, with Jazzercise, Jamnastics, aerobic this or that, Kinetics, Nautilus, even Believercise, a born-again version of the same. Anti-smoking has become a national crusade; nutrition the subject of endless conversation. Themes become entangled: body shape, fitness, strength, endurance, natural living, health, beauty, youth, longevity, disease prevention, wellness, and of course, sex appeal. So do the targets of concern: inside and outside, cardiovascular conditioning and waistline, physical status and social status.

The commercialization of health and fitness is truly astounding. Advertising has attached every conceivable product to the changing physical fashion. A cascade of specialty magazines and books flood the market. Almost every major national magazine and network have run features on one or another aspect of the health and fitness revolution. In short, "health" and "fitness" are being manufactured. The complex ideologies of health are picked up, magnified, and given commodity form by the image makers.[6]

Self-control as a cultural theme

There is another way to approach the questions posed earlier: why is health conceived in terms of self-control? And why does a new health consciousness in which self-control is a prominent theme emerge at this time? I have argued that the practical activity of health promotion can only be understood in the context of culture. Now I would like to explore the proposition that "health" is a moral discourse, an opportunity to reaffirm the shared values of a culture, a way to express what it means to be a moral person (Haley 1978; Whorton 1982). From this perspective, the question is raised whether the emphasis on self-control and discipline in the way we talk about health can simply be understood as following from the practical necessities of achieving health; or, might such a conception also follow from the importance within our culture of the values of self-control and discipline? Self-control, self-discipline, self-denial, and will power may be attempted not only *in order to achieve* health; they may constitute the symbolic substance, the implicit meaning of the pursuit of health. It is possible to say that health is thought about in terms of self-control. It is equally possible that the concept of self-control is "thought" through the medium of health.

Self-control, self-discipline, self-denial, and will power are concepts that are fundamental to the western system of values. Each take on specific meanings in different historical periods and have been connected with various ideologies and social formations. They have appeared in the garb of religious asceticism. They underpin several philosophical systems. Weber (1930) identified these values as key components of the work ethic, a this-worldly asceticism understood as the product of a conjuncture of Protestant and entrepreneurial cosmologies. Norbert Elias (1978) writes of a "civilizing process," whereby controls over bodily expressions were elaborated and internalized as a function of market-defined social relations and class identity. Foucault (1977) describes a new kind of "discipline" in modern society, an epistemological regime bent on the maximum utilization of bodies by dominant powers. Control has been universalized by Freud as an internalized response to the unending war between biological instinct and social necessity, a theory given historical specificity and explicit critical usage by Marcuse (1955) and others. As discussed earlier in this paper, control has been considered the underlying ethic of an instrumental and objectifying mode of symbolization, nature and the body having become in this mode the object of positive knowledge and manipulation (Horkheimer and Adorno 1972; Balbus 1982). In the nineteenth century, self-control became the supreme virtue of a triumphant bourgeoisie, the foundation of "character" and achievement, the bedrock of an ideology of self-determination that continues to function both pragmatically as a guide to action and morally as a legitimation of privilege. A "culture of professionalism" took root in the same soil (Bledstein 1976). These values have become as inseparable from modern individualism as they have from our notions of adulthood, even personhood. It should not be surprising that "health," a concept that gives expression to our culture's notions of somatic, psychic, and social well-being, would provide the perfect metaphor for values that so fundamentally structure our social and cultural life. What I am suggesting is that in contemporary American culture, and particularly for the middle class, to be healthy is to demonstrate to self and others appropriate concern for the virtues of self-control, self-discipline, self-denial, and will power. Talking about health becomes a means by which we participate in a secular ritual. We affirm ourselves and each other, as well as allocate responsibility for failure or misfortune, through these shared images of well-being. The "health" of the physical body – at the same time a social body – validates conventional understandings.

Evidence presented by Haley (1978) and Whorton (1982) demonstrates that self-control and related concepts have appeared prominently in health discourse throughout much of the nineteenth and twentieth centuries. The importance of these categories in western culture would also suggest that their connection to our concepts of well-being may be long-standing. But does the revival of a cultural enthusiasm for health promotion under the sign of self-control indicate an increase in the importance of that sign in contemporary culture? Is there a new mandate for self-control, self-discipline, self-denial, and will power? I believe there are signs that in the last few years the mandate for control has, in fact, grown, that our notions of self and social reality are more infused with symbols of control. Does such a change appear in what we say and do about our bodies?

Historically, at least since industrialization, a primary source of the disciplinary ethic has been the world of work. Despite the celebrated decline of the work ethic and the claim that it has been replaced by a "culture of narcissism" (Lasch 1978), work continues as one of our most fundamental social values and as an experience thoroughly saturated with direct and indirect controls. Capitalist industrialization has brought a disciplining of minds and bodies to the "industrial clock" (Thompson 1967); a regulation of movement in terms of space and speed (Braverman 1976); a mobilization of energies through habituation, training, supervision, inducements, and sanctions (Foucault 1977); a definition of personhood in terms of "badges of ability," achievement, and the symbols of consumption that only success at work can buy. (A system of consumption based on debt financing imposes a discipline of payment). If no longer universally held to be the fount of progress, the bedrock of social obligation, or a sign of righteous self-denial, the work ethic persists through middle-class codes of achievement and professionalism and working-class values of "hard work," "manhood," "craftsmanship" and "sacrifice." Moreover, it is through the discipline of work that the American dream of deserved status and material reward is to be realized. Work is the so-called key to social mobility, the professed means by which one moves up in a putatively open class structure.

In an economic crisis, the discipline, control, denial, and will power associated with work are moved forward on the cultural agenda, an agenda that is both mandated and "chosen" as attempts are made to adapt to worsening economic conditions. A disciplining of labor is imposed. Unions are aggressively confronted. Workers in every sector, from professional to blue collar, must increase their "productivity," reversing the claimed trend toward slack and lack of effort. Job performance and output are formally and informally renegotiated. Wages are held down while the pace of work is speeded up. The new regime is internalized. We discipline ourselves. As unemployment surges, competition for keeping or obtaining jobs requires still greater effort. Those who have jobs work harder to keep them and become more submissive to the demands of management. Labor bites its lip in a discipline of silence.

Moreover, larger numbers of people are forced to live on less. And of those who have so far escaped, more are curbing spending in anticipation that their immunity may be temporary. Vacations are cancelled, retirement put off, optional medical care delayed. In a period of wage freeze or cuts, take-backs in benefits, and slashes in social programs, a discipline of consumption is also imposed. Corporate leaders talk of "cutting out the fat," and political leaders urge sacrifice. Again, we discipline ourselves in response, "tightening our belts" as diminishing personal income either imposes an unfamiliar self-denial or forces second jobs or overtime upon those fortunate enough to obtain them. As heating prices soar, thermostats are lowered and our bodies and spirits are prepared for a long economic winter. We internalize the mandate for discipline because it appears to us as an adaptive necessity.

The cultural reaction to hard times can take many forms. I am suggesting here that one of them is a hardening of bodies. I am not proposing that the new health consciousness is simply a response to the economic crisis. As I have stated, several factors converge to give health its present meanings. The interest in health was growing rapidly before our economic misfortune became fully apparent. I am arguing, however, that as we internalize the mandate for control and discipline, "health" and "fitness" are readily available means by which we literally embody that mandate. Our bodies, "the ultimate metaphor," refract the general mood. We cut out the fat, tighten our belts, build resistance, and extend our endurance. Subject to forces that lie beyond individual control, we attempt to control what is within our grasp. Whatever practical reasons and concerns lead us to discipline our bodies in the name of health or fitness, the ritualized response to economic crisis finds in health and fitness a compatible symbolic field.

It is the professional middle class, however – the social category least pressured by the economic crisis – that most readily adopts and displays the value of self-control, including its physical expressions.[7] But this too, I would argue, can be understood in part as a response to the economic crisis. For the middle class, the evocation of self-control is a ritual of identity and justification.[8] And in the face of class insecurity, the conspicuous pursuit of health – jogging, not smoking, health fashion, etc. – becomes a rite of belonging. Although a substantial segment of the middle class is still relatively protected, almost everyone is affected by the mood of foreboding and "getting down to business." Many of the familiar signs of being middle class – home ownership, steadily rising income, job security – are no longer so prevalent among those (especially people in their twenties and thirties) raised to expect them. When both class identity and perhaps an even more general sense of control are threatened (through, for example, the progressive instability of personal relationships, the increasing anxiety about nuclear annihilation),[9] it is reasonable to expect that the symbols of self-control may become more important, especially among those who have grown up believing that self-control is the foundation upon which everything they will accomplish in life depends. The body and "personal responsibility" for health is, I believe, the symbolic terrain upon which both the desire for control and the display of control is enacted.[10]

Health as release

Q: How would you define health?
A: It's being able to do what you want to do when you want to do it. It's nice to be able to do things. It's nice to be able to eat and drink what you want, not worrying about being overweight or sticking to the diet that the doctor told you to stick to.

Logically entailed in any discourse of self-control is its opposite. A disciplinary regime in the name of health is opposed by a belief in the salubrious qualities of release.[11] One discourse does not exist without the other. And as will be discussed, the interplay between them, apparent within individuals as well as within society, reveals an underlying symbolic and structural order, a logic of "freedom" and constraint which in advanced capitalist societies is inherent in the contradiction between production and consumption.

The releasing motif suggests pleasure-seeking rather than ascetic self-denials, the satisfaction of desire instead of the repression of desire. Release is the antithesis of discipline, a disengagement or extrication from imposed and internalized controls. Instead of a language of will power and regulation, there exists a language of well-being, contentment, and enjoyment. There is a resistance to changing lifestyle, a defiance of renunciatory health promotion models or an attempt not to worry about the multiple threats to personal well-being. Health is not rejected as a value, but it is often repudiated as a goal to be achieved through instrumental actions. In this conception, health is more likely to be understood in psychosomatic rather than purely physical terms. It is understood more as an outcome of the enjoyment of life and the positive state of mind derived from such enjoyment. Whereas in the dominant, control orientation, releases – such as food, drink, or various "excesses" – are viewed as antithetical to health, the source of bodily decline against which controls must be mounted, those who emphasize release celebrate these pleasures on the altar of health. "If it feels good, it can't be all bad." Finally, people speak of release when expressing a concern about stress, such as the competing pressures of over-work, family obligations and problems, and the emotional tensions arising from some life crisis, such as the death of a loved one, divorce, or a career disapointment.

Within the release modality, the most important ingredient for health is the psychological capacity for "not worrying." It is not so much the external threats themselves that are considered dangerous, but one's personal reaction to them. These externals are often taken as givens; risks are inescapable. In the absence of a capacity to control one's life situation, more characteristic of working-class experience, what is important is to have another stance toward it, a positive and easy-going attitude. "Enjoy it. Shoot, you only go around once," pronounces one man in rejecting health-motivated renunciations. "I'd rather party," claims another in disdain of hygienic moralizing:

> It's hard to crack a joke. They take it too seriously. Some doomsday device is hanging over their head. Maybe it is, I don't know. There's other things. I'd rather party. I work all the time and, you know, somehow there are other things more entertaining than listening to someone spout off their view of health.

The discipline of work is likened to the discipline of health-mandated controls. Leisure time, for these hardworking men, will not be invaded by still more disciplines. Neither can present self-denials be justified by their future effects. Here, again, is the steel worker quoted earlier:

> I'm saying that I'm not going to worry about when my time is up. I just worry about when my time is here. When my time is up then I'll probably be ready. I'm not going to worry about it in the least, in the least, you know. That doesn't mean I'm going to run out in front of a car; I'm not going to rush it. But as far as smoking and drinking and all of that – smoking hasn't made a real effect on my life other than I kind of enjoy smoking a cigarette too.
>
> It's that enjoyment thing again. You want to get something out of it. . . . You got every right in the world to satisfy yourself. So I say do it. . . . I'm going to work and I'm going to enjoy the fruits of my work and I'm going to be happy and I'm going to lead a full and productive way of life.

While for this man physical control is necessary in order to work, the self does not appear to be constituted through such control. Work, although necessary for a "full and productive" life, is subordinated here to the value of immediate enjoyment. There is no value in delaying gratification.

If for some, ignorance is bliss ("Years ago we didn't know about all these things and we lived a happier life"), for advocates of a worry-free existence the problem of health is precisely a public discourse that instills fears and demands more controls over behavior:

Q: So what do you think they should do about the cancer problem?

A: I think they should keep their damn mouths shut about it. If you get rid of cancer there is going to be something else. There is always going to be plagues in this world. There always was. . . . I've got to bring fear into it again because you listen to the news and it says if you drink three cans of beer a day it is like smoking two packs of cigarettes. That is the new thing they have come out with now. And then you are told, "don't use saccharine; don't use this; don't use that. Don't eat junk foods; don't do this; don't do that." It's always *"Don't."* "This is bad for you; that is bad for you." Now if you are thinking I'm not going to eat that because so and so said it is no good for me then that can cause a lot of fear. It would cause fear in me if I thought that way. With that kind of thinking I'm going to be scared to death. And if I'm afraid and full of fear, I'm not going to be healthy.

Here again is the perception of lack of control. Rather than intensify controls over the body, the adaptive response is release. Attempting more controls itself becomes a hazard.

This impatience with the growing list of proscriptions on pleasurable activities is echoed by those who feel that what is most threatened is their freedom, defined as pursuing a "lifestyle" with no restraints on consumption. This man reveals a deep resentment of the imposition of controls that would in any way constrain "living the good life:"

Q: You don't change your behavior in any way in response to health warnings?

A: No, I don't. And the people who do that, I think they might be more healthy than I am, but I don't know, they just worry about everything under the sun. Worry itself can cause more problems than actual illness.

Q: Why is that?

A: When you hear about something causing a problem – a doctor comes up with a study and says you shouldn't have
   coffee any more, and people keep responding to all these
   things – "You shouldn't eat; you shouldn't have butter;
   you shouldn't have starches; you shouldn't have" – your
   whole lifestyle becomes prone to – You become a reactionary. Instead of a person living your own life, you are
   living a life where people are saying you are being threatened by this or that. . . . You live in a shell; you don't enjoy
   life. The fact is that I want to live a certain lifestyle. I don't
   want to be forced by any kind of worry about health that is
   really not based in reality of fact. . . . Now they start coming out with everything under the sun is going to cause
   cancer. What does that do to people? I just say to hell with
   it. If I've been eating it, I'm going to keeping eating it. I'll
   get check-ups, sure, but I'm not going to worry about it.

Despite the tenor of some of the preceding remarks, each of
these men could not be said to simply disregard health. The
emphasis on feeling good involves a psychosomatic conception. A perfectly healthy body will do no good if its achievement
demands a punishing disciplinary regime. Health is enjoying
life without worry and without a self-denying load of constraints. Health is pursuing a free "lifestyle," individually
chosen and externally obstructed by no one: "Ideal health is
being able to do my own thing." Or again, "Health is being able
to do what you want to do when you want to do it." Health in
this conception cannot derive from controls, denials, and disciplines; they only interfere with the positive experience of
enjoyment. Perhaps overwhelmed by the endless proliferation
of threats, these individuals refuse to get on what they see as a
health hazard merry-go-round. Worrying about health will
undermine one's sense of well-being, may induce illness ("I
have a whole slew of relatives to prove that"), and at the very
least will interfere with the pleasures that make life worth-
while. The attitude is best summarized in the following comment from a salesman:

Q: Are men healthier than women or are women healthier
   than men?

A: I think men are on the whole healthier than women due to

the fact that I think they feel better. I think they feel healthier. They may have the same aches and pains, but if a man doesn't notice it, or doesn't want to notice it, I would tend to think that that's healthier. The woman may live longer because she does notice it and maybe takes care of if, *but if he feels better, who is healthier?* It gets back to what my interpretation of being healthy is: if you feel healthy, you are healthy. You may kick the bucket next week but you're healthy. Now a doctor may have a different interpretation than that. You have a foreign body invading your system, he would say you are not healthy. And from his reality he is right. But not from my reality. Because I don't go to a doctor every day and ask him, do I have a foreign body invading my system? From day to day it is how do I feel? And if I feel healthy, I'm healthy. If I feel sick, I'm sick.

This remarkable statement also reveals one dimension of an anti-medical discourse found throughout the interviews. The cosmology of instrumental, future-oriented control is rejected in favor of an immediate, experiential ethic. Here the contrast between a reified, objectifying concept of health and a definition of health grounded in everyday, social–emotional experience is clearest. The physical body (the reality of the doctor) is opposed to the social body ("day-to-day" reality). The comment highlights the distance of the release conception of health from the language of control and its underlying ethos of inner-directedness goal-seeking, and self-creation. Health as release sits uneasily with both medical discourse and with the medicalized conceptions of health found in everyday life.

Just as those who conceive of health in terms of self-control and discipline often complain of being unable to achieve their objective, people who regard health as a matter of release also frequently talk about how they are unable to relax or "let go." As with the value of self-control, there is a difference between principle and reality. In fact, many of those who prescribe "not worrying" as the key to health are preoccupied with worries, revealing an ongoing struggle to attain the desired freedom from "pressures:"

Q: How do you account for your high blood pressure?
A: Well, I say one thing, I say pressure causes high blood pressure more than anything. You can be pressured like if you

worry, you can be pressured with your family, and if you have a job, and being a woman you've got pressure. There's three things you've got pressure from. You got pressure at home; you got pressure on the job; and you got pressure away from home. You might be working and you get to thinking about what to fix. You go out shopping and you have to pick and pick and pick and see what you can get to last until the next paycheck comes in. A woman is under a whole lot of pressure.

Q: Tell me more.

A: Oh brother, if you've got a husband you got pressure (laughing). That's the biggest pressure of all. And when you got kids – that's pressure. A mother never gets through worrying about kids, whether they are little, big, or grown. I am more worried about them now than I was when they were little, because out there I don't know where they are. It's a sick society out there. You don't have to do nothing now that somebody do something to you. So that's pressure.

But I don't worry. This is the way it is with me. Sometimes the kids go out and they don't come in at the time they say they're going to come in. I might lay there and just see things happening to these kids but then I catch hold of myself and say, "Lord, whatsoever your will, protect them, it's going to be done." So I don't worry about it; but I don't rest so well. I just don't lie down and worry. What's going to happen is going to happen. It's hard to accept these things, but what's ever going to happen is going to happen, regardless if I worry or if I don't worry. So when I come to that state of mind, I don't worry.

This comment deserves much more attention than can be given here. One can see, for example, how the whole language of sickness and the body reflects and reproduces the contradictions of her social world. Here also is a clear example of release as an adaptive response to the experiences of uncontrollability – and the difficulty of achieving a sense of well-being under such difficult circumstances. Also notice that the attempt not to worry, turned into a struggle, begins to sound like a discipline. Not to worry under circumstances in which pressures are intensely felt requires will power. "Don't worry!" becomes a command:

I like to wipe any bad thought out of my mind. When my mind goes astray on me and says, "Hey, you know, what's that pain?" it came back twice; or "I don't feel too good," I like to wipe it aside. You attack it mentally and say, "it's not there;" or "I feel good." So I can continue whatever I'm doing without worrying about it.

If health is equated with feeling good, as distinct from following rules of health medical authorities say will reduce chances of illness or early death, a mind-over-matter psychosomatics is frequently the conceptual vehicle by which health is to be achieved.

Q: How do you account for why you are healthy?
A: Well, I want to be healthy. You know, I don't want to be ill. That may be the most important factor of all.

The strategy proposed for maintaining health is a determination to maintain a healthy attitude, a positive mental outlook, an assertion of the power of the mind. Health can be had by wanting it. In the mind-over-matter formulation, one discipline is substituted for another.

Health as release – an interpretation

Power would be a fragile thing if its only function were to repress, if it worked only through the mode of censorship, exclusions, blockage and repression, in a negative way. If, on the contrary, power is strong this is because . . . it produces effects at the level of desire.   (Foucault 1978: 59)

In the limited space remaining I can only suggest the directions that an interpretation of the release modality might take. First, it is important to note that although there are people who speak mostly one or the other language, a significant number of those I interviewed speak both, at one point declaring the importance of controls, and at another expressing a longing to be free of disciplines.[12]
As with self-control, there are practical or instrumental reasons why health is understood in terms of release. Health, this time defined more generally as well-being or "feeling good" (almost always involving a somatic as well as a psychological

component) may be maintained or improved through releasing activities and states of mind. Listening to people talk about health is to hear of considerable pressures in their lives, often cited as the source of physical tension, pain, or exhaustion. Several people talked about emotional strain, distress, or apprehension. Frequently, these and other emotional–social problems were linked with specific diseases or illness episodes, or were seen as threats to physical health. Repeatedly, I heard the lists of anxieties we have come to expect: money and future security (most frequently), employment, job or school performance, personal safety, concerns about children. As one low-income woman speculated with regard to the relationship between anxiety about money and hypertension, "Everybody has the same thing – frustration. . . . We got to worry trying to get money; they got to worry about trying to keep it." Many complained about not being able to relax, citing factors such as being too busy, too much work, the difficulties of managing both work and domestic responsibilities, their own personality, or simply "too tired". Most of these people would probably find absurd the suggestion that they find time for health-promoting activities such as jogging. Finding time for "the self" may be an impossible dream for some of these highly pressured people (for example, single working mothers).

This is not the place to review the voluminous literature on the social and psychological factors increasingly being linked to various measures of physical health. There is considerable evidence, however, that the imposition of extensive or "surplus" controls, including the internalization of the cultural mandate for self-control, or conversely, perceptions of uncontrollability or helplessness, are an important source for what one writer (Freund 1982) calls "bodily deregulation:" endocrinological and neurological changes, muscular tension, and the inhibition of physical expression. These physiological changes have in turn been connected with several diseases, sleep problems, and painful physical conditions such as low back pain. The "fetishization of self-control" may itself become a destructive coping pattern:

> Self-control can become a fetish and "freeze" or inhibit a person so that letting go (even in situations in which "letting go" is functional) becomes impossible. This type of internal

control is an expression of "bourgeois individualism" that denies the need for supportive social contexts and imposes a stigma on those who either temporarily or permanently display an inability to function or cope, as in the cases of mental patients and alcoholics.
(Freund 1982: 61)

Numerous psychological and physical therapies – Reichian, gestalt, and several now called holistic – are largely aimed at helping the individual (of course, almost always middle class) achieve release from these embodied controls.

Like the public discourse on physical hazards, there has also been an escalating public discourse on the importance of release for achieving health. In the last few years stress has become an important word in our vocabulary. As psychologists and social scientists have turned their attention to the body, the profusion of professional literature is popularized in portrayals of the "type A personality," the "cancer-prone personality," and stress-inducing lifestyles. Stress has become a public enemy no longer confined to ulcers and heart attacks. Stress is now held responsible for everything from an outbreak of herpes to a general undermining of resistance to any disease. Advertisements for stress-reducing products are inescapable. The American Cancer Society features stress in its list of warnings. Stress "management" has become a component of employee relations and "burnout" a growing concern in the professions. The popular discourse on stress is a rich one and requires a careful examination (see Young 1980). Is there, for example, an ideological and political context shaping the emergence of stress as a concept and model of prevention similar to the model of prevention emphasizing the physical hazards of individual lifestyle? In the stress paradigm, how is the problem defined (where is stress located?) and what solutions are proposed? I have argued elsewhere that the contribution of holistic health to the discourse on stress is characterized by a psychological reductionism that reinforces individualistic solutions (Crawford 1980). Here I would simply point out that when people talk about stress, or some related concept like pressure, they are usually talking about health in terms of release. (I do not, however, want to argue the reverse, reducing the release concept of health to the experience of stress. Some who talked about health in terms of release expressed absolutely no concern about stress, but only the desirability of feeling good or living the good life.)

Release as a cultural theme

The question raised earlier about the metaphorical features of
health as self-control can be asked about release as well. Is
release simply a practical orientation toward achieving psychosomatic health? Or is talking about health in this way an
opportunity to give expression to one of our culture's most
fundamental symbolic categories, one of our most widely
shared values? Again, the latter kind of interpretation is not
opposed to nor does it exclude the former.

Every culture organizes releases from its normal renunciations or "moral demand systems" (Rieff 1966). Festivals, holi-
days, ecstatic and orgiastic religious experience, a variety of
intoxications, war, pogroms, and sport and games are a few of
the more important forms. Dionysus and Bacchus are deities
that have persisted through the ages. If culture normally
represses sexual expression, it also provides for its de-
sublimation (Foucault 1978). Occasionally, celebrations of
release can turn against the social order, but typically release is
a means by which societal tensions are managed.

In contemporary American culture, release is not only an
essential mode of relieving pressures that otherwise might not
be contained, it is also the indispensable creed of its economic
system. Release has been appropriated to the requirements of
consumption. For an economy that normally requires ever
greater levels of consumption, a symbolic order based on self-
control is ruinous. Rather than delay gratification, the imperative is to indulge. Rather than deny the self, the premise is
instant contentment. Social institutions are mobilized to produce a personality structure compatible with consumption.
Whereas production requires a structuring of time to the industrial clock, consumption must reorganize non-working time
into "leisure" and "lifestyle" – a transformation into time
available for buying and using an endless array of products. The
sign of our culture, projected on billboards and television
screens, is unambiguous: the "good life" means a life of consumption. The freedom to consume has become the image of
the "free world" (Berger 1972). And if it is true that we now
inhabit a "culture of narcissism," it is in large part a culture of
consumption that has pushed aside the older values rooted in
community, family, and communal moral purposes (Ewen

1976; Lasch 1978). In Rieff's terms, we have entered an "appetitive mode," a culture "based on the automaticity and ease with which an infinity of created needs can now be satisfied" (Rieff 1966: 239).

The problem with Rieff's analysis is his claim that the new culture based on release is an "anti-culture" in which controls disappear. The release modality cannot be understood in terms of the disintegration of the cultural mandates for controls as individuals enter a realm of detached, a-cultural abundance. The detachment from one set of controls, to the extent that it actually occurs (and the first part of this essay can be read as an argument that Rieff and his successors (e.g. Lasch) vastly underestimate the persistence of cultural mandates for controls), is the opportunity for the imposition of another. These new controls constitute an unprecedented and powerful cultural mandate of their own. The traditional ethics of denial and delay *must* be abandoned. A disciplined consumer *must* be pried loose from outmoded restraints and non-commodified enjoyments. Along with the scientific management of work, there is now a management of needs and pleasures – a science of satisfactions. Along with a design of disciplines there is a logic of desire. Needs must be attached to commodities. Rieff fails to understand that the surface individuality of our era hides a dictatorship of needs, a credal structure that molds the desire for individuality to conformist social ends. Consumption itself must be understood as a moral demand system, with its own controls, internalizations, and modal personalities. Our notions of self, fulfillment, and even health are substantialized through the "gorgeous variety of satisfactions" that the new system both offers and demands.

I have argued that health is a symbol through which various concepts of individual and social well-being are given expression. Here I am suggesting that the discourse of health as release can be understood in part as a representation of historically specific values of and mandates for release. The assumption is that cultural mandates, particularly crucial ones such as the one that yokes release to consumption, are internalized and reproduced through key concepts such as health; concepts which thus function as metaphors for those mandates. I am not arguing that *the* meaning of health as release can be understood in these terms, any more than health as self-control can be interpreted as merely a reflection of the cultural mandates for discipline and control. None the less, these dominant cultural meanings are a good place to begin one's interpretation. But it is only a beginning. Symbols are appropriated for a multitude of individual purposes that in turn the analyst must attempt to understand in specific historical and subcultural contexts.

The opposition

"All of my self-control is used up not smoking cigarettes; therefore I don't have self-control for anything else. All my energy is used up . . . so I treat myself to everything I always wanted to eat."

Contemporary Americans are the objects and subjects of two opposing mandates, two opposing approaches to the attempt to achieve well-being. The opposition is structural. At the level of the social system it is a principal contradiction. The culture of consumption demands a modal personality contrary to the personality required for production. The mandate for discipline clashes with the mandate for pleasure. The managers of labor complain that the American worker has become hedonistic and undisciplined, that we have become too comfortable in our abundance; while the managers of consumption incite indulgence. Advertising, in offering a version of the good life "aimed at those who [are] despairing of the possibility of well-being in their immediate industrial environment" (Ewen 1976: 108–09), contributes to the erosion of discipline on which production depends. "Put a little weekend in your week!" reads the beer advertisment. Employers in industries experiencing high levels of on-the-job or lunch-time drinking are not likely to be happy with alcohol promotions that undermine the symbols of self-control and discipline associated with the work ethic (the week) with symbols of release from those controls (the weekend). Release extended to the shop floor is subversive. Self-control and self-denial extended to the market is equally subversive. Moreover, the disciplining of labor in terms of wage freezes and cuts comes up directly against the socially engineered expectations of abundant and expanding levels of consumption.

The contradiction in structure leads to a conflict in experience. As in the soft drink ads that portray young, athletic bodies, one must consume and stay thin at the same time. The omnipresent command, "Eat!" is countered by the moral imperative to control eating. Indeed, food becomes a central metaphor for our dilemma. Indulgence in eating is infused with guilt while denial of food elicits the feeling of deprivation. Constant dieting engenders a persistent desire to "indulge one's appetite." Both feast and fast become images of health and disease. No wonder that bulimia emerges as one of our most common eating disorders. It has become a key cultural statement of the contradiction. There is a "tyranny of slenderness" but there is also a tyranny of consumption. Like shopping, the desire to eat is a favorite form of coping. And for those who don't throw up or fast, exercise has become our most popular attempt to resolve individually the contradiction. If one of the meanings attached to smoking is relaxed control, one of the implicit codes of drinking is controlled indulgence. Some diseases are attributed to loss of control (especially those connected with obesity) while others are believed to be caused by too much control (cancer). Some psychologically-oriented cancer therapists urge their patients to take control of their lives and their bodies, while for a host of other diseases the message is to slow down. We starve a fever and feed a cold. Sexual "frenzy" and sexual repression are both considered pathogenic. Holistic health advocates prescribe a full array of programs emphasizing both control and release as the secret to "high level wellness."

The new health and fitness consciousness is also an embodiment of the opposition. The standard fare in most health clubs is an elixir of pleasure and pain. "We'll work you out and then we'll pamper you," advertises one Chicago club. "Fitness can be fun!" proclaims another. A growing number of clubs provide bars as well as barbells. Sexercise competes with exercise. (Some of my students assure me that health clubs are the best place these days to meet a potential sexual partner.) The body is reconstructed to the rhythms of your favorite music – "Jamnastics is a fun way to get your heart beating and your body toned." Advertisers of products that have been the subject of health warnings are not insensitive to the opposing values: "If you're still drinking de-caffeinated coffee because you should, here's one you'll drink because it tastes good." My favorite illustration of the attempt to manage the contradiction is a book entitled *Fitness Through Pleasure: A Guide to Superior Health for People Who Like to Have a Good Time* (Shimer 1982). The jacket, quoting the author, proclaims,

> Living to 100 doesn't have to mean no more parties. . . . We're not going to tell you to quit anything or even cut down if you decide you really don't want to. . . . We live with enough stress as it is. . . . We don't need burdensome health routines to weigh on us even more.

"Keep one thing in mind," the author counsels, "if it feels good, it can't be all bad."

The new health consciousness belongs to neither control nor release. People often speak of the necessity for "balance" or the avoidance of "extremes." And certainly, each symbol and its corresponding experiences find their power in opposition, an opposition that is perhaps basic to human life. The specific content of these forms, however, a product of living cultures, raises questions as to their easy integration. The contemporary mandates for control and release, reflecting a basic contradiction in the social body, mitigate against such a balance. The pursuit of health is bound to reproduce that contradiction.

Vertical oppositions: some notes

I have argued that health is a metaphor for generalized well-being. It is a concept that references key aspects of our cultural order. Concurrent with practical reasons for our conceptions of health, which are themselves symbolically ordered, other socially structured systems of meaning are given expression through "health." Americans find themselves astride two opposing mandates, one calling for self-control, the other for release. Both mandates appear as specific historical forms. Both mandates are internalized in varying degrees and are variously experienced depending on person and context. And both are central to our ideas of personal well-being.

But the foregoing commentary oversimplifies. The cultural modalities of control and release that play themselves out in our bodily experience should not be understood in a unitary fashion. Our concepts of our bodies and our understandings of health do not simply replicate cohesive or unitary cultural categories. Dominant cultural notions shape our concepts of health in complex relations with meanings that emerge from concrete physical–emotional–social experiences. These experiences do not simply conform to cultural mandates. The body is not only a symbolic field for the reproduction of dominant values and conceptions; it is also a site for resistance to and transformation of those systems of meaning. Cultural meanings are not only shared or given; they are fragmented and contested. They are contested because social life is divisive as well as cohesive. The body is a social body and the social body is fractured. Not only are systems of domination themselves contradictory, experiences of class, sex, race, and age also rupture meaning. Modes of perception and symbolic forms common to the entire society are filtered through hierarchically arranged social relations and the concrete experiences associated with one's position within them. Because of those experiences, we not only internalize dominant codes, values, or categories; we resist them, substituting our own meanings, transforming them, often putting to "subversive" use symbols intended for quite another purpose. Thus, the body and the concepts we use to describe our bodily experience represent a dynamic distribution of power, with all the contradictions that such a distribution produces in social life (see Comaroff, forthcoming). A symbolic modality like self-control or release is thus polysemic. The opposition of control and release is itself fractured by other oppositions. In attempting to account for the meaning of control and release in health discourse and in our culture the question is not only what kind of body does society require (Foucault 1980: 55–62)? It is also what kind of body emerges in opposition? As one commentator on the women's fitness movement recently put it, what is "the politically correct body" (Pollitt 1982)? I conclude this essay by raising some of these questions.

What, for example, are the political implications of the women's fitness movement? Is it a manifestation of cultural resistance or the continuation of a "tyranny of slenderness," a "Coming On Strong" to meet male expectations of a "New Ideal In Beauty" (*Time* 1982)? Jane Fonda claims that "Discipline is Liberation!" She argues that body consciousness is the first step toward an anti-corporate, environmental health consciousness. Similar claims have been made for the self-help movement; that it is the essential, prior step to empowerment. This stage theory of politicization is problematic, although I am not prepared to say that Fonda or the self-helpers are wrong. Stating the political connection, as Fonda and others do, may contribute to the eventuality. Interpretation is itself a political act that occurs in an everyday context.

Do women achieve some political benefit from becoming more physically fit? Do physical activity and strength, for example, bestow a new assertiveness and self-confidence? To what extent might rape, battering, and physical intimidation of women by men be reduced by women shedding the traditional images of vulnerability and physical submissiveness? Or is the attempt to gain control of one's body a diversion from the real political tasks that women face, an "illusion that control of the body's shape and appetites will resolve their dilemma" (Chernin 1981:107)? Is "taking responsibility" for one's own body – through "health" or "fitness" or "self-care" – a political act in itself? Or are individual lifestyle changes precisely what "power" requires of us at this historical moment?

These questions cannot easily be answered. Individual lives do not readily lend themselves to the analyst's categories of interpretation, perhaps especially those we call "political implications." There is an attitude among much of the left and many critical observers that the individual pursuit of health or fitness is by definition narcissistic, diversionary, or hopelessly encumbered by a reified medical discourse and practice. I have at times shared these sentiments (Crawford 1977, 1980). But at this writing I am still not sure. The opposition of control and release, which remember is only one dimension of a highly differentiated and complex health discourse, does not point to a clear political direction. Even though I have emphasized in this essay the hegemonic meanings that can be found in these clearly individualistic conceptions of health, it is also possible to see liberatory aspects in both modalities. Even if repressive cultural mandates are unavoidably internalized, the categories of self-control and release have no inherent ideological content. They can be and are appropriated for ends that are not wholly conformist.

I do not think it is a romanticization to suggest that in our individual attempts to achieve self-control and release there is *often* an element of resistance. Resistance occurs when cultural mandates and the concrete experiences they represent are perceived as injurious or as obstacles to well-being and an effort is made to do something about them. The political implication of such "resistance," however, is very much an open question. I have attempted to demonstrate how a key structural contradiction is expressed in conflicting notions of well-being. Our concepts of health unmask the horns of a dilemma: resistance to the "health"-denying aspects of one mandate will often take the form of the opposing mandate. But when mandates are appropriated to the act of resistance, they no longer simply function to achieve dominant ends. The meaning of symbols is transformed in everyday practice. Both consumption and disciplined work and self-denial can be put to counter-hegemonic use. Contemporary capitalism and perhaps all industrialized societies must now promote both mandates – and by doing so, a readily available symbolic framework for resistance to the opposing mandate is provided. True, by so providing, power reintegrates and co-opts resistance. In our unending search for the sources of liberatory change, we should not neglect this sobering reality. Neither should we ignore, however, that society's own contradictions contribute to and reinforce the inherent instability of relations of domination as expressed and promoted within each sphere.

Self-control and release understood as resistance, like their function as cultural mandates, must be seen as two sides of the same coin. It is the same society that paradoxically makes it difficult for us to attain control over the conditions that shape our everyday lives while concurrently undermining our capacity for "healthful" release from imposed and internalized controls. That the body is the site for resistance should not be surprising. The mandates of control and release are experienced physically. Power imposes its agenda and achieves its objectives through our bodies. Certainly the political struggle for well-being must extend beyond our individual bodies. But to ignore the effects of power on our bodies is to miss a crucial arena for the exercise of power and for its transformation. Our bodies are social bodies. We need to become more aware of how our bodies are both the metaphor and the substance of our struggle against domination. Only then will we be able to move our submerged and individual gestures of resistance toward more collective and consciously political ends. "Health" is but one dimension.

Notes

1 In his essay on contemporary western cultures, Rieff concludes: "That a sense of well-being has become the end, rather than a by-product of striving after some superior communal end, announces a fundamental change of focus in the entire cast of our culture – toward a human condition about which there will be nothing further to say in terms of the old style of despair and hope" (Rieff 1966: 261).

2 Foucault identifies "the emergence of the health and physical well-being of the population in general as one of the essential objectives of political power. . . . Different power apparatuses are called upon to take charge of 'bodies,' . . . to help and if necessary constrain them to ensure their own good health. The imperative of health: at once the duty of each and the objective of all" (Foucault 1980: 170).

3 Blame is also a frequent by-product of psychosomatic conceptions of health (Zola 1972). In my interviews people expressed the belief that others have a hidden desire to be sick, that worry or "negative" thinking is the cause of illness, or that the lack of good health flows from some personality defect, a literal "fatal flaw." One man I interviewed blamed his inability to control his anger and disappointment over career reversals for his cancer. A woman traced her polio to her childhood truculence. Also see Sontag (1977) and Davis (1963) for popular conceptions of moral culpability for cancer and polio respectively.

4 These events, in turn, can be read as symptoms of a more fundamental change in American society, the physical location of a wider cultural crisis along with its attendant anxieties. The secular religion of capitalism – unlimited growth and continual improvement in living conditions – came up against the objective reality of "limits" – an environment that could no longer support without irreversible damage the weight of unrestrained industrial production. The 1970s was also a decade of deteriorating public services, stagnating real income, and slowing rates of growth. Following on top of the urban rebellions of the 1960s, Vietnam, and then Watergate, the environmental and economic crises of the past ten years have shattered the serenity of America's post-World War II secular meliorism. Cancer, acid rain,

and Love Canal are macabre signs of the end of a dream, the symbols of a social body wildly out of control. The changed mood is captured by the advertisement for a popular pain reliever: "Life Got Tougher – We Got Stronger!"

5 These occurrences also are expressions of an underlying loss of confidence in established institutions and professions that developed in the late 1960s and throughout the 1970s. The etiology of this decline in confidence is complex, but again, one must surely cite the Vietnam war, Watergate, and not least of all the student and youth revolts of the 1960s which raised basic and enduring questions about the fabric and core institutions of American society (see Skolnick and Currie 1979).

6 One important sub-current in this complex ideological stream is that significant numbers of middle-class young people who had been involved in varying degrees in the political issues and "counter-culture" of the 1960s turned to health as a kind of extension of their political and social protest. "Natural living" and "taking reponsibility for one's own health" have been perceived by many as ways of making less collective, but none the less political statements. Nuclear power and toxic chemicals reinforced the perception. The idea of a "holistic" health outside the medical establishment, health food stores (in which one could experience a sense of instant community), and the health sub-culture in general, offered the symbols of a continuing nonconformist identification. For this portion of the middle class – the 1960s generation, now largely in their thirties – "health" is a tie that continues to bind. Of course, for many others health (and the "human potential" movement) became an attractive vehicle for the journey from a politics of confrontation with which they may never have felt very comfortable, or with which they became extremely disappointed. The distance so many have traveled is perfectly captured by the term, "the me generation." Of those who see the pursuit of health as a political statement, one must question what political has come to mean. Alternatively, what we too often simply conclude is narcissistic may also co-exist with submerged political understandings.

7 This point should not be overstated. The internalization of controls occurs throughout the social structure and is likely to appear in different forms in lower economic strata. Not only is there a dissemination of middle-class values of self-control, internalized body controls emerge directly from working-class experience. Highly regulated body movements in factory and assembly line work, for example, or the demands on the body of overtime and shift work; or the constant repression of anger and aggression when such expression would result in retaliation from supervisors

or other authorities – these mandated physical controls may easily become a generalized physical style (see Freund 1982). As discussed earlier, the value of physical control is more likely to be linked directly with the requirements of job performance. It is the *display* of self-control that may be more distinctly middle class. And because they have more time, flexible schedules, money, are less likely to be drained by strenuous job requirements, and are more exposed to media–medical reports about health hazards, the middle class are more likely to choose health and fitness as an arena for such display.

8 Note the open anger and hostility expressed by a large portion of the middle class towards the poor, the unemployed, and the homeless. Economic misfortune is explained by lack of control (having too many babies), lack of discipline (too lazy to find work), lack of will power (unwillingness to work at whatever job is available), and lack of self-denial (inability to save for hard times).

9 A growing number of people cite the threat of nuclear destruction as a primary concern and worry. The ultimate power over our bodies – the power to inflict mass, violent death – is more imposing than ever. Is it surprising that in such a climate of terror we should rediscover our bodies? The daily workout is the perfect antidote. Again, it is a ritual of control.

10 Mary Douglas (1966) contends that any group that feels its identity threatened will expand the number of controls that regulate the group's social margins. The passageways of the body, the points at which the outside may "pollute" the inside, become the points at which controls are imposed. Thus, dietary and sexual taboos are elaborated. The body is literally "closed off" from other social groups; external threats are neutralized. Thus, group identity is protected. The morality of health is a middle-class morality. Prohibitions against smoking, unhealthy diet, and at-risk sexual promiscuity are the signs of "responsibility" and respectability. The reputed "internal locus of control" of the middle class may thus not simply be a matter of a social experience that imparts a sense of controllability; it may also be essential to middle-class self-image.

11 The term release is drawn from Phillip Rieff (1966). Rieff advances an argument that appears to be the exact opposite of my interpretation that contemporary health discourse is largely about control. Controls, Rieff believes, have practically given way to releases. In his interpretation of contemporary culture as a release-dominated "anti-culture" (culture, for Rieff, is equivalent with controls), Rieff sees the triumph of an individualistic society in which the unattached person seeks a personal salvation. The

bedrock of the new culture is a "gospel of self-fulfillment." "For the culturally conservative image of the ascetic, enemy of his own needs, there has been substituted the image of the needy person, permanently engaged in the task of achieving a gorgeous variety of satisfactions" (Rieff 1966: 241). My use of the term release is somewhat different from Rieff's. At times Rieff essentially equates release with the decline of community and its "moral demand systems" through which the individual had previously sought personal salvation. Thus, he would include my own category of self-control in his category of release since it involves a pursuit of individual well-being apart from communal purpose. I am using the term to refer to a particular set of notions about how to achieve individual well-being. However, as I have already contended with regard to self-control and will argue as well about release, I believe that these individual pursuits of well-being represent cultural imperatives or, in Rieff's terms, "moral demand systems."

12 The two are perhaps inseparably linked, after all. Discipline and denial, understood as a restraint on desire, generate an intensification of desire. In turn, that intensification appears to engender its own tendency toward confinement. (Is there not pleasure in denial and control? Or a hidden discipline in pleasure?) We seem to carry within us an opposition that, however long its historical genesis, or however deeply rooted in an eternal opposition between biological instinct and social necessity, finds profuse expression in contemporary American culture.

References

Balbus, I. (1982) *Marxism and Domination*. Princeton, NJ: Princeton University Press.

Berger, J. (1972) *Ways of Seeing*. Harmondsworth: Penguin.

Bledstein, B. (1976) *The Culture of Professionalism*. New York: W.W. Norton.

Braverman, H. (1976) *Labor and Monopoly Capital*. New York: Monthly Review.

Chernin, K. (1981) *The Obsession: Reflections on the Tyranny of Slenderness*. New York: Harper & Row.

Comaroff, J. (forthcoming) Symbolic Healing: Medicine as a Socio-Cultural System. In F. M. Ricci (ed.) *The Social History of the Bio-Medical Sciences*, vol. V. Milan: F. M. Ricci.

Conrad, P. and Schneider, J. (1980) *Deviance and Medicalization: From Badness to Sickness*. St Louis, Missouri: Mosby.

Crawford, R. (1977) You are Dangerous to your Health: The Ideology and Politics of Victim Blaming. *International Journal of Health Services* 7: 663–80.

——(1980) Healthism and the Medicalization of Everyday Life. *International Journal of Health Services* 10: 365–88.

Davis, F. (1963) *Passage Through Crisis: Polio Victims and their Families.* Indianapolis: Bobbs-Merrill Publishers.

Douglas, M. (1966) Purity and Danger: An Analysis of Concepts of Pollution and Taboo. London: Routledge & Kegan Paul.

——(1970) *Natural Symbols: Explorations in Cosmology.* New York: Pantheon.

Elias, M. (1978) *The Civilizing Process: A History of Manners.* New York: Urizen Books.

Ewen, S. (1976) *Captains of Consciousness: Advertising and the Social Roots of the Consumer Culture.* New York: McGraw-Hill.

Foucault, M. (1977) *Discipline and Punish: The Birth of the Prison.* New York: Vintage.

——(1978) *The History of Sexuality: An Introduction.* New York: Pantheon.

——(1980) *Power/Knowledge: Selected Interviews and Other Writings.* New York: Pantheon.

Freund, P. (1982) *The Civilized Body: Social Domination, Control and Health.* Philadelphia: Temple University Press.

Haley, B. (1978) *The Healthy Body and Victorian Culture.* Cambridge: Harvard University Press.

Horkheimer, M. and Adorno, T. (1972) *Dialectic of the Enlightenment.* New York: Herder & Herder.

Illich, I. (1975) *Medical Nemesis: The Expropriation of Health.* New York: Pantheon.

Lasch, C. (1978) *The Culture of Narcissism.* New York: W. W. Norton.

Marcuse, H. (1955) *Eros and Civilization.* Boston: Beacon.

Pollitt, K. (1982) The Politically Correct Body. *Mother Jones* (May): 66–7.

Rieff, P. (1966) *Triumph of the Therapeutic: Uses of Faith after Freud.* New York: Harper & Row.

Sahlins, M. (1976) *Culture and Practical Reason.* Chicago: University of Chicago Press.

Shimer, P. (1982) *Fitness Through Pleasure: A Guide to Superior Health for People Who Like to Have a Good Time.* Emmaus, Philadelphia: Rodale Press.

Skolnick, J. and Currie, E. (1979) *Crisis in American Institutions.* Boston: Little, Brown.

Sontag, S. (1977) *Illness as Metaphor.* New York: Farrar, Straus & Giroux.

Taussig, M. (1980) Reification and the Consciousness of the Patient. *Social Science and Medicine* 14B: 3–13.

Thompson, E. P. (1967) Time, Work-Discipline, and Industrial Capitalism. *Past and Present* 38: 56–97.

Time Magazine (1981) The Fitness Craze: America Shapes Up. 2 November: 94–106.

——(1982) The New Ideal in Beauty: Coming on Strong. 30 August: 72–7.

Turner, T. (1980) The Social Skin: Bodily Adornment, Social Meaning and Personal Identity. In J. Cherfas and R. Lewin (eds) *Not Work Alone*. London: Temple Smith.

Weber, M. (1930) *The Protestant Ethic and the Spirit of Capitalism*. London: Allen & Unwin.

Whorton, J. (1982) *Crusaders for Fitness: The History of American Health Reformers*. Princeton, NJ: Princeton University Press.

Young A. (1980) The Discourse on Stress and the Reproduction of Conventional Knowledge. *Social Science and Medicine* 14B: 133–46.

Zola, I. (1972) Medicine as an Institution of Social Control. *Sociological Review* 20: 487–504.

Acknowledgements

A special thanks to Jean Comaroff who at several points in this essay suggested extensions of my argument. Also, I owe much thanks to Ike Balbus for his careful criticisms.

Part Two

Capital interests and

the role of the state

Three

The crisis of the international capitalist order and its implications on the welfare state

Vicente Navarro

This chapter[1] analyzes the current crisis of the international capitalist order and its consequences for the welfare state policies of developed and underdeveloped capitalist countries. Special emphasis is given to the impact of the crisis on state health care policies in those countries. The first part discusses capital's and labor's response to the crisis, with special focus on (1) capital's political and ideological interventions in the areas of production, consumption, and legitimation; and (2) their realization as health care policies. The second part analyzes (1) the major capitalist responses to the crisis, that is, the "market" and the "social contract" strategies; and (2) their consequences in health care policy. The last part critically evaluates the call for a new economic order and its limitations.

Introduction: the crisis and the welfare state

Fifty years after "The Crash," the *Wall Street Journal* (the mouthpiece of financial capital in the United States), published an article on the US economy which concluded, "not since that time has the western system of power been under such stress as now . . . the US and other western economies are in deep trouble . . . the western capitalist order is being questioned" (1979: 5). It is the intention of this paper to discuss the nature of that stress, of that trouble, and of that questioning, and to analyze their implications for the welfare state policies of the capitalist world.[2] Let us first clarify that the capitalist world is not merely an aggregate of capitalist countries, but is an international system with an overall structure of definite interrelated parts. This overall structure can best be understood in terms of core capitalist countries (usually referred to as developed capitalist countries) and peripheral countries (usually referred to as underdeveloped or developing capitalist countries) (Sweezy 1979).

The crisis in the core capitalist countries appears in many economic, political-juridical, and ideological dimensions. On the economic level, we find that the current crisis is characterized by (1) extremely high levels of unemployment, with the number of unemployed in 1977 climbing to a staggering 17 million people for all the Organization for Economic Cooperation and Development (OECD) countries (Sweezy 1978); (2) unprecedented levels of inflation; (3) an economic slump, as indicated by the fact that the combined GNP of the OECD countries fell by 5 per cent from 1973 to 1975; (4) a dramatic decline of 14 per cent during the same time period of world trade with substantial balance of payments deficits in most OECD countries; and (5) an alarming growth of public debt in most of the western core states (Gough 1979: 132). The existence of all these negative economic indicators during the same time period makes the current economic crisis of capitalism unique. Never before have all these indicators appeared at the same time.

Why is there this crisis? An important point that has to be stressed here is that these negative economic indicators – such as unemployment, inflation, slow growth, and others – are not the *causes* but, rather, the *symptoms* of the crisis. The actual cause of the crisis is the decline in the profitability of the largest industrial and commercial companies of the capitalist world. In popular parlance, the propelling industries of western capitalism have not been making enough profits and they have triggered the present crisis in order to recreate the conditions for those profits to rise again. *The objective of this crisis is to reorder and recreate a new international social division of labor that would allow the rate of profit to increase.* Contrary to what is usually believed by current "orthodox" schools of economic thought, capitalism is not a harmonious system that exists in equilibrium but, rather, is a system based on most profound antagonistic contradictions (the key one being capital/labor) which requires brutal crises for its continuous reproduction (de Brunhoff 1977: 163).

Why is there such a crisis at this particular time? At the end of the 1960s, the undisputed leadership of US capital began to be challenged. For over a quarter of a century, the hegemony of US capital over the international capitalist economic system was undisputed. That hegemony, however, was weakened by (1) the strength of the working class in western capitalist countries, including the US; (2) the appearance of other economic powers within the capitalist system, such as Germany and Japan, that bargained and competed with US capital to get more "room at the top;" (3) the appearance of forces in the peripheral countries that demanded a higher share of the plunder in those countries; (4) the existence of revolutionary antiimperialist and anti-capitalist movements in the peripheral countries that represented an actual threat to the overall capitalist world system; and (5) the existence of ever-growing areas of the world under the control of socialist forces that represented alternative models to the capitalist world system. All these forces – at work for more than a quarter of a century – have threatened and substantially weakened the international capitalist order in which US capital has been and continues to be the hegemonic force.[3]

The response by international capital to this threat has been the creation of one of the most profound crises that the capitalist world has ever known. *Central to that response has been a stepped up class warfare by capital against the working class and popular masses of the core and peripheral countries.* Even Lane Kirkland, the head of the AFL-CIO in the United States, and a person not known for radicalism, has expressed alarm that big business in this country is involved "in an unprecedented class warfare" (Ruskin 1979). A primary aim of that warfare is to cut the level of individual and collective consumption of the working class most dramatically.[4] Indeed, the boom of the 1950s and 1960s exacerbated the contradictions within capitalism. The dramatic growth of capital accumulation exhausted the reserve army of labor, thereby strengthening the labor movements in core countries. Those movements in core countries were able, through an active class struggle, to increase the percentage of national income going to wages and to decrease the percentage going to profits. Also, those movements forced the establishment and extension of social expenditures, such as pension schemes, health benefits, disability programs, and many other programs which were provided to a large degree by the state. This growth of social expenditures, however, was considered by capital to be at the root of the capitalist crisis. It was thought that capital was being spent in social consumption, contributing to what was called the shortage of capital, that is, shortage of capital that could be invested in productive or profit-making endeavors (for an excellent reply to this argument, see Gough 1979: 102–27). Consequently, the response by capital in this conjuncture has been to stimulate, through its hegemony in the state, *substantial cuts of collective consumption*. In the US, the Reagan administration has drastically cut the social expenditures in the Federal budget, cuts that were already initiated during the Carter administration (United Automobile Workers of America 1981). In West Germany, the Social Democratic government has severely cut expenditures on education, hospitals, and health services (Gough 1979: 131). In France, the government of Barre had cut most substantially social security payments and pension benefits (Gresh 1981). In Great Britain, social expenditures were also cut from 1975 to 1980 with the heaviest cuts taking place under Thatcher's government (Bleaney 1979).

This cutting of social expenditures has taken place concurrently with an *increased privatization of services*, that is, a switch from direct state provision of services to public subsidization and purchase of privately produced services. Examples of this intervention are the provision of social services, publicly financed but privately run, according to contract arrangements between state agencies and private capital (*New York Times* 1979b). The closing down of public hospitals in the United States and the subsidization of private care is another instance of that policy. Similarly, in Great Britain, the increased emphasis on private beds, with care subsidized by public funds, translates into a similar type of intervention. In all these cases, the purpose of the shift from public to private is to optimize profits in the private sector. In that shift, a preferred scenario for capital is to have the public sector pay for the private provision of services. An example of the power of capital in the United States is that all proposals for national health insurance, including the one sponsored by Senator Kennedy (the left alternative within the Democratic Party), foresee the taxpayer as paying for the delivery of health services provided by the private sector.

The cutting of social expenditures, and the privatization of benefits and services is accompanied by calls for *changing the character of public services in order to make them more amenable to capital's specific need for accumulation.* Education, for example, has to be made more relevant to the need for skills in the labor market. Thus, vocational and training components are stressed over other types of knowledge not so immediately relevant. State regulations and programs on occupational medicine cannot interfere with the needs of capital accumulation, and so on. As part of that approach, it is worth noting that health, education, and other services are increasingly evaluated and considered less as social consumption and more as social investment, that is, their contribution to the process of capital accumulation.

A last point that needs to be stressed is that the cutting of state expenditures is not uniform across the board. While there are dramatic cuts in health and social expenditures, there are more *substantial increases in funds for state military expenditures, state agencies of law and order, and state aid to private enterprise.* An example of this transfer of funds in the UK is found in the latest social policies of Margaret Thatcher's government. While education was cut by 4.3 per cent, defense was increased by 3.5 per cent, and expenditures for "law and order" agencies were increased by 3.5 per cent (El Pais 1979).

In the US, the transfer of funds from social consumption to military expenditure is put quite dramatically in Edward F. Snyder's testimony before the US House Budget Committee on the 1979 Federal budget proposed by President Carter's administration.

Six surveillance and command planes added for an additional cost of $120 million; Head-start programs (pre-school training) cut $20 million . . . One submarine tender to support nuclear attack submarines added for an additional $262.5 million; maternal and child health services cut $112 million . . . An additional $89 million for the Army XM-1 tank program; mental health centers cut $88 million . . . An additional $141 million for A-10 attack aircraft; cancer research cut $55 million.   (Navarro 1980: 961)

The transfer of funds has been further augmented during the Reagan administration, whose cumulative cuts on social consumption until 1984 total $214 billion, while military expenditures are supposed to increase four times that amount (Johnson 1981).

In summary, what we are witnessing is not so much a *dismantling but a restructuring of the welfare state* with the intention of reducing the level of collective consumption and supporting the process of capital accumulation by actively intervening in the restructuring of capital to enable it to better respond to the international capitalist crisis. This restructuring of the welfare state takes place by (1) large transfers of funds *within* the public sector and also from the public to the private sector; (2) changes in the internal management and control of certain state apparatuses; and (3) changes in the criteria by which decisions are made and funds allocated.

The ideological offensive of capitalism

The restructuring of the state cannot take place only by repression but has to rely on an active ideological offensive that could create a new consensus around a new set of values, beliefs, and practices.[5] Thus, capital mobilizes all types of ideologies and ideologues to explain, rationalize, and justify the restricting of individual and collective consumption. Consequently, a series of ideological positions appear on all sides of the political spectrum emphasizing the importance of people lowering their expectations. In the United States, a most recent voice added to that chorus is the one of Governor Jerry Brown (the Ivan Illich of politics). As London's the *Economist* (1979) approvingly indicates, Governor Brown represents one of the clearest voices in saying that "America needs to adapt to a more frugal way of life." According to bourgeois ideologists, such as Eli Ginzberg, the main danger that the US had to face in the 1960s and 1970s was the rise of people's expectations caused by the growth of the welfare state (Ginzberg 1977). The inability of the capitalist system to meet those expectations triggered a level of popular frustration that could threaten the stability of the social order. Thus, Ginzberg and others believed it vital for the reproduction of the capitalist system to lower people's expectations.

In addition to stressing lowering expectations, there is an emphasis on self and individual care as the best strategy to resolve one's own problems. This self and individual ideology appears in all areas of endeavor accentuating the belief that people's own health, welfare, wealth, and future depend primarily on what people do for themselves and not on what others do for them. As stated by Mrs Thatcher, "we have to get away from collectivism . . . Democracy is people taking care of themselves" (*New York Times* 1979a). In medicine, that self-centered approach appears in the strongly pushed message that most health improvements will come from individuals changing their own patterns of behavior. The assumption made in that position is that individuals are responsible for their own health or disease. Whether people are sick or not is their own fault. This victim-blaming philosophy reaches extreme forms in some branches of medicine, such as in occupational health with the current genetic screening programs carried out by the largest petrochemical industries among their workers. The aim of those programs is to detect those workers whose genetic structure assumingly makes them particularly sensitive to certain toxics. The assumption made in these programs is that a worker gets sick primarily because of his or her genetic liability rather than exposure to the toxic. As Anthony Mazzocchi, Director of Health and Safety for the Oil, Chemical and Atomic Workers International Union said, "I think that in the 1980's we are going to see a lot of victim blaming. The emphasis will be not so much what you work with, it will have to do with who your mother and father were" (*New York Times* 1980).

This call for individual responsibility is accompanied by an increasing emphasis on the sphere of private life. Personal life becomes "intimate" life where the self-centered sphere is the primary axis of one's own realization. The "me" generation is

also supposed to be the "narcissist" and "hedonist" generation. Ideology and culture are used to individualize, atomize,
and depoliticize the population, emphasizing the individual
and not the collective political response as the answer to
people's problems. In summary, capital uses all forms of
ideological codes and messages, including those generated from
cultures of protest, to avoid the creation of a political consciousness capable of going beyond the capitalist system. We
find, then, a long list of movements – from "counterculture"
to "holistic medicine" (among many others) – that are presented as anti-establishment but all of which share the same
road to political unconsciousness. All of them arose in the
United States and are presented both nationally and inter-
nationally as "avant-garde" movements. The fact that they are
presented in those terms, however, reflects (as Samir Amin
(1975) has indicated) more on the political immaturity of
American society than on its avant-garde-ism. The appearance
of these movements in periods of crisis is not the cause but
rather the symptom of the crisis of the dominant bourgeois
ideology. These movements become components in the process of restructuring bourgeois ideology, a restructuring that is
needed to retain its dominance. In the same way that economic
crisis is capital's intent of regaining its dominance, ideological
crises can also represent the restructuring of that ideology to
regain and strengthen its dominance.

The ideological interventions in the world of production and legitimation

In addition to those ideological interventions in the world of
consumption (such as lowering collective expectations and
increasing individual responsibility and self-care), there are
also other ideological interventions that focus on the world of
production, tracing the current crises to not only the expansion
of social consumption, but also to the decline of productivity in
the sphere of production. The crisis of productivity is considered due to the decline of labor's productivity (caused by absenteeism, turnover, sick leaves, low motivation and other
worker-related characteristics) and to the excessive demands
made on management to protect the health and safety of the

workers and consumers, and of the environment. A characteristic of that interpretation of crisis is that in spite of the
evidence to the contrary (*Monthly Review* 1980), it is continuously presented not as an ideological position, but, rather,
as a factual and unquestioned reality: that is, the fault of the
crisis is because of the workers and their excessive demands on
the bosses. Consequently, and in order to increase productivity,
the bourgeoisie intends (1) to gain more control over the work
process and the workers; (2) to obtain tax breaks and government subsidies; (3) to reduce expenditures on health and safety;
and (4) to use its political power to weaken and/or dismantle
government regulations and intervention in areas of health protection. With that intent, the medical institutions are called to
do their part. Witness the American Medical Association's current call to physicians, both occupational doctors and general
practitioners, to reduce the period of convalescence of workers,
putting them back to work as soon as possible.[6] Similarly, The
Robert Wood Johnson Foundation (1980: 10–20), the main private grantor of funds in health care research in the US, consid-
ers the most troublesome problem in the US to be the decline of
America's productivity. Thus, it establishes as a top priority
the funding of medical interventions aimed at increasing
labor's productivity whose decline is considered to be one of the
major contributions to that crisis.

The other side of the ideological interventions in the worlds
of production and consumption are the interventions in the
sphere of legitimation that take place by excluding within the
realm of debate any anti-capitalist explanation of the crisis and
by denying possible alternative modes of production and consumption as solutions to the crisis. These ideological interventions guarantee the success of the capitalist system, making
the possibility of its alternatives unthinkable. Indeed, the
inability of bourgeois ideologies (presented as social sciences)
to explain and solve present realities, together with a most
profound crisis of legitimation of political institutions, represents a clear threat to the stability and reproduction of the
world capitalist order. Thus, all types of ideological messages
appear to avoid the attractiveness of Marxism as an alternative
explanation to people's daily realities and as a guide for revolutionary practice. Marxist analyses of current realities are
quickly dismissed as "rhetorical," "predictable," "dated,"

etc. by the asphyxiating pattern of orthodoxy in today's US. Terms such as capitalism, imperialism, class struggle, and working class rarely appear in general and academic discourse, except to be quickly dismissed in an introductory note. These terms are quickly cast into exile, generally being placed between quotation marks to alert the reader that they should be subject to suspicion, a matter for ideologues perhaps, but irrelevant for serious people. Meanwhile, capitalist rhetoric appears as unideological and remains unmolested in the general and academic media. Let me stress here that this brutal ideological discrimination is even more accentuated in the sphere of medicine whose lack of diversity is well known. Witness recent collections and reviews of US contributions to social sciences in health and medicine written by leading sociologists in the United States (Brenner, Mooney, and Nagy 1970; Mechanic 1980). Nowhere are the many Marxist contributions in medical and health sociology even mentioned. The diversity of those reviews and collections stop within the boundaries of the established order!

Let me further clarify here that while Marxist views are silenced, the anti-Marxist views are given great prominence in overall discourse. Recently, this anti-Marxist discourse also appeared as part of a radical position among the ''new philosophers'' in France and in its American version, the ''new radicals.'' Although defining themselves as anti-establishment, they focus most of their attacks on Marxism. Beginning as ''orthodox Marxists,'' they quickly become ''neo-Marxists,'' and, more recently, ''post-Marxists.'' All of them share some basic beliefs. One is that Marxism is irrelevant to explain today's realities. One of the leading theorists among them, Castoriadis, wrote as late as 1974 that Marxism was wrong because, contrary to what Marxists believe, ''periodical crises of overproduction are not at all inevitable under modern capitalism, except in the extremely attenuated form of minor, passing recessions.''[7] Seventeen million unemployed in the OECD countries and one of the largest and most profound slumps ever known in production reveal who was irrelevant: Marx or Castoriadis.

The other belief that ''new philosophers'' and ''new radicals'' share is that Marxism is not only irrelevant or wrong but is negative and dangerous since its praxis leads to totalitarianism. Castoriadis, for example, opposes the Marxist revolutionary movements (such as the hegemonic forces within the Sandinista movement) that are leading the struggles in peripheral countries, because they are carriers of future totalitarian states.[8] Perhaps it is not surprising that former Secretary of State Kissinger is on record (after having been visited by Henry Levy, another ideologist of that position) as indicating that the "new philosophers" have much to offer. Certainly, but to whom?

In summary, an entire array of old and new bourgeois ideologies are presented to explain and justify interventions in the worlds of production, consumption, and legitimation aimed at reproducing the bourgeois social order, both within and outside medicine. *Figure 3.1* summarizes those ideological interventions. It is important to clarify that the presentation of those ideologies and their reproduction through the value generating systems in society do not respond to a conspiracy. There is no need for that. The bourgeoisie reproduces those messages as part of their own vision and understanding of reality, presenting them as logical and reasonable, required not for the defense of their specific "class interest" but, rather, for "national interests." As Marx said, the bourgeoisie believes that their vision is the universal vision and their interests are the national interests.

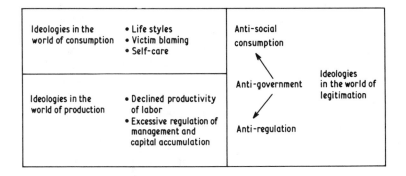

Figure 3.1 The ideologies of the crises

Class struggle in the core capitalist countries

The offensive strategy by capital against labor that appears in all economic, political, and ideological dimensions, is more or less successful depending *on the strength of the working class and the forms in which class struggle takes place.* During the 1950s and 1960s, the struggles carried out by the working class took place on two different levels. One, at the economic level, primarily included demands by the unions for higher wages and compensation for damages created at the workplace. The other level of struggle was the political one and contained demands by political parties for higher social consumption. The late 1960s and early 1970s, however, witnessed the initial steps of bringing together the economic and political struggles in core countries (Magri *et al.* 1975: 11–36). Substantial changes in the process and structure of capital accumulation in the 1960s, with unprecedented levels of productivity and social dislocation, led to strong rebellions by the working classes in the majority of core capitalist countries – rebellions that demanded, not only higher wages and compensation for damages created at the workplace, but, most importantly, changes in the process and pattern of control of production and of social consumption. Struggles appeared at the workplace in the 1960s in many core capitalist countries demanding changes in the pattern of control of work (in such areas as rhythm of work, work environment, and definition of personnel categories) and in the extension of work (such as refusal of night shift labor, overtime, etc.) (Crouch and Pizzorno 1978; Marshall 1978). All of these struggles challenged the control of the work process by capital and demanded a redefinition of the power relations of production. Thus, these struggles, by questioning power relations at the point of production and thus in society as a whole, were and are intrinsically political.

Also, during this period – late 1960s and early 1970s – new mass-based movements appeared, such as neighborhood and community movements, environmentalist movements, and feminist movements that questioned the nature and control of social consumption. The strength of the working class and popular masses in the post-World War II period had determined a substantial increase in collective consumption. Services that were initially provided by separate units of capital, the entrepeneurs, were increasingly being provided by the state. This provision not only meant a substantial expansion of state intervention in people's lives, but also a large involvement by the working class and popular masses in the apparatuses of the state (Castells 1978: 15; Ingrao 1979). This massive involvement meant the expansion of class struggle *within* the state apparatuses, with the development of antagonistic relations between citizens' groups, recipients of state services (public housing, health services, education, etc.) and the administration of those programs run under the hegemony of capital. Here again, struggles took place around the control of state services as well as the expansion of those services. Consequently, new forms of struggle appeared in the community which represented new forms of direct participation and control.

The bourgeois response to the crisis: "the market strategy"

These struggles continue to take place, both in the world of production and of consumption, and represent important threats to the stability of the capitalist order. To those threats, the bourgeoisie has been promoting two alternative responses in each core country. One, exemplified by forces behind Mrs Thatcher in Great Britain, Barre in France, Strauss in Germany, Calvo Sotelo in Spain, the "dorotheos" in Italy, and Reagan in the United States, includes a frontal attack on the service side of the welfare state with a monetary economic policy that relies on "market forces," enhances profits, and heavily disciplines the working class, both directly by creating high unemployment and, indirectly, by instituting such repressive measures as limiting workers' rights, like the right to strike. This strategy – the "market strategy" – assumes that the expansion of state services is responsible for the current economic crisis, hindering the process of capital accumulation by shifting capital from investment to unproductive social consumption. Moreover, supporters state that this expansion is based on a great deal of public borrowing and public debt, taking money away from the private sector and thus generating inflation. Consequently, their answer is to call for more substantial cuts of social and unproductive expenditures.

Needless to say, this discourse masks class interests. The dramatic cuts in social consumption entailed in that strategy aim at weakening the working class most substantially. Simultaneous with those cuts, there is a most substantial growth of government intervention favorable to the interests of the hegemonic strata of the capitalist class, that is, monopoly capital. *Tables 3.1* and *3.2*, for example, compare some of the cuts in the US government expenditures that affect the working class *(Table 3.1)* with the expansion of government subsidies, via tax cuts, to the hegemonic strata of the capitalist class *(Table 3.2)*.

Table 3.1   *The social consequences of the Reagan budgets: budget cuts that primarily affect the working class*

budget cuts	$ billion
Social security Eligibility tightened and minimum benefit eliminated for 3 million elderly people.	11
Medicare Elderly required to pay more for medical services.	4
Unemployment insurance Reduced ability to trigger extended benefits except for short-term, high unemployment situations.	3
Trade adjustment assistance Eliminated original payment levels; provided reduced benefits available to fewer workers.	3
Federal employees Pay increases held to below comparability and full inflation adjustment for retirees eliminated.	17
Comprehensive employment and training Eliminated all public service jobs.	16
Higher Education Needs test applied for some Guaranteed Student Loans and grants to students from low-income families reduced.	3
Elementary and secondary eduation Reduced aid where federal facilities place burden on community.	2
Medicaid Reduced payments to states, causing higher costs or reduced medical care.	3
Food stamps Strikers' families and 1 million working poor eliminated.	6
School lunch Costs to children from near-poor families increased.	5

Energy assistance Assistance to low-income people with high fuel bills reduced.	2
Assistance families dependent children (AFDC) Benefits reduced, primarily those available to the working poor.	4
Housing Subsidized housing reduced, rents increased, and funds for repairs reduced.	1
Rail AMTRAK subsidies cut, CONRAIL to be sold in whole or in part.	2
Highways, airports and mass transit Funds reduced for construction and purchase of equipment	5
Maritime Eliminated funds to rebuild merchant marine.	0.1
Economic development Funds for urban and rural economic development reduced.	2
Postal service Postage costs for non-profits, such as labor, religious and education groups increased. Some Post Offices may be closed.	3
Other social service, health, education, nutrition, economic development and energy programs.	48
total specified cuts in 1983 and 1984	140.1
unspecified cuts in 1983 and 1984	74
total cumulative cuts by 1984	**214**

Source Adapted from United Automobile Workers of America (1981: 2–3).

Table 3.2 *The social consequences of the Reagan budgets: tax cuts that benefit the capitalist class*

tax cuts	$ billion
Tax cuts for wealthy persons About one third of total rate cuts go to those now earning over $50,000 – yet they equal only 6 per cent of all taxpayers.	55
Estate and gift tax cuts Raise combined limit on estates and gifts subject to tax from $175,000 to $600,000.	3
Slash the tax rate on net estates in excess of $2.5 million from a 70 per cent top marginal rate to a 50 per cent rate.	1
Widen special gimmicks for valuing for estate tax purposes for wealthiest farms, woodlands, and other business real estate.	1
Increase annual exemption from gift tax from $6,000 to $20,000 for married ($3,000 to $10,000 for single)	0.6

Oil tax cuts $2,500 windfall profit tax credit for oil royalty owners, replaced by 2 barrels per day exemption in 1982–84.   2.9

Phased in reduction of windfall profits tax rate on ''new'' oil from 30 per cent to 15 per cent.   0.4

Exempt tax on stripper oil production by independent producers.   0.7

Continue percentage depletion deduction for oil and gas production at a 22 per cent rate, instead of scheduled phasedown.   2

Foreign earned income   Phased-in exclusion from taxes of $95,000 for Americans working overseas by 1986 plus additional special deductions for housing costs and a shortened overseas residence period to qualify.   1.5

Extension of so-called Targeted Jobs Tax Credit   Subsidizes employers. Would have otherwise expired at the end of 1984.   0.5

Depreciation   Provides enormous across-the-board speed-up for businesses whereby government absorbs costs of buildings, equipment, and vehicles. Greatest benefactors of these provisions are electric and gas utilities and oil companies.   55.8

Retirement funds   Increase and extend individual retirement account provisions which primarily benefit upper income persons.   3.5

Double deductions for self-employed individuals (from $7,500 to $15,000) that they can take annually by setting up a retirement for themselves.   0.3

Unearned income   Cut top rate on capital gains to 20 per cent and shorten holding period for long-term capital gain treatment.   0.6

Create special exemption of $2,000 from tax for savings certificates ($1,000 for single).   4.7

Tax straddles   Continue to exempt from tax the income of professional commodity traders (would have resulted in a revenue gain for Treasury of $400 million).

giveaway cuts by 1984	133.5
additional cuts by 1984	152.6
total cumulative cuts by 1984	**286.1**

Source: Adapted from United Automobile Workers of America (1981: 2–3).

In addition to government subsidies, there are other government interventions which strengthen the capitalist class such as (1) the growth of military expenditures; (2) the growth of repressive state apparatuses; and (3) the active regulation of social and individual morality, strengthening the public virtues convenient for the reproduction of the social order.

Contrary to their own rhetoric, *the "market" strategy does not mean a lessening of the state's role in economic and social spheres but, rather, a reorganization of the way in which the state intervenes in people's lives.* An example of the growth of state intervention in the economic sphere favored by the "market strategy" is the enormous growth of military expenditures. As indicated by the current US Secretary of Defense, Casper Weinberger (Cypher 1981: 15), a welcome effect of the overwhelming growth of military expenditures (over $1 trillion in the coming five years) proposed by the Republican administration will be the *reindustrialization of the American economy* which will take place under the direction of the US Department of Defense defined by Sherman and Wood as the "largest planned economy" in the world outside the Soviet Union. (Sherman and Wood 1979: 90)

Yet another example of strengthening rather than weakening state intervention in the political and social spheres is the Reagan government's intervention to reduce political and civil rights of the population. As stated by Salvatori, a key member of the Reagan transitional team,

In the history of man everyone has talked about expanding rights, having more and more freedom. But we have found that if you let people do what they want to do, you have chaos. We can't restore moral values, that's hopeless. What we have to do is restructure society, set minimum standards of respect and order. Frankly, *we need a more authoritarian state.* (Emphasis added)   (NACLA 1981: 10)

In brief, the Reagan policies do not diminish state intervention in people's lives but, rather, change the nature and form of that intervention.

The major beneficiaries of these policies are the main constituencies of the Reagan administration: financial and corporate capital and the old *petite bourgeoisie* (such as small business and self-employed professionals), the main components of the "old right" and the "new right," respectively. This latter group is also the main promoter of legislating morality, stimulating a most significant growth of government intervention to assure the reproduction of those values favorable to current power relations.

In the health sector, the most dramatic cuts of federal health expenditures are complemented with a substantial shift in funds from the public to the private sectors, with the privatization and commodification of medical services. Also, the weakening of the regulatory powers of the state apparatuses is complemented with a strengthening of business influence over the planning apparatuses (as witnessed by the current call for the health insurance companies to fund the Health Systems Agencies – the major planning agencies in the health sector of the US (DHSS 1981) or over the regulatory apparatuses, an influence that in the case of OSHA (Occupational Safety and Health Administration) is tantamount to control. We also find in the health sector an alliance between the old right, (for example, Secretary Schweikert) who represent the interests of hegemonic sectors of corporate and financial capital, and the new right (like Dr Koop, new Surgeon General of the US Public Health Service) who represent the interests of the largest sectors of the medical profession and, very much in particular, of the practitioners (as different from the patricians or academic-based physicians). Thus, there is in the federal health establishment under Reagan a confluence of two different types of discourse that run parallel in different degrees of unease. One, the discourse of the old right which stresses the need for competition and for weakening government constraints, a discourse that conceals a strategy for further facilitating economic concentration in the medical sector to the benefit of the major insurance companies in the health sector. The other is the discourse of the ''new right'' which focuses on social issues such as anti-abortion, anti-women, anti-black, and other related issues that are presented as ''shock issues'' to heighten the strategy of social tensions.

In summary, the Reagan administration *represents not a weakening but a further strengthening of the authoritarian state required to deal with the weakening of capitalist hegemony and legitimacy.* This authoritarian state is characterized by (1) intensifying state control over every sphere of socio-economic life; (2) austerity offensive against the working class and other popular forces; (3) a tendency to dismantle many of the social and institutional forces of the Keynesian welfare system; (4) an intensified concentration of power within the state's executive branch; and (5) the all-sided curtailment of civil liberties and rights.

The bourgeois response to the crisis: the social contract theory

Another strategy envisioned by capital to resolve the current crisis is the "social contract" alternative represented by the forces behind Healey in the United Kingdom, Mondale in the United States, Schmidt in West Germany, and Rochard in France, among others. It is important to stress that I include in this alternative individuals representing currents within social democratic and socialist parties or their equivalents rather than the parties themselves, since those parties are not uniform. The current crisis is radicalizing sectors of some of those parties, questioning, for example, the commitment by the social democratic and socialist parties to the capitalist system (for example, Tony Benn, currently within the UK Labour Party). The social contract strategy that has typified the practice of the social democratic parties in Europe and, to lesser degree, of the Democratic Party in the US includes the intent of integrating segments and instruments of the working class (the larger and stronger unions) in the state apparatuses, and developing planning structures in which government, business, and labor jointly plan for the size and type of social consumption. In this tripartite arrangement, the restructuring of state policies and expenditures is, or would be, done in theory with the collaboration of labor but in practice under the dominance of capital. Let me add here that this alternative of bringing labor into this *tripartite arrangement* requires labor to have a centralized power center that can implement the policies adopted in the tripartite arrangement and that can discipline the rank and file membership that might deviate or rebel against that "social contract" arrangement. A clear example of the disciplinary role that this centralization plays in the "social contract" arrangement is seen in the Swedish trade unions, some of the most highly centralized unions in the western capitalist world (Israel 1979; Navarro 1979: 92). The current capitalist offensive aims at either destroying the unions (the monetarists' strategy) or at strengthening them at the top and weakening them at the grass roots levels (the "social contract" strategy).

The "social contract" strategy, the most frequently used strategy by governments in core capitalist countries during the post World War II period, appeared in response to the growing strength of the working class. Its purpose was to integrate the strongest unions within state apparatuses. A function of the state is to mediate the conflict between capital and labor, a mediation that takes place under the hegemony of capital. Important instruments to represent class interests have been the political parties and very important forums at which that mediation can occur are the western parliaments or the United States Congress. The increased strength of working class and popular movements and of capitalist non-hegemonic sectors in those forums has led the hegemonic sector of capital to shift its main area of struggle to the administrative apparatuses of the state, bypassing to an increasing degree the political parties and the electoral process. Consequently, a general characteristic of the western states has been its increased centralization with the establishment of *ad hoc* government agencies that are directly accountable to the executive. As an example of this trend, the "social contract" approach has aimed at establishing those tripartite arrangements whereby social consumption is agreed upon and planned by government, big business, and labor outside the public political arena.

Further characteristics of this social contract strategy have been (and still are) that they (1) assume a consensus between capital and labor; (2) encourage the involvement of labor representatives as junior partners in schemes of co-management and co-participation in the political and economic institutions; and (3) aim at rationalizing the state apparatuses by increasing their control and efficiency; and (4) depoliticize the nature of social problems, seeing them as merely technological problems amenable to technical solutions.

In the health sector that social contract strategy has meant (in addition to expansion of health expenditures) the development of planning and regulatory agencies and of other agencies of rationalization in which all parties – financial capital (health insurance) and providers, together with labor and other users' representatives – were supposed to reach decisions by compromise and consensus. In the words of Rashi Fein (a representative of that position in the US), the health planning agencies were supposed to be *citizen dominated local advisory mechanisms* in which all parties participated in a collective decision-making process with the citizens (by which Fein means the non-providers) having the dominant voices (Fein 1981: Preface). The reality, however, has been rather different. As in other "social contract" arrangements, the partners have not been equal. The senior partners in those planning agencies were the insurers and providers, with labor and other users being not the dominant but, rather, the dominated junior partners in that partnership. Moreover, the failure of those agencies was due not to the lack of understanding and know-how (as Fein assumes) but, rather, to their articulation within a set of class power relations that inhibit the possibility of planning for the benefit of the users rather than financiers and providers. Under those conditions, the assumed consensus was not more than the crystalization of power relations with a dominant/dominated dichotomy built in it.

The crisis of the social contract strategy

The social consensus between capital and labor, while easy to reach in moments of economic boom like the 1950s and 1960s, is difficult to develop in situations of slumps like those in the 1970s and 1980s where the contradictions of capitalism appear more clearly. In the United States, for example, the New Deal coalition that constituted the social base for the "social contract" strategy and which dominated politics until recently has practically collapsed. In response to the crisis of the 1970s, the senior partner of that coalition, represented by President Carter, decided to put first the needs of the economy (that euphemistic term used in bourgeois discourse to define the capitalist system) and put aside those promises for larger social consumption (such as for national health insurance) on which basis he had been elected in 1976. Actually, it is usually forgotten that the most important Reagan policies, such as dramatic cuts of social consumption and growth of military expenditures, were started by the Carter administration. In brief, Carter's policies of austerity disenchanted and demoralized the junior partners in that coalition – the trade unions, and the new *petite bourgeoisie* (such as salaried professionals and civil servants) – as well as the black, feminist, and environmental movements, which explains his defeat in the 1980 election. This disenchantment was reflected in (1) an enormous abstention with only half of the American electorate voting; (2) a protest vote, with 40 per cent of those who voted for Reagan doing it as a protest against Carter rather than as an agreement with Reagan (Brenner and Brenner 1981; Wunsh 1981). Reagan's victory was not so much an indicator of growth of the Republican alternative (Reagan got 27 per cent of the electorate, practically the same percentage that President Ford did in 1976) but, rather, a collapse of the Democratic one (Carter's vote declined most substantially, from 27 per cent in 1976 to 22 per cent in 1980). Needless to say, the hegemonic forces of capital on whose behalf the austerity policies of Reagan are taking place, deny this interpretation of the last election, arguing that those policies reflect an overwhelming mandate from the electorate to implement them. Nowhere is the fallacy of that position clearer than in the health sector. While the Reagan administration is (1) cutting federal health expenditures most dramatically; and (2) weakening the federal power to protect safety and health of workers, consumers, and the environment, the majority of Americans would be willing to pay even higher taxes if those taxes were spent on health services; feel that there is a need for a national health insurance which would require larger government intervention; think that the benefits of government regulation of costs of medical services and drugs outweigh the drawbacks; and support federal control of doctors' fees, hospital costs, and prescription drugs.[9] No less than 34 per cent of Americans want all doctors to be on the federal payroll and paid on a salary basis, and over one-third of the American people are supportive of a national health service, an alternative that rarely, if ever, is reasonably discussed in the corporate controlled media (*Boston Globe* 1978: 8) The overwhelming evidence shows that it is not a popular mood but corporate will that is responsible for those cuts.

The bourgeoisie's strategies and labor

Whether capital favors the market or the social contract strategies depends on many factors of which the correlation of forces between labor and capital is a key one. Indeed, in those situations in which labor is very weak, it is likely that capital will favor the "market" strategy or capitalism without gloves. Whenever labor is a factor still worth reckoning with, then capital will most likely adopt the "social contract" strategy.

In the United States, the cuts of social consumption and the strengthening of the authoritarian state has further weakened the working class, dividing its different strata in competition for the benefits of whatever is left of the welfare state. The political practice of the US labor movement has been that each one of its components behaves like an interest group struggling to defend its own specific interests. Needless to say, the intervention by the state has aimed at strengthening the sense of competition among "interest groups," thereby further weakening and dividing the class interests of labor. The absence of any socialist ideology and culture and its concomitant class consciousness has been in the US the best guarantee of the capitalist order. As Irving S. Shapiro, head of the Dupont chemical empire, indicated recently, "This country [the US] is fortunate to have a reasonable responsible labor movement rather than what we see in [the labor movement] of Europe" (Ruskin 1979: 92). Because of this "reasonable responsibility," the US is the country among the major capitalist core countries where the dismantling of the already limited welfare state has gone furthest and fastest.

In the health sector, the United States – the only major capitalist country without a national health service or insurance – is suffering substantial dismantling of federal health interventions, a dismantling that also aims at presenting the needs of specific sectors of the working class, such as the elderly, the disabled, and the working poor, as being in contradiction with the needs of other sectors of the same class, such as the young and able, or the white against the black and Latinos, or women against men. These divisive policies are accompanied with a rekindling of chauvinist, racist, and sexist ideologies that reproduce and sustain those divisions. A climate of social hostility, tension, and suspicion is thus created that, side by side with the tensions triggered by the arms race and threat of nuclear war, accentuates the feeling of crisis of national survival and security, a public feeling that is required for people's acceptance of the authoritarian state and its austerity policies. Complementing this set of interventions, the Reagan administration and its allied forces stress the twin ideologies of (1) *denial of rights*, an ideology that denies – as David Stockman, a leading spokesperson for the Reagan administration, has indicated – any collective responsibility for the sick, disabled, aged, infant, or weak, and (2) *self-care*, accentuating the individual responsibility for one's own health, wealth, and future. Witness, for example, the wide distribution and promotion of the works of one of the main theorists of self care, Lowell S. Levin (Levin and Idler 1981), by the American Enterprise Institute (one of the ideological centers of the most reactionary segments of monopoly capital and the intellectual center of the Reagan administration, which counts among its financial supporters the Howard Pew Freedom Foundation, a main supporter of the John Birch Society (a quasi fascist group); the Sarah Scaife Foundation, closely linked to Gulf Oil; and the Lilly Foundation, a family fortune based on pharmaceuticals (NACLA 1981)).

To the degree that a labor response may be built and a larger coalition of labor with other forces may be established, it is possible that the "social contract" strategy may be recalled. Already within the Democratic Party there are forces calling for a renovated "social contract" that may be less traumatic to the working class and enable a new partnership between labor and capital under the hegemony of capital (Rohatyr 1981). In the absence of labor's response, however, the hegemonic fractions within the bourgeoisie will continue the more extremist policies of the "market" strategy. Needless to say, the corporate controlled media tries to present those extremist policies of Reagan as actually being "moderate" (that reassuring and approving term which the US media uses as a sign of reasonableness). It is continuously being said that regardless of the ideological extremisms of the candidates during the election parade, they are always forced afterwards to cool down and become "moderate" and "center," terms and expressions that give most US administrations a stamp of "maturity" and "moderation." This maturity and moderation, incidentally, have led us to Vietnam, Watergate, Cold War II, global counter-insurgency supporting the most repressive regimes in the world, bloated military budgets, a regressive tax burden, large corporate subsidies, and the promise of a rigorous repression of dissent, all in the name of "moderation" and "stability." And, of course, the same media rushes to define as "ideological extremists" all those who are against any or all of the above. The events presented in this article, however, show the willingness of the hegemonic forces of the United States capitalist class to use *authentically extremist policies to resolve the current crisis on their own terms.*

The international mobility of capital and the welfare state

Mass struggles in the core capitalist countries force capital to move to other parts of the world where the working class is weaker. In this respect, the gains of individual and collective consumption by the working class in core countries, and the increased political constraints that environmental and occupational health struggles represent for the process of capital accumulation in those countries, has forced the movement of capital both among core countries and between core and peripheral countries (Castleman 1979). Actually, a large percentage of that capital has moved to peripheral countries searching, not so much for new markets, as for cheap labor. A growing proportion of foreign investment (and especially US investment), is allocated to manufacturing industries rather than extractive industries or services (Poulantzas 1975: 52). Both light and heavy industries are either partially or completely moving to peripheral countries. In both cases, the manufactured products are for export to the international market and for internal consumption by a very small percentage of the peripheral population, that is, the national bourgeoisie. Needless to say, the great mass of people in those countries – workers, peasants, and unemployed – do not have a capacity for consuming those products. Those masses are seen by capital not as consumers but as actual and potential producers, that is, very cheap labor. While the cost for one hour of labor power in the United States in current and constant US dollars in 1974 was $4.07, the labor costs were for example 92¢ in Argentina, 47¢ in Brazil, and 8¢ in Chile (Chossudovsky 1979: 61). These low wages go side by side with an over-exploitation of labor. For example, while the "formal" working week (without counting extra time) in most developed countries is 40–44 hours a week, in South Korea it is 50–58; the Philippines 45–50; Singapore 49; and in Thailand 47–51. In Hong Kong the working week is 60 hours with 58 per cent of the labor force working seven days a week (Navarro in press).

Working classes in the peripheral countries rebel against those conditions of exploitation, forcing the national bourgeoisie, supported by international capital, to establish repressive regimes whose primary objective is to reduce the level of individual and collective consumption of the working class and popular masses and to destroy any constraints to capital accumulation. Regarding the former, the examples are many. In Argentina, the fall in the real industrial wage that followed the 1976 military coup was of the order of 50 per cent. In Chile, after the 1973 military coup, real purchasing power declined by 60 per cent in the first few months of the Pinochet regime and by more than 80 per cent after one year. These shifts in purchasing power obviously imply important changes in the structure of income distribution. In Chile, for instance, at least 25 per cent of total income has been transferred from the lower- and middle-income groups to the upper 5 per cent income bracket. The upper 5 per cent income bracket controls more than 50 per cent of total income. In Brazil, the minimum wage has fallen by more than 50 per cent since 1964. According to the Departamento de Informacao e Estudos Estadisticos Socio-Economicos, a worker receiving the minimum wage in 1972 would have to work over 132 hours to purchase the monthly minimum food bundle as opposed to 87 hours in December 1965. This fall in purchasing power has tended to be accompanied by *de facto* increases in the length of the working day (an 8-hour working day is insufficient to meet the costs of subsistence). In the metallurgical industry in Sao Paulo, the working week has been extended to 66 hours (Chossudovsky 1979: 67).

A point that has to be stressed here is that the dramatic lowering of individual consumption in those countries appears also as underconsumption of food with the increasing malnutrition that we see in today's Latin America. That low food intake serves two purposes. First, it means cheaper "nontraditional industrial exports" (that is, the cost of maintenance of labor power is lower); second, the reduction in internal food consumption allows a reallocation of land use patterns, thereby favoring the parallel consolidation of agro and agro-industrial export crops. Underconsumption in food and undernourishment constitute the necessary ingredients for the development of a commercial export-oriented agriculture (Chossudovsky 1979: 63).

In conjunction with this reduction of individual consumption, we find a profound reduction of collective consumption with an *intent of restructuring the "welfare state."* Indeed, in many Latin American countries, we also find cuts, rationalizations, and privatization of social services. For example, social expenditures have, both in absolute and percentage terms, declined substantially in Brazil, Chile, and Uruguay. In Brazil, the percentage of state health expenditures declined from 4.6 per cent of total state expenditures in 1969 to 2.4 per cent in 1977; in Chile, from 8.5 per cent in 1969 to 6 per cent in 1977; and in Uruguay from 16.6 per cent in 1970 to 6 per cent in 1977. Similarly, in state education, the decline in Brazil was from 8.7 per cent in 1969 to 7.6 per cent in 1977; in Chile from 18.6 per cent in 1971 to 15.5 per cent in 1977; and in Uruguay from 29.9 per cent in 1971 to 15.4 per cent in 1977 (Cesar *et al.* 1979). This cutting of social consumption is accompanied by a deterioration of the infrastructural services which, with the beforementioned factors, account for a most dramatic increase of malaria and other conditions in the peripheral countries, particularly since the 1970s. A frequent purpose of that deterioration is put quite clearly by M. A. Farid, the former chief of the Malaria Control Program of WHO in the following quote: "I am inclined to believe that various sectors of business and governments found that the time had come to re-establish an underdevelopment strategy in the Third World utilizing the resurgence of malaria as the best natural repressive tool against social conflicts" (Farid 1980: 8).

In conclusion, the new redefinition of the international division of labor is characterized by a highly sophisticated and centralized "brain and nervous system" placed in core countries capable of coordinating the distinct elements of worldwide processes of production and distribution, placed in different areas in the periphery. Moreover, the international mobility of capital through their main instruments – the multinationals – and the implicit capacity to relocate production from one country to another, have greatly enhanced the power of capital over labor, already weakened by the imposition of strong repressive measures brought to extremes, as in the military regimes that constitute the maximum expression of the authoritarian state. This great weakness of labor in the peripheral countries explains that the "market" strategy is the most frequent strategy followed by capital in those countries. In the health sector, we find substantial cuts in government health expenditures with privatization and commodification of medical services, accompanied by the ever present ideology of self-sufficiency and self-care brought to those peripheral countries by transmission belts of dominant core ideologies, such as the international agencies of aid. Witness, for example, the current emphasis on self care in WHO's publications (Levin et al. 1981), publications that, for the most part, exclude Marxist interpretations of world realities.

The new international economic order

The increased concentration of capital in manufacturing industries geared to exports has created an unprecedented crisis in most peripheral countries. The negative economic indicators discussed for the core countries appear in the periphery with a brutal dimension. For example, while consumer prices in core countries have increased by 65 per cent since 1972, those prices have increased nearly 800 per cent in Latin America (DeCormis 1979). This dramatic reality reflects the dependency of those countries. established by the international social division of labor, where the capital of core countries is hegemonic.

Recently, a call for change in a New International Economic Order (NEO) has been made. Calls for this NEO appeared in most statements and declarations of United Nations agencies including WHO. In this call, an international redistribution of wealth is being asked for with the poor countries demanding more of a share in the world's wealth (Loraire 1981). Let us analyze the main assumptions of that call. A key one is that the world is divided into two primary blocs of countries: the wealthy countries and the poor countries. Class struggle is being redefined and is supposed to take place primarily between ''bourgeois'' nations and ''proletarian'' nations. Two political consequences may arise out of that understanding. One is that the internal national class struggle is supposed to be either transcended or subsumed by the international one. Consequently, the national bourgeoisie and the proletariat and peasant masses are supposed to have similar interests in their struggle against the core countries. Thus, an assumed anti-imperialist discourse appears in official pronouncements of national bourgeoisies. In those discourses, however, the redistribution of international wealth is asked while maintaining the existing parameters of power in each country. But, as Magdoff and many others have indicated, it is precisely these internal power relations, strengthened by the external power relations at the international level, that are the actual cause of underdevelopment (Magdoff 1978). To believe that the external forces are the *determinant ones* may well lead to the conclusion that until those international imperialist power relations that link core with peripheral countries change, there is no possibility for internal relations of power in the peripheral countries to change. Many experiences, however, show the possibility for breaking with international imperialist relations, once the working classes, peasantries, and popular masses break with those internal power relations in each country. Obviously, anti-capitalist and anti-imperialist struggles are clearly intertwined, due to the close dependency between the national bourgeoisies and international capital. And the international imperialist system heavily conditions the focus and possible direction of national class struggles. However, the point that has to be repeatedly stressed is that the primary condition for breaking with underdevelopment is to break with those *parameters of power given at the national level*. The class struggle is fought at the national level. To think otherwise is to fall, as Rossana Rossanda has indicated, into a type of determinism where nothing can occur in the peripheral (and even in some semi-core) countries, unless the core of imperialism is destroyed (Magri *et al.* 1975). That ''Third World'' position leads to an immobilism and demobilization of class struggle at the national level.

In summary, the current call for a new economic order does not touch upon the key contradiction, that is, the class struggle at the national level which takes place within a set of international power relations that condition but do not determine it. It is because of the silence about class struggle that this discourse on NEO has become so prevalent in the corridors of power of national and international bourgeoisies.

Conclusion

In summary, we are witnessing today a most profound international capitalist crisis in which the hegemonic forces of the United States and international capital are involved in active warfare against the working class and popular masses of this and other countries. The aim of that warfare is to restructure the different components of the welfare state of these countries in order to solve the crisis in terms favorable to capital. Of course, the working class does not remain passive but fights back to avoid further reduction of its individual and collective consumption. The degree of success of the working class response depends on the strength of the working class and on its political consciousness and awareness.

Needless to say, it is quite likely that the analysis of the capitalist crisis and its consequences for the health and social policies of western states presented in this paper will be dismissed by the asphyxiating pattern of orthodoxy existent in today's United States. Still, the dramatic underrepresentation of Marxist positions in the United States is not innocent. There is a continuous discrimination of these positions aimed at avoiding their possible attractiveness to the growing numbers that are disenchanted with conservative and liberal positions and that may represent a threat to the current established order. It is the intention of this paper to offer an alternative interpretation of the current crisis and its impact on welfare state policies. I am aware, of course, that this paper is a mere first step that will, undoubtedly, require further elaboration and corrections. Still, the validity of this interpretation will not be measured by its acceptability in the corridors of power, (likely to be nil) but, rather, by its explanatory value for those readers who are disenchanted with prevalent explanations of present reality. To them, this paper is dedicated.

Notes

1 This chapter is a modified and expanded version of an article by Vicente Navarro entitled, "The Crisis of the International Capitalist Order, Class Struggle, and the Welfare State," published in *Catalyst* 1980, No. 7: 9–25.
2 By welfare state policies, I include two sets of state interventions: (1) state provision of collective and social services to individuals and families (either in cash or in services in kind); and (2) state regulations of private activities (of individual and corporate bodies) which directly alter the conditions of life of specific groups within the population.
3 There is a very extensive bibliography on each one of the points raised in this article. To avoid academic ponderosity, the references have been kept to a minimum.
4 Individual consumption is consumption purchased with the private wage. Collective consumption is the consumption of state benefits and services consumed and used by individuals. It includes the provision of cash benefits and subsidies to individuals (social wages) plus the delivery of social services in kind, such as education and personal health services.
5 I am using ideology in the Gramscian sense, including the set of ethical, juridical, political, aesthetical, and philosophical ideas about social reality as well as a set of customs, practices, and behaviors that consciously or unconsciously reflect that vision of reality.
6 Resolution 149 submitted by the American Occupational Medical Association and the American Academy of Occupational Medicine to the American Medical Association's House of Delegates and approved on 22–8 July, 1979.
7 Castoriadis, "L'institution imaginaire de la société" (p. 22). Quoted in N. Poulantzas *State, Power, Socialism*, London, New Left Books, 1978, p. 165.
8 Interview with Castoriadis. *El Viejo Topo* 38(1979): 4.
9 Gallup Poll, August, 1979, quoted in *Health Law Newsletter* 105 (Jan. 1980): 1; and Harris Poll, 1979, quoted in *Medical World News* (7 Jan. 1980): 9.

References

Amin, S. (1975) Toward a Structural Crisis of World Capitalism. *Socialist Revolution* 5(1): 41.

Bleaney, M. (1979) The Tories' Economic Strategy. *Marxism Today* (November): 12.

Boston Globe (1978) Analysis of Harris Survey. 2 January, p. 8.

Brenner, H., Mooney, A., and Nagy, T. (1970) *Assessing the Contributions of the Social Sciences to Health.* Boulder, CO: Westview Press for the American Association for the Advancement of Science.

Brenner, J. and Brenner, R. (1981) Reagan, the Right and the Working Class. *Against the Current* (Winter): 30.

Castells, M. (1978) *City, Class and Power.* New York: Macmillan.

Castleman, B. (1979) The Export of Hazardous Industries to Developing Countries. *International Journal of Health Services* 9(4): 2.

Cesar, J. *et al.* (1979) State Medicine in Latin America. Present Problems. Paper presented at the II Conference on the Political Economy of Health, Rome, August.

Chossudovsky, M. (1979) Human Rights, Health and Capital Accumulation in the Third World. *International Journal of Health Services* 9(1): 61, 67.

Crouch, C. and Pizzorno, A. (eds) (1978) *The Resurgence of Class Conflict in Western Europe Since 1968,* vols I and II. New York: Macmillan.

Cypher, J.M. (1981) Rearming America. *Monthly Review* 33(6): 15.

de Brunhoff, S. (1977) Crisis Capitalista y Politica Economica. In N. Poulantzas (ed.) *La Crisis del Estado.* Barcelona, Spain: Ed. Fontanella.

DeCormis, A. (1979) Inflation: Don't Blame OPEC. *The Guardian* 28 November, p. 2.

DHHS (1981) Health Planning Provisions of the Budget Reconciliation Act of 1981. *Health Resources News* 8(5): 1.

Economist (1979) California Dialectics. November, p. 32.

El Pais (1979) The British Government Reduces the Public Expenditures by 5% 3 November, p. 33.

Farid, M.A. (1980) The Malaria Program – from Euphoria to Anarchy. *World Health Forum* 1(1 and 2): 8.

Fein, R. (Chairman) (1981) *Health Planning in the US.* Report of a Committee of the Institute of Medicine, National Academy Press.

Ginzberg, E. (1977) *The Limits of Health Reform.* New York: Basic Books.

Gough, I. (1979) *The Political Economy of the Welfare State.* New York: Macmillan.

Gresh, H. (1981) The Impact of the Crisis on French Medicine. Paper presented at the International Conference on Health and the Economy, sponsored by the Center of Social Studies, Rome, 9–12 November.

Ingrao, P. (1979) *Las masas y el poder.* Barcelona, Spain: Critica.

Israel, J. (1979) Swedish Socialism and Big Business. *International*

Journal of Health Services 9(3): 5.

Johnson, J. (1981) The Reagan Budget. *Economic Notes* 49(3): 5. Labor Research Associates.

Levin, L. and Idler, E. (1981) *The Hidden Health Care System.* Cambridge, MA: Ballinger Press, sponsored by the American Enterprise Institute.

Levin, L. S. *et al.* (1981) Round Table on Self Care. *World Health Forum* 2(2).

Loraire, J.A. (1981) Doctors and the Brandt Report. *The Lancet* 20 June.

Magdoff, H. (1978) Limits of International Reform. *Monthly Review* 30(1): 1–11.

Magri, L., Rossanda, R., Claudin, F., and Quijano, A. (1975) *Movimiento Obrero y Acción Politica.* Serie Popular Era.

Marshall, D. (1978) The Miners and the UMW: Crisis in the Reform Process. *Socialist Review* 40/41: 65–115.

Mechanic, D. (ed.) (1980) *Readings in Medical Sociology.* New York: The Free Press.

Monthly Review (1980) Editorial: The Uses and Abuses of Measuring Productivity. 32(2): 1.

NACLA (1981) Reagan Policy in Crisis. *NACLA Report* 15(4): 10, 14.

Navarro, V. (1979) Union Policies and their Social Costs. In *Workers, Community, and Popular Participation. An International Review of Forms of Democracy.* Baltimore, MD: The Johns Hopkins University. Mimeo.

——(1980) The Social Costs of National Security or Insecurity. *American Journal of Public Health* 70(9): 961.

——(in press) The Labor Process and Health. *International Journal of Health Services.*

New York Times (1979a) Mrs Thatcher's Declarations. 12 November, p. A.2.

——(1979b) Towns Seeking Private Service of Public Needs. 23 November, p. 1.

——(1980) Genetic Screening by Industry. 3 February, p. 36.

Poulantzas, N. (1975) Internationalization and the State. In *Classes in Contemporary Capitalism.* London: New Left Books.

Robert Wood Johnson Foundation (1980) *Annual Report.*

Rohatyr, F. (1981) If Reagan Fails? *Economist* 19–27 September, p. 31.

Ruskin, A.H. (1979) Lane Kirkland, A New Style for Labor. *New York Times Magazine* 28 October, p. 91, 92.

Sherman, H. and Wood, J.L. (1979) Military Spending. In *Sociology: Traditional and Radical Perspectives.* New York: Harper & Row.

Sweezy, P. (1978) The Present Stage of the Global Crisis of Capitalism. *Monthly Review* 29(11): 3.

——(1979) On the New Global Disorder. *Monthly Review* 30(11): 2.

United Automobile Workers of America (1981) The Winners and the
   Losers under Reaganomics. *The Washington Report* 21(33): 1–3.
Wall Street Journal (1979) Editorial: The Current Crisis. 10 November,
   p. 5.
Wunsh, M. (1981) Has the Working Class Moved Right? *Against the
   Current* (Summer): 22.

Part Three

Selected issues

Four

Organizing medical care for profit

J. Warren Salmon

Over this decade, nationwide and multinational corporations will become prominent providers of health services, with their primary purpose being profit. The rapidity and scope of this trend in the organization of health care is phenomenal in that proprietary corporate forms only began in the US in the late 1960s.

While the American economy is generally characterized by a few concentrated corporations in each sector, the health care system has, until recently, remained based upon thousands of practitioner entrepreneurs and smaller-scale provider organizations. Except for firms in the peripheral *supply* role (for example, pharmaceuticals, medical equipment and supplies, construction), large capital has not been a major factor in the delivery of services. Urban teaching hospitals, organized "not-for-profit," have dominated here as the largest, and most costly, institutions. An analysis of the relationships between hospitals and the drug, medical technology, and other supply firms reveals lucrative profit streams in this "medical industrial complex," especially since the federal subsidization of providers through Medicare and Medicaid. Today, a vigorous and varied "new medical industrial complex" of investor-owned entities is transforming the delivery of services through "modern business organization and technology."

The editor of the prestigious *New England Journal of Medicine*, Arnold Relman, sees the "*new* medical industrial complex" as "the most important recent development in American health care" (Relman 1980: 963). Surprised at the rapid growth of proprietary providers, he estimates that investor-owned hospital and nursing home corporations, diagnostic labs, mental health and home health care agencies, hemodialysis centers, free-standing ambulatory and emergency centers, and a variety of other services produced between $35–40 billion in 1979, or 25 per cent of personal health care expenses. Another estimate puts the gross revenues of for-profit health care providers at $40 billion for 1981 (Gray 1983). Both figures have climbed greatly in subsequent years.

For-profit hospital systems presently own 15 per cent of non-government acute general hospital beds in the United States (but more than 50 per cent of non-government psychiatric beds). Their growth in numbers and beds over the past fifteen years constrasts dramatically to the contraction of the "not-for-profit" and government segments of the industry. Estimates range between 25–30 per cent for their *ownership* by 1990 – though there is a good chance it will be higher. (This does not account for the increasing number of "not-for-profit" voluntary hospitals under management contracts with the national for-profit firms.) Spurred by rising demands for nursing home care, these proprietary hospital systems are rapidly diversifying to compete with or acquire nursing home chains. More significantly, they are posed to take over a major portion of ambulatory care, as well as already entered into a wide range of other health-related services found in the "new medical industrial complex."

The entire development of the corporate proprietary thrust supports the emergence of a new organization form – the multi-institutional provider. This form allows for the escalation of the concentration process in the delivery of services. Investor-owned health care corporations have become transnational in scope. Moreover, their integration with finance capital (that is, commercial insurance companies that are quickly diversifying themselves) may predictably give them the dominant position in policy formulation. Analyzing these trends outside of a clear consideration of capitalist development presents an incomplete, inaccurate, and often apologetic review. In order not to overlook the implications for the health of the population, it is necessary to have this perspective of the larger and long-term forces impacting on health and health care.

This chapter focuses upon developments surrounding the advent of the organization form that profit-making is taking in services delivery. Specific attention is given to historical tendencies that have set the stage for its extension under conditions of a continuing general economic crisis, conservative health policy redirections, and continued industrialization of the health sector. Rapid scientific and technological advances have reshaped professional roles and relationships and increased the bureaucratization of providers. Coinciding with these are major actions by the corporate class in health policy and planning, and an impending demographic shift where aging population cohorts give rise to expanding ''markets'' for proprietary health care firms. The situation in Great Britain bears some similarities, though the presence of the National Health Service limits prospects for organizing medical care for profit there.

The medical industrial complex

Typological analyses of the array of health care providers and institutions has usually been by ownership: the largest, being the voluntary, private ''not-for-profit'' segment; the fastest growing, being the proprietary segment; and the severely contracting government segment, including local, state, and federal programs. The private practice of physicians represents the bulk of ambulatory care. As with proprietary institutions, profitability governs, though the scope and content of small-scale physician entrepreneurs differs from the national corporate forms. Before expanding on this point, a brief historical review of the growth of profit extraction from health care is in order.

From the turn of the century onward, dramatic advances in medical sciences and key policy developments yielded an elaborate hospital organization central to what became defined as "health care." The American uniqueness to the latter included voluntary health insurance, federal support for hospital construction, and hospital-based postgraduate medical education and allied health training. The Great Society programs of the federal government stimulated the expansion of the hospital-centered industry. Medicare and Medicaid were grafted onto the structural arrangement for hospital care, both of which had been consolidated under retrospective Blue Cross and Blue Shield payment programs (Kelman 1971). Thus, the mode of payment (and its large capital flows to peripheral supply firms) affected the forms of care. Overmedicalization and dependent care-seeking behaviors resulted (Renaud 1975; Illich 1976) in disease-focused, technological interventions. Under such a system propelled by profit – not the preservation and maintenance of people's health – the commodification of the human needs associated with chronic illness became represented in costly "technological fixes" which by their nature are generally ineffective.

By the late 1960s the large urban hospitals affiliated with medical schools – Health Policy Advisory Centre (PAC) called them medical empires – served as the entry point for a stream of new products and services, from the hospital equipment, pharmaceutical, and medical supply firms to construction and computer companies, bankers, lawyers, accountants, and management consultants (Ehrenreich and Ehrenreich 1970). McClure (1979) reports that no change occurred in the market share of medical schools and teaching hospitals between 1970 and 1980. Of the total hospitals in the US, 12 per cent account for 50 per cent of hospital industry expenditures and 50 per cent account for 90 per cent of expenditures. Labor costs comprise about 60–70 per cent of the typical hospital budget, and the bulk of the remaining $136 billion spent on hospital care in 1982 (Davis 1983) remains available to firms from the old medical industrial complex. McKinlay lists several of the attractive features in the profitability of medical care:

(a) There exists a large and often captive (literally) market. (Everyone is sick some of the time, and some people are sick all of the time).

(b) The public often give primacy to medical care over

other commodity consumption, and this demand appears insatiable.

(c) An association with medical care facilitates a strategic control over a near total consuming public.

(d) It fosters control over valued technology and skilled workers, thereby enhancing competitive position.

(e) It is an arena where the state acts as guarantor of profits.

(f) It enables institutions, threatened in other spheres (e.g. the environment), to project the false image of conspicuous benevolence.   (McKinlay 1977: 39)

Because of these features, a rapid proliferation of health-related products fashioned around a technological medicine have come from large corporate supplies.

Strelnick (1982) notes that these corporate firms are highly concentrated, often with a few major ones dominating market share for most product lines. American Hospital Supply Corporation is an example. Pillsbury writes:

> In the past decade the company's annual sales have climbed from $610 million to $2.9 billion, and American has moved up from sixth place to number one, grabbing nearly 20 per cent of the highly fragmented national market and growing to three times the size of its nearest competitor.
>
> (Pillsbury 1982: 56)

Though the actual net profit figures from corporate accounts estimated from 1972–75 remained low, Stevenson (1976) maintains the influence of peripheral supply firms has been great, in that approximately 35 per cent of all health expenditures flow through strictly large corporate entities. The importance of this finding is underscored by a 277 per cent increase between 1962–75 in US health expenditures, not adjusted for inflation. It is interesting to note that the for-profit hospitals and nursing homes were the fastest growing component at this time. In 1975 one third of proprietary hospitals were in corporate chains holding only 3 per cent of general care beds; in 1982 this figure was 15 per cent. Of note also is the fact that health expenditures by 1981 had doubled the 1975 level. *The US – Industrial Outlook* published by the Department of Commerce estimated sales by hospital suppliers at $11.6 billion in 1981 and *Standard and Poor's* puts the figure at $13 billion (Strelnick 1982). These tabulations do not count all profit-making activities as Stevenson attempted.

The HMO strategy and corporate inroads to delivery of care

Given the promising health care market (growing at approximately 15 per cent annually across the 1970s), it was reasonable that corporate capital would eventually extend beyond the supply role. In fact, the Nixon administration attempted to achieve its greater penetration into the delivery of services through the health maintenance organization (HMO) strategy (Salmon 1975). At this time in 1970 total health expenditures were $69.2 billion and 7.2 per cent of GNP, prompting President Nixon to proclaim a "health care crisis." Adding to the involvement of the "private sector" in peripheral supply and insurance companies, the HMO strategy was designed to redirect capital flows within delivery institutions and raise the overall profitability of the industry. Federal contracts to consulting firms were to secure "private sector funding for HMOs" in the amount of $300 million, while appropriations for other federal health programs were shuffled into simulating HMO development across the country. However, the unavailability of substantial federal financing (alongside the Nixon administration's cutbacks and impoundments of health funds) created a situation of almost total reliance on private capital for HMO growth and expansion – investment which was not forthcoming in the economic recession of 1973–75.

Paul Ellwood of Interstudy, a Minneapolis health think-tank, was the chief architect of the Nixon administration's HMO strategy. HMOs were conceived to be the organizational building blocks for a rational, corporate-run delivery system. Being designed for profit-making, the HMO's costs of rendering services contracted in the benefit packages are deducted from prepaid subscriber revenues. Since profitability is key to their survival, Ellwood invited large corporations to lend their "industrial know-how" because "they are experienced in the application of management and have the ability to generate and effectively use capital resources" (Ellwood 1971: 291). A major article by Ellwood and Herbert in the *Harvard Business Review* detailed the benefits of corporate-run profit-making HMOs and suggested that industrial medical departments should be converted to HMOs to "realize a substantial saving over present expenditures for employee health care benefits" (Ellwood and Herbert 1973: 105). The hope of the HMO strategy was to transform the system to where the "number of health care organizations in the United States would be reduced to as few as 1,000 with each HMO serving from 5,000 to several million persons" (Ellwood 1972a: 363). Local HMOs were expected to "function either as autonomous units or branches of larger national or regional organizations with several subsidiaries" (Ellwood 1972b: 97). Ellwood carried on extensive consultations with large corporations in the development of employee health programs, which led him to understand concerns of executives and employee benefit managers:

> Clearly, fundamental changes are underway in the relationship between medicine and business. Physicians can no longer expect businessmen to accept, without question, the way in which medical care is delivered . . . But some businessmen are beginning to grumble that medicine imposes a serious threat. In their view, rising employee health costs are no longer a minor concern, for expanded employee health programs, coupled with medical inflation, have become a critical element in a pattern of climbing production costs and rising prices, eroding both corporate profits and the competitive position of US business in the international marketplace. (Ellwood 1974: 13)

In 1970, the same year as Nixon's pronouncement of the HMO strategy, the US Department of Health, Education, and Welfare listed fourteen major corporations, twenty "entrepreneurial organizations," and fifteen private insurance companies actively investigating HMOs for investment purposes. By July 1974, there were 177 "operational" HMOs, with 204 in the "formational" stage and 88 in the "planning" stage. A compilation of large firms active in exploring HMO development read like the *Fortune* 500. Several of the more successful HMO ventures were due to local business involvement. In California, proprietary HMOs stimulated by the then Governor Ronald Reagan under the Medi-Cal program wound up with several exploitative firms generally discrediting the program (Health PAC 1975).

Apart from physician and hospital opposition and consumer uninterest and non-participation, the HMO program was also hindered by the Watergate-disrupted federal bureaucracy and the economic recession of 1973–75. Nevertheless, the HMO strategy tended to legitimize profit-making through corporate entities in the delivery of health services. More importantly, it became a means to educate the corporate class in problems of health care and activate them in health policy and planning (Salmon 1977). As purchasers of health services through fringe benefit packages for their workers, business has experienced rampant inflation in health insurance premiums, crimping their profit margins. Moreover, the questioning of the effectiveness of medical care led executives to ponder more closely how the health sector should be restructured and services redesigned to increase labor productivity.

Large corporations sought other avenues to expand the business role in relation to the health care system. Richard Egdahl of the Center for Industry and Health Care at Boston University became a chief strategist. Writing in the *New England Journal of Medicine* (Egdahl and Walsh 1977) he detailed three levels for corporate inroads: (1) the in-house programs of medical care, patient education, health protection and promotion; (2) corporate investment in employee health benefits through long-range planning, scrutinizing the cost of benefits administration, monitoring claims, and collecting data; and (3) reforming the external health care delivery system. As examples of "industrial sponsored pre-paid health plans," he extolls the Kaiser-Permanente Health Plan established by Kaiser Industries in the 1930s and the more recent Winston-Salem Health Care Plan, a health maintenance organization opened in 1977 by R.J. Reynolds Company, the tobacco conglomerate. Egdahl consulted with Gillette Company "in the development of a rationalized system of care that permits both greater pluralism than is possible in a closed-paneled pre-paid group practice, and tighter management controls than most open-panel plans have been able to achieve" (Egdahl and Walsh 1977: 1350). This is Egdahl's "hybrid industry-sponsored health plan" which can be established by an individual firm or by smaller and more dispersed firms banding together. With the lack of success of the Nixon–Ellwood Health Maintenance Strategy, Egdahl's more practical conceptualization would combine occupational and family medicine to serve "as a nidus in which the emergent specialty of primary care in industrial clinics can mature" (Egdahl and Walsh 1977: 1352).

Egdahl has produced a series on Industry and Health Care to inform corporate leaders on how to affect major change in the health care delivery system (Egdahl 1977). This series was developed in close association with the Washington Business Group on Health (WBGH), which was created by the Business Roundtable, a corporate planning organization comprised of chief executives of the top 200 major corporations in America. The WBGH's identification of class interests, and its strident attempts to pressure government and provider officials, coincides with efforts of other corporate planning bodies, such as the US Chamber of Commerce, the American Enterprise Institute, and the Conference Board (Salmon 1977). These groups have carried out extensive investigations of health care over the past decade, while the business press has publicized activities of various firms in addressing health care issues for their workers (Salmon 1978).

Extending beyond the national arena, are more practical interventions by corporate purchasers. In several communities across the nation, providers are bracing for a fight with "employers (who) are banding together, hoping to meld their market power as large-scale purchasers of health care services in order to keep costs down" (Rhein 1982: 55). Just as the Reagan administration is dismantling the nationwide system of health system agency, approximately eighty business coalitions on health care have been started to watch over their $55 billion outlays in 1981. The point should be made that many of these coalitions, particularly ones whose creation was sparked by the WBGH, exclude doctors as well as hospitals. This raises fears among medical specialty groups and certain hospitals who might be targeted for "excessive" utilization, prodding *Medical World News* to run a cover story entitled "Will Big Business Run The Show?" (Rhein 1982).

While most of these coalitions will probably seek to avoid outright antagonisms with local health providers, businessmen in general are ideologically committed to the "free enterprise" embodied in the Reagan administration's proposals for interjecting "competition" into health care. They also are geared to managerial solutions for problems in hospitals where they serve as board members. The influential Robert Wood Johnson Foundation has funded business involvement in various communities, and Ellwood's Interstudy has worked with several business groups rearranging local services (Iglehart 1982d).

Since there has been a general corporate inability, and from some quarters an unwillingness, to control professional and institutional behavior, "managerial solutions" by using "marketplace economics" have come into vogue. Reducing the federal health role, setting financial limitations on care, and creating profit "incentives" now make up the strategy. This "reform from within" includes "not-for-profit" rationalization, selected federal cutbacks, stiffer consumer co-payments, and proprietary systems growth and amalgamation – all orchestrated through conservative federal policies.

Corporate spokespeople argue their interest is to curtail their outlays for employee health, to reduce absenteeism and to improve worker productivity: all directly affect the level of corporate profits. However, the business interest in reorganizing the health sector is rarely portrayed in its full intent and implications. It is important to grasp that workers' health extends beyond the productivity and maintenance issues – people should not be treated as capital. Moreover, other population segments (whom the business press calls the "unproductive") will increasingly suffer from inadequate services in the planned reallocation of health resources.

Over a longer period of economic stagnation, the corporate class may realize the strategic necessity of integrating health services under tighter control for maximizing their profitability and planning. There are surely different dimensions of corporate involvement in health care, with diverse capitals often taking conflicting positions to the larger class interest. Navarro analyzes:

What we are witnessing is not so much a dismantling but a restructuring of the welfare state, with the intention of reducing the level of collective consumption actively intervening in the restructuring of capital to enable it to better respond to the international capitalist crisis. This restructuring of the welfare state takes place by: (a) large transfers of funds within the public sector and also from the public sector to the private sector; (b) changes in the internal management and control of certain state apparatuses; and (c) changes in the criteria by which decisions are made and funds are allocated   (Navarro 1982a: 172).

Even in Great Britain under Prime Minister Margaret Thatcher, similar dynamics can be observed, fundamentally modifying the course of social welfare policy.

Cost containment effects on health providers

The Reagan administration when it arrived in Washington, DC in 1980, ushered in a dramatic alteration in American domestic as well as foreign policy. Promises of a reduction in government role, regulatory reform, and private sector involvement have been fulfilled with the full effects of this redirection in health policy not completely realized. Massive cutbacks in nearly every public health program and the phasing out of the two regulatory programs (the Professional Standards Review Organizations and the Health Systems Agencies) has been attempted. Funding for Medicare and Medicaid has been slashed, with higher co-payments and stricter eligibility requirements being instituted, along with a proposed federalization of Medicaid. Medicare reimbursement rates to hospitals have been reduced below their cost figures, and prospective payment according to diagnostic-related groupings (DRGS) is being implemented. While the rhetoric for "competitive health plans" has somewhat diminished, aspects of this proposal seek greater health provider reductions and higher consumer out-of-pocket expenditures as a means to contain costs (Salmon 1982). In the face of the Reagan administration's shrinkage of the health care system, large-scale entities, which are claimed to be more economical, have staked out opportunities for profit. The president of the Federation of American Hospitals, the lobbying group of the proprietary hospital chains, explained that for the first time there is:

an administration opposed to government regulation of our industry, opposed to comprehensive national health insurance, opposed to cost controls, opposed to planning, and receptive to new ideas . . . We have never been in a better position in our history.

                                    (Federation of American Hospitals 1981: 2)

Even before the enactment of Republican policies, federal and corporate constraints on health expenditures brought upheaval to the hospital industry. In the face of deterioration of the public hospital system and financially-distressed urban voluntaries, "not-for-profit" hospitals have sought survival strategies through the financial crunch by mimicking their proprietary counterparts.

Between 1974–77, eighty-five public hospitals closed. Twenty-one county hospitals in California were closed or sold during the last six years of the past decade. In New York City alone, twenty-nine hospitals were closed between 1976 and 1980, and seventeen were considered "financially distressed" in 1982 along with a total of 160 hospitals nationwide according to the US Department of Health and Human Services. Over the six years up to 1980, the American Hospital Association (AHA) showed a net loss of 186 hospitals (Rhein 1982), and this was before the Reagan administration health budget cutbacks. The AHA reported a continuing decline in the total number of hospitals in 1981 to 6,933 and approximately 1,362,000 beds – a decline of thirty-three hospitals and more than 3,000 beds less than 1980 (Federation of American Hospitals 1982).

An article in the *Wall Street Journal* mentions that "by 1990 the money crunch will force about 1,000 hospitals to shut their doors forever" (Waldholtz 1982: 1). It described rivalries in Dayton, Ohio which forced a local hospital to set up a profit-making holding company over its several diversified businesses in response to an aggressive expansion by the national Seventh Day Adventist Health System chain. Needless to say, this "competition" provoked business purchaser concerns because of higher short-term costs, and expected later higher system-wide costs if other local health providers go under.

Brown (1981) sees the rate of closures accelerating, particularly in public hospitals now that the Reagan administration has downgraded health systems agencies. Previously, access, quality, and cost issues surrounding closures could be reviewed within the context of local health planning. Of the number of hospital admissions eliminated after a closure (estimated at 24–38 per cent), how many people with serious medical problems will no longer gain access to other facilities because of financial reasons? Further, can it be readily assumed that hospital closings mean reduced aggregate cost? More sophisticated, higher level institutions that remain open, find their caseload heavier, and with more patients who have inadequate means for paying for their care! While teaching hospitals have historically been the "provider of last resort" to the disadvantaged, many voluntaries are no longer able to afford being "humanitarian" to the uninsured indigent (including the unemployed), or to the Medicaid population whose reimbursement is lower than private health insurance. To achieve real savings, teaching institutions would have to reduce their case-mix intensity, utilization, and the number of costly procedures, along with instituting preventive and other out-of-hospital services – actions unlikely in the current climate. Indirectly complicating the fiscal dilemmas of teaching institutions, numerous community general hospitals are reducing their mix of services (often out-patient services) to cut losses and maximize reimbursement. This internal restructuring is a necessary adaptation for "economic success" according to Feldstein (1981), notwithstanding community health needs. Many voluntary hospitals, particularly those serving minorities and low-income populations, hold options of either bankruptcy, relocation, or conversion of facilities. Even before these changes however, Wennberg and Gettelsohn (1982) found that quality and cost of hospital care were linked more directly to the number of physicians, their specialties, and the number of available beds than to the health needs of community residents. In the absence of any system-wide assessment of local health needs in the entire population, continuous disruption of hospital services in many cities holds severe consequences for the poor, aged, and disabled who are being denied access to quality hospital services. The ramifications of these unplanned tendencies may turn out to be more detrimental than the apparently innocent extension of a hospital-centered system with technological priorities.

In the current climate, the "not-for-profit" voluntaries have become more obviously profit-seeking. Their true organization behavior is now unveiled, reflecting a convergence to that of the proprietary competition. Etzioni and Doty (1976) found that budget surpluses of voluntaries went mostly into exotic technology and duplication of facilities in their communities, which is partly to blame for cost inflation. More specifically, the generation of surplus by a voluntary hospital is realized by its medical staff (mostly indirectly), administrative personnel (in high salaries and expense accounts), trustees (and their business associates who furnish services or products to hospital operations), and, as mentioned previously, an array of medical industrial complex suppliers (Health PAC 1979). Past behavior of voluntaries has significantly been due to the conditions for their development, including the advent of Medicare and Medicaid, physician and administrator desire for increased technology and growth in size, changes in their labor force, government regulation, and even community and consumer influences. With philanthropic funds now inconsequential, the problematic ethical issues surrounding the profit motive apply only to governmentally provided services. *Medical Care News* has reported:

> The corporate chains' success has elicited a compliment from the non-profit sector: imitation. Non-profit hospitals are also forming multi-hospital systems, and there are now 225 non-profit systems that manage 1,131 hospitals. "The same ingredients that propel such companies as Sears, McDonald's and Exxon are also applicable to the institutional health care sector," [comments an officer of Hospital Corporation of America].   (Rhein 1982: 58)

Over the past several years, the hospital industry's trade magazines have extolled the necessity of changing their historical role through diversification into new "markets." Forward-looking hospital executives are urged to partake in long-range strategic planning, set up "profit centers," and seek out "captive distribution systems" to guarantee patient flow.

In order to cope with lagging revenues from unfilled beds, voluntaries have engaged in acquisitions, mergers, and a variety of diversification schemes. Several across the nation have offered stock in these new services. Corporate restructuring is common, to set up a holding company or parent corporation and to spin off "new lines of business" in, for example, hospice care for the terminally ill, occupational medicine programs, sports medicine clinics, biomedical engineering businesses, mobile diagnostic units, alcoholic recovery centers, clinical labs, surgi-centers, dialysis centers, nursing homes, home health care, housing for the elderly, restaurants, parking lots, health spas, flower shops, shopping centers, and more. Some diversification is only remotely related to the original mission of health care, contributing to the blurred distinction between the "not-for-profit" and proprietary segments.

Writing in the *Harvard Business Review*, Goldsmith (1980) urges hospitals to analyze and adapt to the "new health care market" or face severe difficulties and be absorbed. For a more "cost-effective, business-like basis" to voluntary hospital operations, multi-institutional arrangements have become prevalent in medical facilities and care; staffing resources; administrative and other services; continuing education and inservice training (Warren 1981). Over the last two decades, there has been a trend toward combining various clinical services (for instance, blood-banking), as well as a range of administrative services, just as proprietaries have done to achieve "economies of scale" (for example, group purchasing, management information systems, personnel, laundry and linen).

Whether the financial squeeze on the hospital industry necessitates the new organizational response, or the economic successes of proprietary chains are the model, hospital executives have not become outspoken critics of the Reagan administration's health policy redirections. David Stockman, Office of Management and Budget Director, predicted that the "health care market," once put back on competitive terms to "normally" handle "supply and demand," will force voluntary hospitals to become part of larger for-profit marketing operations; if they fail to make good investment decisions in beds or equipment, they can go bankrupt, or be taken over by more efficient concerns (Rhein 1982). Huff and Sharrer (1982) maintain that the Economic Recovery Tax Act of 1981 and reimbursement policies for Medicare and Medicaid have created a competitive imbalance for the "not-for-profits." Since "government resources are increasingly being channeled into the for-profit health sector . . . and voluntary hospitals' ability to survive is jeopardized," these authors urge conversion to for-profit status by voluntaries. The future picture of competition is full of conflicts not only between proprietaries and "not-for-profits," but also between teaching and non-teaching hospitals; among medical specialty services; between physicians and other practitioners challenging their domains; between hospitals and their communities, nowadays described as "target markets" (if they happen to be people with insurance or other means to pay); and between hospitals and their regulators and "adversaries" (including federal and state governments, local business coalitions, and insurance companies).

The growth of multi-hospital systems

Only four of the thirty-nine proprietary hospitals listed in the first US Hospital Census in 1873 survived into the twentieth century. By 1928, 2,435 were in operation, constituting about 36 per cent of hospitals of all types in the country (Relman 1980). Many were extensions of group practices of physicians and surgeons, serving either small towns or catering to well-to-do patients who wish not to be admitted to large urban centers.

Last decade, a university hospital representative expressed concerns that were echoed throughout the health care system:

> There is considerable evidence to indicate that many of the institutions owned by such corporations seek to gain their profit margin through the exclusion, by one technique or another, of patients who cannot pay the full cost of their hospital care; by using methods of patient selectivity to ensure that the institution does not care for the more complex type of medical and surgical conditions; through the exclusion of such services which have traditionally been money-losers for hospitals; or through a combination of all the above factors. This obviously brings the profit motive of the proprietary hospital directly into conflict with the total community medical needs in a particular locality.
>
> (Cannedy 1970: 65)

In a policy report on proprietaries, Blue Cross summed up:

> The provision of health care has traditionally been considered a social undertaking . . . In recent years, lack of confidence in the ability of profitable enterprises to maintain quality in health care has helped maintain dominance by non-profit hospitals.   (Stewart 1973: 5)

Today, arguments questioning the proprietaries' qualities of care, "cream-skimming" practices, and whether they achieve their purported efficiency have, for the most part, subsided with the acceptance of "competition" conditions. The convergence of hospital behavior in both segments of the industry has led the proprietaries to criticize the tax-exempt status of their counterparts. Representatives of the corporate chains claim that their hospitals are more efficient and cost effective (Eamer 1978), but evidence suggests that they have slightly higher costs and charges. Lewin, Derzon, and Marguiles (1981) found that proprietaries have a higher income per day and higher total operating costs per case; their Medicare and Medicaid reimbursement also tends to be a little higher per day. (Medicare pays an additional return on equity to for-profit firms.) Pattison and Katz (1983) found California proprietaries having higher total operating expenses, but only slightly higher costs per patient stay. Both studies showed not only higher costs and charges in the investor-owned hospitals, but also higher profit levels.

Medical education and postgraduate training are absent in proprietaries, though a couple hospital management corporations have identified selected teaching institutions as new ventures. They generally avoid the most sophisticated and costly technological care, emphasizing profit-laden services to usually more affluent, growing communities in states with fewer regulatory constraints. Thus, teaching institutions have argued that they have an exclusive burden for training future professionals and for the provision of care to the most severely ill and the inadequately insured.

The investor-owned hospital chains have clearly become the phenomena of the 1970s and 1980s, dedicated to aggressive growth and resourceful managerial practices. From 1968 to 1975 the number of proprietaries in corporate chains increased from fifteen to 300. By 1978, there were 399 hospitals with 84,000 beds owned by thirty-one major entities ("The Chain" 1978). While the hospital industry recently as a whole was shrinking, proprietaries expanded rapidly (see *Table 4.1*). From 1977–82, the total number of owned and managed hospitals in the US and abroad increased by 42 per cent, with beds jumping 62 per cent (Federation of American Hospitals 1982: 6). In 1981 alone, the ten largest proprietary hospital corporations expanded by an average of 42.5 per cent (Johnson and Punch 1982). In 1982, a total of 120,848 beds in 1,045 hospitals were

Table 4.1   *Multi-hospital systems in the US*

| type of system | Total | | | | | | Owned and leased |
| | beds | | | units | | | beds |
	change %	1981	1980	change %	1981	1980	1981
Investor-owned (30)*	27.4	107.765	84.560	32.3	795	501	73,110
Secular non-profit (64)	10.3	66.467	60.244	15.0	421	366	52,373
Catholic (46)	1.2	80.737	79.787	4.9	320	305	74,929
Other religions (21)	7.2	23.658	22.070	9.5	162	148	19,791
Public (11)	– 4.6	18.453	19.339	– 2.2	44	45	17,502
Total (172)	11.7	297.000	266.000	18.9	1,742	1,465	237,705

*Number of systems reporting in parenthesis   Source: *Modern Healthcare* (1982, May: 68).

held by investor-owned firms (Federation of American Hospitals 1982) (see *Table 4.2*). Nineteen investor-owned systems increased their revenues over the year in 1982, by 34.2 per cent and their profits by 51.7 per cent (Johnson 1983). The largest, Hospital Corporation of America (HCA) based in Nashville, Tennessee, is a $3.9 billion concern (1983), owning 355 hospitals in the United States, United Kingdom, and several other countries. (This transnational health provider manages another 35,303 beds in 294 hospitals under contract, an increase of 11.4 per cent over 1981). With the Reagan administration's prospective reimbursement for Medicare, HCA plans to acquire 1,200 additional beds in 1983 and expects a substantially increased demand for its contract management services – about $8 million profit on $27 million in 1982 revenues (Johnson 1983).

The growth strategies of the proprietary chains have been altered with great flexibility. In the late 1960s, they raised equity capital in the stock market for the construction of new facilities. Later, contract management became predominant with higher interest rates, capital shortages, and escalating construction costs. More currently, voluntaries and public hospitals with financial problems are targeted for acquisition. Hull (1983) reports that twenty-three public hospitals have been absorbed since 1979. Punch (1982) states that "Catholic hospitals are prime acquisition targets" as religious orders rethink their mission when confronted with financing difficulties. HCA, the leader in the "public-to-private" conversion,

			Managed			
	units		beds		units	
change from 1980 %	1981	change from 1980 %	1981	change from 1980 %	1981	change from 1980 %
23.7	517	28.3	34,655	36.2	278	40.4
5.1	266	3.1	14,094	35.1	155	43.5
0.3	275	3.4	5,808	14.2	45	15.4
3.9	109	7.9	3,867	28.0	53	12.8
− 4.9	35	− 2.8	951	1.0	9	0
7.5	1,202	13.0	59,375	32.1	540	34.7

bought sixteen city or county hospitals between 1975–80 (Lancaster 1980). American Medical International (AMI) (1983 sales of $1.57 billion and $130 million profit) owns over ten former public hospitals; it recently acquired Hyatt Medical Management Services, which had managed Cook County Hospital in Chicago, the teaching affiliate of the University of Illinois. The proprietaries have been particularly aggressive in obtaining psychiatric hospitals: HCA has twenty-five and National Medical Enterprises (NME) has twenty-two. Of non-government psychiatric beds in the US, 50 per cent are owned by proprietaries.

Concentration and centralization characterize the investor-owned hospital chains. Within the past few years, a wave of mergers has reduced the number and dramatically increased the size of the top firms. HCA bought Hospital Affiliates International; Humana merged with American Medicorp to become the $1.9 billion second largest; and NME ($1.765 billion of 1983 sales) acquired National Health Enterprises and Hill-Haven Corporation of Tacoma, Washington, two nursing home chains. The Forum Group, Inc. of Lexington, Kentucky, now controls American Medical Centers, Somerset Corp., Medical Corporation of America, National Psychiatric Institute, Excepticon, Inc. (home for the retarded), and Retirement Living of Wilmington, Delaware. American Medical International and Lifemark merged in 1984, yielding a combined 12,000 beds for hospital care, besides alcoholism treatment and ambulatory care facilities. The top ten chains now operate over 70 per cent of all proprietary hospitals, with each diversifying

Table 4.2 *Major proprietary hospital management companies, 1982*

Company		Owned Hospitals	Beds	Managed Hospitals	Beds
AHS	Advanced Health Systems Irvine, California	21	762	25	841
AHM	American Healthcare Management Dallas, Texas	11	833	3	608
AMC	American Medical Centers Nashville, Tennessee	12	1,007	2	140
AMI	American Medical International Beverly Hills, California	73	9,480	1	100
		10*	1,012	9*	1,591
AEB	Brim & Associates Portland Oregon			36	2,189
CMD	Charter Medical Corporations Macon, Georgia	30	3,607	2	261
		1*	49	1*	130
CPC	Community Psychiatric Centers Santa Fe, California	18	1,656		
		2*	168		
CCC	Comprehensive Care Corporation Newport Beach, California	7	594		
GHI	Greatwest Hospitals, Inc. Santa Anna, California	5	579	7	378
HCI	Healthcare International Austin, Texas	6	951		
HGI	Health Group, Inc. Nashville, Tennessee	13	1,161	3	374
HCA	Hospital Corporation of America Nashville, Tennessee	202	31,265	146	17,872
		17*	1,678	2*	750

		Hospitals	Beds	Hospitals	Beds
HMP	Hospital Management Professionals Brentwood, California			10	1,445
HUM	Humana, Inc. Louisville, Kentucky	88 3*	16,259 465		
HMMS	Hyatt Medical Management Services Encino, California			17	5,331
LMK	Lifemark Corporation Houston, Texas	25	4,025	8	784
NME	National Medical Enterprises Los Angeles, California	43	6,206	16 3*	1,816 575
PIA	Psychiatric Institutes of America (NME Subsidiary) Washington, D.C.	17	1,459	1	26
PHC	Paracelsus Hospital Corporation West Covina, California	11 7*	764 1,729		
QLC	Qualicare, Inc. New Orleans, Louisiana	10	900	5	594
UHS	Universal Health Services Bala Cynwyd, Pennsylvania	11	1,488	1	100
USHC	U.S. Health Corporation Clearwater, Florida	5	586	1	34
WLS	Whitaker Corporation Los Angeles, California			5*	1,250

* = foreign

Sources: Federation of American Hospitals 1983 *Directory*, p. 8–9; *Modern Healthcare* (1982, May: 68).

into other areas, mostly nursing home chains and free-standing ambulatory care centers. This concentration trend follows a series of financial advantages that accounted for their rapid growth.

During the inflationary 1970s investor-owned firms were able to service their long-term debt in cheaper money. The use of tax-exempt industrial revenue bonds greatly aided construction projects, which have lessened with the subsequent rise in contract management and "not-for-profit" acquisitions. Wall Street found their stocks glamorous (Loeb 1982). Other debt instruments have included bank and insurance company loans, commercial paper, subordinated debentures, and Eurodollar financing. These firms are one of the most highly leveraged industries in the US according to Siegrist (1983). Compared to the stock market as a whole, the stock of hospital chains sold at higher price earnings multiples, which aided equity building. Given these favorable conditions, they can move much more quickly than "not-for-profits" who experience significant delays in funding expansion – delays that make higher costs and increasingly a scaling down of the planned expansion.

The proprietary chains have searched out viable markets in the southwest, midwest, California, and Florida, virtually abandoning the northeast. By positioning themselves in these regions, they not only have found greater acceptance of for-profit systems by consumers, voluntaries, and third-party payors, but also usually have avoided hospital unions and stiffer state regulations. It must be remembered that the expansion by proprietaries has also been supported by public funds in cost-plus reimbursement with an added amount for building equity. For example, HCA received 37 per cent of its revenues in 1977 from Medicare and Medicaid (Fortune 1978).

The chains have also found more lucrative profit opportunities in managing voluntaries and public hospitals without tying up much capital. In the last decade, these hospitals needed numerous improvements in financial management, management information systems, credit and collection, industrial engineering, and materials management. Investor firms provided management consulting in these areas for individual hospitals, which often led to management contracts replacing the hospital administration. By 1981, investor-owned firms managed 278 hospitals, an increase of 40 per cent over the previous year (Johnson and Punch 1982). Between 3–8 per cent of gross hospital revenues is usually charged for the chain to institute revenue-enhancing and cost-cutting measures. What this means is that the hospital is brought into the chain's purchases of drugs, supplies, and insurance, and higher reimbursement from third parties and increased collections from self-pay bills are sought. *Business Week* (1975) reports that savings to the managed hospital can be three to five times the contract cost; however, critics maintain that the real savings come from lowering staff/patient ratios and eliminating services (Dallek 1981).

The proprietary hospitals have undertaken foreign expansion for similar reasons to other multinational corporations: profit margins usually exceed those in the US, besides tax advantages and less regulation. Nine chains operate hospitals overseas in seventeen different countries, with the most rapid investment being in the last few years. Even with its National Health Service, Great Britain is not exempt from this proprietary penetration. AMI owns and manages seven hospitals in Great Britain and has two more under construction. HCA has six British hospitals with several other countries being studied as potential targets for development. Whitaker Corporation gained 50 per cent of the top rating profit from foreign work, including Saudi Arabia (Hull 1982). Mannisto reports that:

> American health care expertise not only upgrades the quality of health care in the countries that these corporations serve, but foreign operations also provide the opportunity for U.S. companies to become familiar with different medical philosophies and techniques that can be applied to their domestic operations. (Mannisto 1981: 52)

The proprietary hospitals are still dwarfed by the "not-for-profit" segment, which is itself concentrating on multi-institutional provider systems. The formation of hospital coalitions and alliances by voluntaries, as well as local governments, present a parallel to the nationwide proprietary chains (14 per cent of not-for-profits are owned or leased by MIPs). They are likewise poised to benefit from the Reagan administration's alterations in health care financing. *The Modern Health Care survey* (Johnson and Punch, 1982; Johnson 1983) reported a 10.3 per cent and 11.5 per cent respective growth in the number of beds owned, leased, or managed by the secular non-profit chains in 1981 (66,476 beds) and 1982 (80,159). While not growing substantially in 1981, Catholic chains controlled 80,737 beds, and other religious chains grew 7.2 per cent to a total of 23,658 beds. This growth, besides the 27.4 per cent increase of the investor-owned system, was in constrast to the 4.6 per cent decline in the public hospital systems reported in the survey (see *Table 4.2*). The Seventh Day Adventist Health System, with three regional networks, ranked second to the Kaiser Foundation, the $2.4 billion HMO as the largest "not-for-profit" system. The Sisters of Mercy Health Corporation in Farmington Hills, Missouri, is the largest Catholic system, with 5,750 beds in 1982. Several other religious systems have combined under Catholic orders and Protestant sects. An example of a hospital coalition is the Voluntary Hospitals of America, Inc., based in Dallas, Texas. It is owned by thirty large tax-exempt hospitals and expects to be an $8 billion holding company of 100 share holders by 1985. In the public sector, the New York City Health and Hospital Corporation held 8,027 beds in 1981, and the County of Los Angeles Hospital had 3,754 beds, though both are continuing to close hospital units due to severe fiscal problems.

The immediate outlook is for substantial growth in these inter-organizational arrangements among the voluntaries along with a continued contraction of public hospitals. Johnson maintains: "The standard forecast is that more than 50 percent of the nation's hospitals will be part of systems in five years" (1983: 93). The brokerage firm Drexel, Burnham, Lambert, Inc. predicts that by 1990, 80 per cent of all hospitals will have joined chains (Rouse 1983). The supposed economies of scale and greater availability of clinical and managerial expertise for participating units are reasons given for this tendency toward the multi-institutional provider. Their larger operating and monetary-base strengthens their political power and increases access to private capital markets. Moreover, prospective reimbursement payments will force independents rather quickly into this pattern of consolidation.

Concentration disguised as competition

The Reagan administration has tightened the reimbursement climate for hospitals to intensify "competition." According to Wennberg (1982), local hospital areas have varied extensively in reimbursement rates by Medicare and Blue Cross, and in per capita expenditures for hospital care. Part of these variations are due to fixed costs from past expansions and differing intensities of services to more ill-patient populations; however, corporate sources have urged a modification of physician behavior as a means to curbing climbing costs in hospitals (*Wall Street Journal* 1976).

Toward this end, the Reagan administration's prospective hospital payment for public beneficiaries by diagnostic-related groupings (DRG) will reallocate hospital expenditures and force administrators to police their medical staff. DRGs promote incentives for profit when patients are promptly discharged and ancillary services utilization is reduced. In effect, the DRG system, like "vouchers" to allow Medicare patients to join prepaid arrangements like HMOs and PPOs, allows for greater profits to providers most able to control their marginal costs (that is, multi-institutional systems). Of note, the Federation of American Hospitals, which had opposed the Carter administration's proposal for a "cost cap" over hospital expenditures, was one of the staunch backers of DRG legislation. Seeking assurance that federal policy further aids FAH members, FEDPAC contributed $200,000 to the 1980–81 Congressional races. By making profit incentives central to promoting provider efficiency, current health policy has favored concentration, not withstanding the adverse effects on the unplanned larger system of care. In effect, the multi-institutional provider systems have emerged as the foremost contender for arranging for a fuller range of personal health services; their domination of the delivery system is virtually assured.

Besides this transformation of hospital care, dramatic developments in ambulatory care have begun, as physicians and health care organizations anticipate the Reagan administration initiative on "competitive health plans." The greater number of medical graduates each year presents an employee pool to multi-hospital systems and medical entrepreneurs who are setting up free-standing clinics (Weiss 1982). Humana operated fifty-five MedFirst centers in 1981, with twenty-five more to start by mid-1983 (Punch 1983); and over the next five years Humana plans to build 500 (Rhein 1982). National Medical Enterprises and American Medical International are also participating in this trend of making the group setting the dominant form of medical practice. HCA has associated with PruCare, the health maintenance organization owned by Prudential Insurance Company. HCA also runs an HMO in Brazil serving 650,000 people.

Several other multi-state HMOs are expanding rapidly (Iglehart 1984). Regional and national networks include the Kaiser Foundation Health Plan, CIGNA Health Plan (the largest investor-owned HMO), MaxiCare Health Plans (which acquired CNA in 1982), US Health Care of Pennsylvania, Health-Plans of Nashville, Tennessee, John Hancock, and PruCare of Prudential Insurance Company of America. The *Modern Health Care* survey lists eight investor-owned firms and four secular "not-for-profit" (Kuntz 1983). As with hospitals, there have been significant mergers and acquisitions, and the largest "not-for-profit" HMOs (Group Health Plan, Minneapolis; Harvard Community Health Plan, Boston; Group Health Corporative of Puget Sound, Seattle; and Health Insurance Plan of Greater New York) have signed an affiliation to set up a profit corporation and market to large corporate purchasers and develop HMOs in other areas. Blue Cross–Blue Shield Plans have likewise taken steps to do nationwide marketing.

For the explicitly for-profit HMOs, little upfront capital is actually required if these corporations take over HMOs that were originally set up as non-profit entities (e.g. Philadelphia Health Plan by John Hancock; Health Service Plan of Pennsylvania by Health-Plans; North-Care in Evanston, Illinois, by Prudential, among several others). Relatedly, insurance companies and proprietary hospital chains are beginning scaled-down hybrid HMOs known as Preferred Provider Organizations (PPOs). In a PPO, the consumer is allowed to choose his or her own primary care physician, but must use prescribed hospitals and their specialists for referral care. Besides the rapid extension of Humana Care Plus, the state of California has seen many PPO beginnings (Punch and Johnson 1984).

Whether the evolving form is a competitive health plan, an

HMO, or a PPO, it seems evident that these larger proprietary entities and commercial insurance companies will easily dominate the out-of-hospital territory soon. The Washington Business Group on Health has been backing HMO development and favors these "private sector initiatives" to arrange coverage in coordinated ambulatory and hospital care. These multi-state HMO providers are thus seeking to capture enrollees from large corporate purchasers. Moreover, if the past predicts future dynamics, combinations of these HMO health plans, proprietary hospital chains, and large insurance companies are on the horizon of health care delivery.

Implications from competition

By looking at other industries that have become concentrated, it can be seen that larger firms have distinct advantages over others. They possess ready organizational and financial resources to systematically search out possible modifications in their activities to reap big cost savings. By virtue of their domination of the market, these larger corporate entities can also risk the installation of more efficient, but expensive new systems and technology because of their ability to sell their product lines. The larger and more dominant the firm, the greater its marketing strength and the greater its manipulation of the market to its terms.

Of course, corporations in concentrated industries, particularly in times of economic downturn, have little incentive to pass their cost savings on to consumers. Rather, innovations in production, and reductions in labor costs, will just increase profits. In health care, concentration may tend to work *against* organizational innovations and advances in science that are not profitable, but are in the interests of improved health.

Relman (1980) had urged the American Medical Association to "act defensively in separating physicians from the commercial exploitation of health care" (1980: 965), though he does not see similar issues in the private practice of medicine, nor in the pharmaceutical, hospital equipment, and supply industries: "no one has seriously challenged their social usefulness" (1980: 963). As in the response in the 1930s by the medical profession to the "corporate practice of medicine" under the prepaid group practice form, Relman's principal concern may lie in the increasing control over physician behavior by these large organizational structures managed by non-physicians. He resounds a narrow self-interest for the profession in that "the physician alone has the expertise and authority to decide which services and procedures should be used in any circumstance" (1980: 965). Expressing his academic medical perspective, Relman questions "whether competition from profit-making providers is really threatening the survival of our teaching centers and major urban hospitals" (1980: 963). However, by pitting for-profit against "not-for-profit," he fails to note similarities in their respective organization behaviors, most notably that both segments are interested in "increasing its total sales," and both are now "cream-skimming," "over-emphasizing procedures and technology," with "excessive fragmenting of services."

Two recent encroachments into academic medicine have come from proprietary hospital systems with more to come. Humana signed a management contract for the University of Louisville Medical Center in 1983, and Harvard Medical School's Massachusetts General Hospital considered selling the prestigious McLean Psychiatric Hospital to HCA. Evidently, these firms' corporate strategies include obtaining arrangements for teaching and research. Relman remarks about the Harvard-HCA association,

> Here is the bastion of academic medicine, with the most distinguished teaching hospital in the country, if not in the world, face to face with the biggest, richest hospital company in the world. They want Harvard's imprimatur.
>
> (Butterfield 1983: 24)

Through the twentieth century, physicians as a profession have postponed or minimized their proletarianization, a process inherent in modern corporate society that has quickly and more easily engulfed most other workers (McKinlay 1977). Nevertheless, the nature of this current transformation of the health sector, coupled with the "oversupply" of physicians by the year 2000, appears to be leading a slow reduction of the physician to a proletarian function in large bureaucratic organizations. Given the forthcoming industrialization of health services, small-scale medical practice will become untenable and professional prerogatives will erode slowly in the large structures. Fuchs' (1975) notion of physician as the "captain of the team" seems absurd under the impending changes, as medical activity moves closer to the service of the dominant interest of capital accumulation.

In an article related to Relman's in the *New England Journal of Medicine*, Wilson (1982) examined the private for-profit enterprise in financing construction and renovation of hospitals. Tax exempt revenue bonds have replaced the Federal Housing Administration and Hill-Burton Hospital Construction Program as the principal mechanism for capital financing. The consequence is that:

> A powerful new force has been added to the industrialization of health care: bond investors, banks, and investment firms with a pecuniary interest in increasing hospital use and costs. Since the generation of cash to repay bonds becomes their first obligation, non-profit community hospitals with financial obligations to bond holders are likely over time to differ only slightly, if at all, from investor-owned hospitals similarly responsible to share-holders. (Wilson 1982)

The authors ponder how obsolescent voluntaries who are estimated to require $193 billion for new construction and modernization this decade, might be kept out of financial markets by investment bankers favoring for-profit providers.

Other objections to the extension of proprietary health care have been raised, though in the main, the Reagan administration's advocacy of the private sector as savior has colored the whole political, institutional, and intellectual development. It may become one of the major tragedies in the history of US public health that the infusion of management and finance capital has not been more critically questioned as a tenet of health care reform.

Marginal concerns by some professionals decry health care's "humanitarian" efforts eroding into an exclusively economic endeavor. Summing up what seems to be the prevailing viewpoint from inside provider institutions, Cunningham believes "it is possible to see more common ideas and convictions among investor-owned and non-profit hospitals and less antagonism of their motivating beliefs and concepts than there has been in the past. Responsible owners and managers in the investor-owned system are here to stay" (1982: 818). Unfortunately, given the apparent acceptance, or outright embrace, of a profit-centered health care system by professionals, Americans may come to accept this transformation provided only "reasonable" profits are extracted and certain quality standards are "guaranteed."

Merely describing the trend of organizing medical care for profit is insufficient, as is the assessment of the larger corporate form as just another step in the advance of medicine and its bureaucratization (Starr 1982; Berliner 1983). Basically, all of these predominant observations of the "new medical industrial complex" fail in their analysis by *not* focusing upstream to the process of capital accumulation in American society (McKinlay 1974). The pursuit of profit under capitalism cares not about boundaries of supplying providers and actual services delivery, nor does it respect out-moded designation of proprietary and voluntary. While health care can be exploited by corporate capital, it will be, at least until the rapinous thirst for higher profit levels leads it elsewhere.

The impending industrialization of health care appears ready to subject most professional activity and smaller providers to large corporate entities. Prospects for this decade include: (1) continued diversification of "product lines" as the commodification of health needs expands; (2) increasing concentration in supply firms, delivery organizations, and insurers, predictably with numerous interconnections; (3) entry of non-health corporations into services delivery; and (4) health care systems becoming a major export activity to international markets.

Production for profit in medical care means much less emphasis on equity in the distribution of services and less concern for the individual regardless of class, sex, race, age, and language. Patient–practitioner interactions can be expected to be redesigned. It remains to be seen how mutual trust and respect, which are integral to healing, will be supported in altered economic relationships between patients and their providers of care. Profit maximization tendencies are likely to influence how numerous bioethical issues are viewed and resolved. Future medical research priorities, and ideological orientations in health services research, will likewise be shaped by it, for nationwide provider systems stand poised to benefit from forthcoming advances in biomedicine and behavioral medicine. Moreover, the next decade's "information systems revolution" will enable a concentrated health care industry not only to modify the content of medical practice, but to possess a pervasive power to define health. This prospect is made more ominous given the political nature of the inexorable expansion of socially- and environmentally-generated health problems. It is also doubtful that managerial talent will yield benignly beneficial results in lessening demonstrated ineffective procedures, wasteful use of biotechnology, unnecessary ancillary testing, ritualistic surgery, and the like (McKinlay 1981). Profit has accounted for their embedment in the delivery system; they may be predictably prolonged to recover costs, even while corporate purchasers of care for employees demand efficiency and cost effectiveness. Probably, much of this development will be obscured from public scrutiny beyond what may be presented for acceptability.

Profit-making extensions in Great Britain

The key difference between the health systems in the United States and Great Britain dates back to the war years when social welfare policy in Britain took a distinct departure in creating its National Health Service (NHS) (Adams 1981). Consequently, this administrative structure more forthrightly opposes a reorientation to corporate medicine.

The conservative economic strategy of Prime Minister Margaret Thatcher has employed a tight money supply, high interest rates, and reduced public borrowing to trim British corporations to the realities of the new economic order in the world. While inflation is down from the 1979 level, unemployment of approximately four million characterizes Britain's deepest recession since the 1930s. With one of the lowest growth rates in Europe, a vastly shrinking export economy, and lessening North Sea oil reserves, there appear to be certain imperatives for more draconian reductions in social welfare spending, including selling off government holdings.

During the past decade, the NHS has come under increasing attack as an unmanageable and costly system of acute hospital care. An ideological crusade has been launched to limit the budget and force hospital closures and service cutbacks, even though health expenditures account for 5.5 per cent of economic output, one of the lowest percentages of advanced capitalist nations. The NHS covers 93 per cent of Britain's medical bill, equivalent to $20 billion per year (Newman 1983). While increased demand for medical care implies a need for additional funding, conservatives have found that control over the NHS budget allows reduction of the "safety net," thought to be too high relative to national productivity. Proposals have been made to switch the financing from general taxation to an insurance system with high patient co-payments to shunt one-third of the cases to private medicine (Newman 1983). Such a change would retrogressively burden lower income groups and threaten the NHS's equity basis (Radical Statistics Health Group 1980). NHS policy has been attempting to maximize efficient use of dwindling resources in accordance with cost/benefit criteria, while being designed to obscure the reality of reductions in expenditures by presenting their effects as improvements, rather than deterioration in services (Doyal 1979: 208). The budget crunch has led to greater regional disparities in resource allocations, as well as being less related to morbidity and mortality needs. As in the US, the notions that the individual should be responsible for his or her own health and bear a greater share of costs are being widely promulgated.

Meanwhile, the proprietary medical sector has grown during the NHS difficulties, with government interventions assisting it (Iliffe 1982). The attempts by the Labour government of 1976–79 to reduce the number of private beds in NHS hospitals created the basis for growth by profit-making hospitals. The Thatcher government has supported the private sector by tax concessions and increasing opportunities for physician private practices. Tax breaks have been given to some workers who buy private insurance. In anticipation of a growing "market," American multi-national hospital management companies have staked out England for their greatest foreign investment. The Federation of American Hospitals (1982) claims:

> Selection of a country for hospital development and ownership is a careful, painstaking and often lengthy process for the companies. In addition to the customary feasibility and economic studies, they usually do a political and cultural assessment and other exploratory research that would provide

a good feel for the stability and future direction of the country in question. These steps are regarded as an integral part of the decision-making process.

Companies that are mainly interested in equity investment and long-term development concentrate on countries where there is impetus in the private sector. For example, opportunities are especially bright in countries with ailing national health programs, such as England. Government support for private sector hospital build-up has been especially encouraging for the American companies operating there.   (The Federation of American Hospitals 1982: 24–5)

Six US hospital corporations own and operate fourteen hospitals (1,132 beds), with seven under construction; one other hospital is under a management contract.

To help keep proprietary beds filled, private health insurance increased to $3\frac{1}{2}$ million Britons in 1980, with a projection estimated to be 20 per cent of the population by 1985. Newman (1983) reports that there were 4 million privately insured people who wanted "instant attention" for high-profit surgical procedures, rather than having to queue up for the NHS. He states 151 private hospitals are in operation. Chubb, Haywood, and Torrens (1982) maintain that approximately 6,500 acute beds exist in non-NHS hospitals, with 1,000 planned and another 1,900 soon to be applied for under Thatcher's eased restrictions on the building of private hospitals. More recently Chubb has counted some 160 private hospitals with over 7,600 beds (Chubb 1984). A significant share is controlled by the American hospital chains. Chubb, Haywood, and Torrens warn that the private sector may:

fragment unified social policy and planning; create a two-class health system; divert scarce personnel out of the public into the private sector; increase the total cost of health care without corresponding improvement in the health status of the population; emphasize technology and deemphasize nontechnological services at a time when the latter are becoming the most critical.

(Chubb, Haywood, and Torrens 1982: 187)

Private insurance coverage is built around the NHS and personal social services as a fallback, since entitlement to these government-run programs is maintained by citizenship. Mostly catering to those with upper incomes, non-profit provident associations are increasingly marketing to employer groups to provide a fringe benefit for selected employees. An example is the British United Provident Association (BUPA) which has several profit-making subsidiaries linked to it.

Public support for the NHS remains strong (Howe 1981), making it unlikely that its basic foundations will be dismantled. Nevertheless, the structure has not been immune to trimming at its margins. As the British economy faces further constraints, cutbacks in the NHS will be the private sector's gain. The extent of expansion in the latter depends not only on the Thatcher government's policy decisions, but also upon the private sector generating ample profit levels. The successes of the ''new medical industrial complex'' in the US may influence its extension, both as the model for ''private sector initiatives'' and as a source of foreign investment, to Britain.

Summary and conclusions

This chapter has attempted to demonstrate how the process of capital accumulation is central to health sector developments. In the United States and Great Britain, trends and prospects that are influencing future opportunities for profit in health care have been discussed. Most importantly, the context of the continuing economic crisis of western capitalism portends significant readjustments to the cumulative nature and structural fit of medical care in both nations. The weakness of capital in each country is reflected in retarded growth of investment and significantly lower rates of return than in previous decades. International monetary instability, political realignments among nations, and continued challenges from other advanced and developing countries will influence domestic policies.

President Reagan and Prime Minister Thatcher have eroded previous full employment goals and income redistribution attempts in order to strengthen the material base of corporations. The renegotiation of the social contract between labor and capital is signified by both governments' reductions of social welfare spending and the unilateral revocation of health benefits for certain workers. This erosion of the social wage, and decline in the standards of living of the American and British people, are not short-term aberrations soon to be corrected. To the extent that health in these populations emanates from social structural and ecological conditions arising from the overall process of capital accumulation, the divergence between the social production of disease and for-profit medical care will increasingly indicate limitations in medical interventions (McKinlay and McKinlay 1979).

On the one hand, the proprietary thrust in medical care has been gaining legitimacy by appeal to the corporate class and government with promises of efficiency, cost-controls, and economic returns. These parties may recognize their apparent inability to overcome the disease-producing aspects inherent under capitalist development other than through market creation. On the other hand, there have been deep economic affinities between institutionalized services under the medical model and other ideological characteristics of corporate expansion into the service sectors. The larger corporate entry into medical care has escalated with the rising imbalances between a "socially inefficient" health system and the overall corporate profit squeeze over the last decade.

The probable convergence between the corporate class interest for cost containment and the for-profit reorganization lies in the legitimation of a chaotic system of health care consistent with its principles of economic production; yet antagonisms will inevitably persist. What may come to pass with this entry are new forms of class control, whereby a reorganization strategy will gradually reshape the ideology of medicine and the specific content of health services. The loss of relative autonomy by health sector parties in the economy threatens the medical profession, which is the point that concerns the editor of the *New England Journal of Medicine* (Relman 1980). The growing influence of corporate planning bodies in health policy formulation and numerous local business coalitions signifies a new context for future health sector developments. O'Connor (1973) had maintained that a "social industrial complex" may eventually emerge to organize more "rationally" health, education, and social welfare services, and even other aspects of family and social life. All necessary for the reproduction of labor power under a capitalist economic system, he analyzed it would make sense for class-conscious corporate policy to redesign them to lessen their absorption of the social surplus. Marginally productive and disenfranchised populations serve little purpose in the generation of profit from these services or in the allocation of societal resources in the first place. Thus, the current discussions of "rationing" medical care resources assume a logic beyond the individual clinical level. What may have seemed reprehensible a mere decade or so ago, this topic has only come into vogue recently in both the US and UK (Evans 1983; Aaron and Schwartz 1984).

The imposition of such a framework is being resisted. A changing public consciousness indicates that many people will not be satisfied with their own health level resulting from an economic transaction dependent on the value of their labor. Moreover, Navarro (1982b) presents evidence that no popular mandate exists for the withdrawal of services for the aged and unfortunate, nor for the weakening of government protection for the worker, consumer, and our ecology. As greater numbers of Americans and Britons more broadly define their health, demands for more meaningful and sensitive encounters with health practitioners will surely escalate. Ideologically, the medicalization of a whole array of political, cultural, and personal conditions leading to chronic degenerative illnesses are presently being manipulated to obscure the social and ecological origins of disease. While not always countering this, commentaries from the women's health, self-care, and holistic health movements, and from ecological, spiritual and "New Age" circles, are articulating the political and social issues. From these quarters have come attacks on the "medical model," which has been most amenable to commodified services for repair of acute illnesses (Berliner and Salmon 1980).

If a large enough segment of both populations seek an altogether different orientation in the purpose and meaning of health care; if people demand decentralized health services organized under the democratic control of their community; if communities attempt to relate health services with other aspects of community and social life, profit-making opportunities will be undermined and progress toward collective health will be achieved.

References

Aaron, H.J. and Schwartz, W.B. (1984) *The Painful Prescription: Rationing Hospital Care*. Washington, DC: Brookings Institution.

Adams, P. (1981) *Health of the State*. New York: Praeger.

Anlyan, W.G. and Cohn, V. (1980) Can the Private Sector Lead the Evolution of Medicine in the 1980s? *The New England Journal of Medicine* 303(1): 57–9.

Berliner, H.S. (1983) Starr Wars: A Review of the Social Transformation of American Medicine. *International Journal of Health Services* 13(4): 671–75.

Berliner, H.S. and Salmon, J. Warren (1980) The Holistic Alternative to Scientific Medicine: History and Analysis. *International Journal of Health Services* 10: 133–47.

Blue Cross Association (1973) Blue Cross Reports (9). Chicago, Ill.: Blue Cross Association.

Brown, E.R. (1979) *Rockefeller Medicine Men: Medicine and Capitalism in America*. Berkeley: University of California Press.

——(1981) *Public Medicine in Crisis: Public Hospitals in California*. California Policy Seminar Monograph No. 11. Institute of Governmental Studies: University of California.

Brown, G. (1981) Chains Take Over Public Hospitals. Newsletter of the *National Health Law Program* 121: 1,3.

Brown, M. (1980) Trends in Multi-hospital Systems: A Multi-year Comparison. *Health Care Management Review* 6 (Fall): 9–22.

Business Week (1975) How Outsiders Manage Hospitals For Profit. 24 November: 50, 55–6.

——(1982) The Spiraling Cost of Health Care-Rx: Competition. 8 February: 7–12.

Butterfield, F. (1983) Proposed Sale of a Hospital by Harvard is Raising Fears. *The New York Times*, 4 September: 24.

Cannedy, L.L. (1970) An Historical Analysis of the Viability of For-profit Hospitals. *Hospital Progress* 51 (November): 64–71.

Chubb, P.L. (1984) Managing the Mixed Economy of Health-Policy Options for Health Authorities in the National Health Services, United Kingdom. Paper presented at the American College of Hospital Administrators, 27th Congress on Administration, Chicago, 8 March.

Chubb, P., Haywood, S., and Torrens, P. (1982) Managing the Mixed Economy of Health: Policy Considerations for the National Health Service in Dealing with Expansion of the Private Sector. Occasional Paper No. 42. Health Services Management Centre, Birmingham.

Coffin, T. (1983) Health Care, the "Medical Industrial Complex." *The Washington Spectator* 9(7): 1–3.

Cunningham, R.M. (1982) Changing Philosophies in Medical Care and the Rise of the Investor-owned Hospital. *The New England Journal of Medicine* 307(13): 817–19.

Dallek, G. (1981) The Private (Mis-) Management of Public Hospitals: Feeding at the Public Trough. *Health Law Project Library Bulletin* 6: 62–76.

Davis, C.K. (1983) The Federal Role in Changing Health Care Financing – Part I. *Nursing Economics* 1: 10–17

Deans, J.H. (1976) Investor-owned and Not-for-profit Hospitals Conduct Joint Activities. *Hospitals* 50 (16 February): 49–51.

Derzon, R., Lewin L.S., and Watt J.M. (1981) Not-for-profit Chains Share in Multi-hospital System Boom. *Hospitals* 54 (16 May): 65–71.

Doyal, L. (1979) *The Political Economy of Health*. Boston, MA: South End Press.

Dreitzel, H.P. (1971) *The Social Organization of Health*. New York: Macmillan.

Eamer, R.K. (1978) Why Proprietary Hospitals are More Efficient and Cost Effective. *Modern Hospital Care* 8(4): 60–3.

Egdahl, R. (ed.) (1977) *Springer Series on Industry and Health Care* (5 vols). New York: Springer-Verlag.

Egdahl, R.H. and Walsh D.C. (1977) Industry-sponsored Health Programs: Basis for a New Hybrid Prepaid Plan. *New England Journal of Medicine* 296(22): 1350–353.

Ehrenreich, J. and Ehrenreich, B. (1970) *The American Health Empire: Power, Profits and Politics*. New York: Random House.

Ellwood, P.M. (1971) Health Maintenance Strategy. *Medical Care* 9 (May/June): 291–98.

——(1972a) Testimony before the Senate Subcommittee on Public Health and Environment. Serial no. 97–90, part II. Washington, DC: US Government Printing Office.

——(1972b) Models for Organizing Health Services and Implications of Legislation Proposals. *Milbank Memorial Fund Quarterly* 50 (October): 73–101.

——(1974) Big Business Blows the Whistle on Medical Costs. *Prism* December: 12–15.

Ellwood, P.M. and Herbert, M.E. (1973) Health Care: Should Industry Buy It or Sell It? *Harvard Business Review* 51 (July/August): 99–107.

Etzioni, A. and Doty, P. (1976) Profit in Not-for-profit Corporations: The Example of Health Care. *Political Science Quarterly* (Fall): 433–53.

Evans, R.W. (1983) Health Care Technology and the Inevitability of Resource Allocation and Rationing Decisions. *Journal of the*

American Medical Association (Part I) 249(15): 2047–053; (Part II) 249(16): 2208–222.

Eyer, J. and Sterling, P. (1977) Stress-related Mortality and Social Organization. *Review of Radical Political Economics* 9: 1–44.

Federation of American Hospitals (1981) *Federation of American Hospitals 1981 in Review: Annual Report*. Little Rock, Arkansas: Federation of American Hospitals.

——(1982) *The 1983 Directory: Investor-owned Hospitals and Hospital Management Companies*. Little Rock, Arkansas: Federation of American Hospitals.

Federation of American Hospitals Review (1982) New Law will Strengthen the Positive Aspects of the Peer Review System, Durenberger believes. 15(6): 22–5.

Feldstein, P.J. (1981) Economic Success for Hospitals Depends on Their Adaptability. *Journal of the American Hospital Association* 55(2): 77–9.

Figlio, K. (1980) Sinister Medicine: A Critique of Left Approaches to Medicine. *Radical Sciences Journal* 9: 15–159.

Fortune (1978) Keeping Young in Nashville. 13 July: 14.

Fuchs, V.R. (1975) *Who Shall Live?* New York: Basic Books.

——(1981) The Coming Challenge to American Physicians. *The New England Journal of Medicine* 304(24): 1487–490.

Goldsmith, J.C. (1980) The Health Care Market: Can Hospitals Survive? *Harvard Business Review* (September/October): 100–11.

——(1981) Outlook for Hospitals: Systems are the Solution. *Harvard Business Review* (September/October): 130–41.

Gouch, I. (1981) Poverty in the United Kingdom. *International Journal of Health Services* 11(2): 315–28.

Graham, D. (1981) The Private (Mis-) management of Public Hospitals: The Case of Highland Hospital. *Health Law Project Library Bulletin* 6: 75–82.

Gray, B.H. (ed.) (1983) *The New Health Care for Profit: Doctors and Hospitals in a Competitive Environment*. Washington, D.C: National Academy Press.

Greene, R. and Baker, T. (1981) Paging Dr Adam Smith. *Forbes* (13 April): 152–57.

Havighurst, C.C. (1970) Health Maintenance Organizations and the Market for Health Services. *Law and Contemporary Problems* 35 (Autumn): 716–95.

——(1973) Regulation of Health Facilities and Services by Certificate of Need. *Virginia Law Review* 59(7): 1143–232.

Health and Medicine Policy Research Group (1982) The Corporatization of American Health Care. *Health and Medicine* 1(2).

Health Insurance Association of America (1982) *Major Health Policy*

Issues. Washington, DC: Public Relations Division.

Health Policy Advisory Center (1975) *Materials on Pre-paid Health Plans*. San Francisco: Health Policy Advisory Center.

——(1979) *The Profit in Non-Profit Hospitals*. San Francisco: Health Policy Advisory Center West.

Howe, G. (1981) Health and the Economy: A British View. *Health Affairs* 1(1):30–8.

Huff, J.S. and Sharrer, K.I. (1982) Government Policies Force Non-profits to Go Profit. *Modern Healthcare* 12(6): 81–3.

Hull, J.B. (1982) Hospital Firms are Expanding Foreign Work. *The Wall Street Journal*, 9 July: 19, 33.

——(1983) How Ailing Hospital in South was Rescued by a For-profit Chain. *The Wall Street Journal*, 28 January: 1.

Iglehart, J.K. (1981) Drawing the Lines for the Debate on Competition. *The New England Journal of Medicine* 305(5): 291–96.

——(1982a) The Future of HMOs. *The New England Journal of Medicine* 307(7): 451–56.

——(1982b) Health Care and American Business. *The New England Journal of Medicine* 306(2): 120–24.

——(1982c) Funding the End-stage Renal-disease Program. *The New England Journal of Medicine* 306(8): 492–96.

——(1982d) Report on the Duke University Medical Center Private Sector Conference. *The New England Journal of Medicine* 307(1): 68–71.

——(1984) HMOs (For-profit and Not-for-profit) on the Move. *New England Journal of Medicine* 310(18): 1203–208.

Illich, I. (1976) *Medical Nemesis*. New York: Pantheon.

Iliffe, S. (1982) The Economic and Political Crisis in the British National Health Service. Paper presented at the International Conference on Health Policies in Western Europe, Frankfurt, July.

Interstudy (1978a) *A National Health Care Strategy: How Business Can Stimulate a Competitive Health Care System*. Washington, DC: National Chamber Foundation.

——(1978b) *A National Health Care Strategy: How Business Interacts With the Health Care System*. Washington, DC: National Chamber Foundation.

Johnson, D.E.L. (1983) Multi-units are Ready to Boost Their Market Share. *Modern Healthcare* 13(5): 89–122.

Johnson, D.L. and Punch, L. (1982) Multi Hospital Systems Survey. *Modern Healthcare* 12(5): 74–122.

Kelman, S. (1971) Review of *The Rising Cost of Hospital Care* by M.S. Feldstein. *International Journal of Health Services* 3(2): 311–14.

Kennedy, L. (1981) Hospitals in Chains: The Transformation of American Health Institutions. *Health PAC Bulletin* 12(7): 9–14, 31–6.

Kinkead, G. (1980) Humana's Hard Sell Hospitals. *Fortune* (17 November): 68-81.

Kotelchuck, D. (ed.) (1976) *Prognosis Negative: Crisis in the Health Care System.* New York: Vintage.

Kuntz, E.F. (1982) Systems Scoop Up Nursing Homes. *Modern Healthcare* 12(5): 102-03.

——(1983) HMOs Run Path of Consolidation. *Modern Healthcare* (13)5: 145-47.

Lancaster, H. (1980) More Public Hospitals are Sold to Firms Despite Objections from Poor and Aged. *The Wall Street Journal*, 11 November: 48.

Lave, G. (1981) Health and the Economy: A British View. *Health Affairs* 1(1): 30-8.

Levine, A. (1982) American Business is Bullish on Wellness. *Medical World News* 23(6): 33-40.

Lewin, L.S., Derzon, R.A., and Marguiles, R. (1981) Investor Owned and Nonprofits Differ in Economic Performance. *Hospitals* 54 (1 July): 52-8.

Loeb, M. (1982) Hospital Corp., Similar Stocks Remains Favored by Analysts Despite Medicare Cuts, Trust Suits. *The Wall Street Journal*, 30 August: 31.

Lowrie, E.G. and Hampers, G.L. (1981) The success of Medicare's End-stage Renal-Disease Program. *The New England Journal of Medicine* 305(8): 434-38.

Mannisto, M. (1981) Hospital Management Companies Expand Foreign Operations. *Journal of the American Hospital Association* 55(3): 52-5.

McClure, W. (1979) Conversion and Other Policy Options to Reduce Excess Capacity. In *Interstudy*, Dept of Health, Education and Welfare Publication No. (HRA) 79-14044: 97, Excelsior, Minnesota.

McKinlay, J.B. (1974) A Case for Refocusing Upstream – The Political Economy of Illness. *Applying Behavioral Sciences to Cardiovascular Risk*, proceedings of American Heart Association Conference, Seattle, Washington, 17-19 June.

——(1977) Toward the Proletarianization of Physicians. Unpublished manuscript.

——(1978) On The Medical-Industrial Complex. *Monthly Review* October: 38-42.

——(1981) From 'Promising Report' to 'Standard Procedure': Seven Stages in the Career of Medical Innovation. *Milbank Memorial Fund Quarterly/Health and Society* 59(3): 374-411.

McKinlay, S. and McKinlay, J.B. (1979) Examining Trends in the Nation's Health. Paper presented at the American Public Health Association Annual Meeting, New York, November.

McNeil, D. and Williams, R. (1978) Wide Range of Causes Found for Hospital Closures. *Hospitals* 52 (December): 76–81.

Mechanic, D. (1978) Rationing Medical Care. *The Center Magazine* (September/October): 22–31.

Medical World News (1982) Proprietary Hospitals' Boom: A Boom for MDs – or a Threat? 23(2): 26–9.

Modern Hospital (1969) Big, Bigger, Biggest – For-profit Hospital Chains Continue to Expand. 113: 99–103.

Morris, M. (1981) The Legacy of the Past: The State and Health Care. *Medicine in Society* 8(2): 31–4.

Navarro, V. (1976) *Medicine Under Capitalism*. New York: Prodist.

——(1982a) The Crisis of the International Capitalist Order and Its Implications for the Welfare State. *International Journal of Health Services* 12(2): 169–90.

——(1982b) Where is the Popular Mandate? *The New England Journal of Medicine* 307(24): 1516–517.

Neuhauser, D. (1974) The Future of Proprietaries in American Health Services. In C.G. Havighurst *Regulating Health Facilities Construction*. Washington, DC: American Enterprise Institute for Public Policy Research.

Newman, B. (1983) Frugal Medical Service Keeps Britons Healthy and Patiently Waiting. *Wall Street Journal*, 9 February: 1.

O'Connor, J. (1973) *The Fiscal Crisis of the State*. New York: St Martin's Press.

Pattison, R. and Katz, H. (1983) Investor-owned and Not-for-profit Hospitals: A Comparison Based on California Data. *New England Journal of Medicine* 309(6): 347–53.

Pillsbury, A.B. (1982) The Hard-selling Supplier to the Sick. *Fortune* (July) 26: 56–61.

Punch, L. (1982) For Profit Nursing Homes Systems Consolidate; Beds Grow by 18%. *Modern Healthcare* 12(6): 74.

——(1983) M.D.s, Hospitals Beat Out Systems in the Alternative Service Market. *Modern Healthcare* 13(5): 126–28.

Punch, L. and Johnson, D.E.L. (1984) HMOs Perfect Rapid Enrollee Growth as Consumers' Cost Concerns Mount. *Modern Healthcare* 14(1): 54–8.

Radical Statistics Health Group (1980) In Defense of the National Health Service. *International Journal of Health Services* 10(4): 611–45.

Relman, A.S. (1980) The New Medical-industrial Complex. *The New England Journal of Medicine* 303(17): 963–70.

Relman, A.S. and Drummond, R. (1980) Treatment of End-stage Renal Disease. *The New England Journal of Medicine* 303(17): 996–98.

Renaud, M. (1975) On the Structural Constraints to State Intervention in Health. *International Journal of Health Services* 5(4): 559–71.

Rhein, R.W. (1980) Hospitals in Trouble: Crisis for Doctors? *Medical World News* 21(24): 58–68.

——(1982) The New Cost-control 'Coalition': Will Big Business Run the Show? *Medical World News* 23(3): 54–64.

Rouse, E. (1983) Hospitals Fight for their Lives in an Ailing Industry. *Philadelphia Inquirer* 20(1): 23A.

Ruchlin, H.S., Pointer, D.D., and Cannedy, L.L. (1973) Hospitals that Fail are often the Small Ones. *Modern Hospital* 120(6): 61–4.

Sager, A. (1981a) Survival of the Fattest (Part I). *Health/PAC Bulletin* 12(7): 21–31.

——(1981b) Survival of the Fattest (Part II). *Health/PAC Bulletin* 12(8): 25–31.

Salmon, J. Warren (1975) The Health Maintenance Organization Strategy: A Corporate Takeover of Health Services Delivery. *International Journal of Health Services* 5: 609–29.

——(1977) Monopoly Capital and the Reorganization of Health Care. *Review of Radical Political Economics* 9(12): 125–33.

——(1978) *Corporate Attempts to Reorganize the American Health Care System*. Unpublished dissertation, Cornell University.

——(1982) The Competitive Health Strategy: Fighting for your Health. *Health and Medicine* 1(2): 21–30.

Schneyer, S., Landefeld, J.S. and Sandifer, F.H. (1981) Biomedical Research and Illness: 1900–1979. *Milbank Memorial Fund Quarterly/Health and Society* 59(1): 44–58.

Schwartz, H. (1981) The Decline of the Independent Physician Continues. *Wall Street Journal* 11 August: 23.

——(1982) Can the US Make Hospital Costs Go Down. *Wall Street Journal* 2 November: 28.

Shepard, D.S. (1980) Hospital Closures: Modeling their Impact on Medical Costs. Paper presented at the American Public Health Association Annual Meeting, Detroit, Michigan.

Shonick, W. (1982) Expanding Contracting: Private Management of Public Hospitals in California. *Health/PAC Bulletin* 13(1): 7–10, 22–8, 32.

Siegrist, R. (1983) Wall Street and the For-profit Hospital Management Companies. In B. Gray (ed.) *The New Health Care for Profit*. Washington, DC: National Academy Press.

Simpson, J.C. (1976) More Hospitals turn Administration over to Outside Companies. *Wall Street Journal* 21 July: 1, 17.

Sorenson, L. (1983) Hospitals and Doctors Compete for Patients with Rising Bitterness. *Wall Street Journal* 19 July: 1.

Starr, P. (1982) *The Social Transformation of American Medicine*. New York: Basic Books.

Steinwald, B. and Newhauser, D. (1970) The Role of the Proprietary

Hospital. *Journal of Law and Contemporary Problems* August.

Stevenson, G. (1976) Profits in Medicine. *Health/PAC Bulletin* 72: 1–19.

——(1978) Laws of Motion in the For-profit Health Industry: A Theory and Three Examples. *International Journal of Health Services* 8: 235–56.

Stewart, D.A. (1973) *The History and Status of Proprietary Hospitals.* Research series no. 9. Chicago: Blue Cross Association.

Strelnick, H. (1982) Billions from Bandaids. *Health/PAC Bulletin* 13(3): 7–10, 19–27.

Trafford, A. (1979) Inside our Hospitals. *US News and World Report* 5 March: 33–41.

Vladeck, B.C. (1980) *Unloving Care: The Nursing Home Tragedy.* New York: Basic Books.

Waldholz, M. (1981) Some Hospitals are Entering Diverse Businesses, Often Unrelated to Medicine, to Offset Losses. *Wall Street Journal* 12 August: 56.

——(1982) To Keep Doors Open, Nonprofit Hospitals Act Like Businesses. *Wall Street Journal* 29 December: 1, 5.

Wall Street Journal (1976) Doctors and the State. 16 January: 23.

Warren, B.G. (1981) Economic and Legal Implications of Multi-institutional Arrangements. *Hospital Administration Currents* (Ross Timesaver) 25(4).

Weiss, K. (1982) Corporate Medicine: What's the Bottom Line for Physicians and Patients? *The New Physician* 9: 19–25.

Wennberg, J.E. (1982) Should the Cost of Insurance Reflect the Cost of Use in Local Hospital Markets? *The New England Journal of Medicine* 307(22): 1374–381.

Wennberg, J. and Gettelsohn, A. (1982) Variations in Medical Care among Small Areas. *Scientific American* 246: 120–26, 129–132, 134.

Wilson, G. (1982) Effects of Hospital Revenue Bonds on Hospital Planning and Operations. *The New England Journal of Medicine* 307(23): 1426–430.

Five

The transnational pharmaceutical industry and the health of the world's people

Thomas S. Bodenheimer

An estimated 130,000 people in the United States die each year from adverse reactions to medications (Silverman and Lee 1974: 264). As many as 60 per cent of those medications are entirely unnecessary (Burack 1970: 49). In the world's poor nations, one million children die each year from malnutrition and infection caused by the replacement of breast feeding by commercial infant formulas (*Newsweek* 1981). Physicians all over the world prescribe brand name drugs that cost patients from three to thirty times as much as identical generic drugs (Silverman and Lee 1974: 334). Unsafe drugs that are banned or limited in the US are sold indiscriminately in underdeveloped countries (Silverman, Lee, and Lydecker 1982).

It is evident that the partially realized potential of chemical and biological discoveries to reduce suffering and promote health for the world's people has been pervasively distorted, perverted, and turned into its opposite. Why? Where does the responsibility lie?

The cause for this state of affairs is apparent for all who wish to behold. A small group of extremely rich men – directors of a few giant, world-spanning transnational corporations – control the production, distribution, and knowledge of the great pharmaceutical discoveries. These men have turned life-giving scientific advances into a vehicle for immense profits and power. They have bought and bribed health professionals and government officials to collude in their endeavor. They claim to be the benefactors of mankind, but the facts tell otherwise. In the words of Dr Dale Console, former medical director of the huge Squibb Corporation, "The pharmaceutical industry is unique in that it can make exploitation seem a noble purpose" (Console 1960).

This chapter will proceed as follows: (1) description of the pharmaceutical industry as a transnational enterprise; (2) the pharmaceutical industry's use of patent-protected innovation to survive the current world economic crisis; (3) the pharmaceutical industry and the middle class; (4) the effects of the pharmaceutical industry on the health of the world's people; (5) the pharmaceutical industry and the state; and (6) proposals for reform.

The transnational character of the pharmaceutical industry

The transnational corporation has become the center of power in today's world (Dixon 1982a). Decisions made in the board rooms of Zurich, New York, or Tokyo – far more than the decisions of national governments – determine where people will live, what they will eat, when and how they will die. The largest transnational corporations, exemplified by General Motors, Exxon, Citibank, and IBM, have assets far larger than the gross national product of many of the world's nation-states.

Transnational corporations are defined by their power to plan their production and sales on a global scale; each part of the global enterprise is organized and located so as to maximize worldwide profit (Barnet and Mueller 1974). Thus a pharmaceutical company might have its corporate headquarters in the United States, produce its drugs in Ireland, assemble its capsules in Brazil, and sell the product in Bolivia. The details depend on where raw materials are obtainable most cheaply, where labor costs are lowest, where taxes most easily can be evaded, and where marketing regulations are least strict.

The mobility of transnational corporations gives them an insuperable advantage over the immobility of national governments (Dixon 1980). They seek out areas of lowest wages and thereby have wrested from governments the power to maintain stable employment. By pressing buttons of internal computers or Telex machines, they can transfer millions of dollars from one country to another, thereby depriving governments of the power to protect their money supply. They can manipulate prices and profits among subsidiaries in different nations and they can fabricate their books so that sales or loans generated in high tax countries appear to emanate from low tax havens, thereby evading taxes and denying governments the fundamental power to collect revenues.

With their enormous wealth, transnational corporations can and do bribe politicians, as in Koreagate or Watergate; and transnational banks can force basic policy changes on governments by giving, denying, or extending loans, as has taken place across the world from New York City in 1975 to Poland in 1980.

The pharmaceutical industry goes transnational

The worldwide pharmaceutical industry is dominated by a small number of transnational firms, mainly based in the United States, Switzerland, Germany, Great Britain, and more recently, Japan. The largest pharmaceutical corporations are not nearly as large as the giant oil and banking transnationals. In 1981, the largest US pharmaceutical company, American Home Products Corp., had $4.1 billion in sales compared to Exxon's $108 billion (*Fortune* 1982). In rates of profit, however, the pharmaceuticals are far ahead of most transnationals. For the period 1963 to 1976, with the exception of two years, profit rates in the pharmaceutical industry were at least 45 per cent higher than the median profit rates of the 500 largest US corporations (McCraine and Murray 1978). During most of these years, the pharmaceutical industry ranked first or second in return on investment. American Home Products, ranked ninety-third in sales in 1981, was eleventh in net income as per cent of stockholders' equity (*Fortune* 1982) (see *Table 5.1*).

Of the world's eighteen top pharmaceutical companies,

Table 5.1 The world's top pharmaceutical corporations

RANK (by sales)	CORPORATION[1]	LOCATION OF HEADQUARTERS	WORLD SALES, 1980 (in billions of US dollars)	PROFITS, 1980 (in millions of US dollars)	NON-US SALES AS % OF TOTAL SALES	NUMBER OF COUNTRIES WITH MANUFACTURING PLANTS
1	Ciba-Geigy	Switzerland	5.9 (1979)	196 (1979)	?	40
2	American Home Products	US	3.8	446	34	29
3	Warner-Lambert	US	3.5	193	46	?
4	Hoffmann-La Roche	Switzerland	3.5	394	70	30
5	Bristol-Myers	US	3.2	271	30	40
6	Sandoz	Switzerland	3.0	343	78	32
7	Pfizer	US	3.0	255	53	34
8	Merck	US	2.7	415	51	27
9	Beecham Group Ltd.	England	2.7	198	82	26
10	Eli Lilly	US	2.6	342	28	28
11	Abbott	US	2.0	214	35	28
12	Squibb	US	1.8	127	37	24
13	SmithKline	US	1.8	308	46	?
14	Upjohn	US	1.8	170	37	35
15	Schering-Plough	US	1.7	239	50	?
16	Sterling	US	1.7	123	48	46
17	Searle	US	1.1	98	37	?
18	Glaxco	England	1.1	72	?	36

Note: 1 Huge chemical/pharmaceutical corporations whose drug products are not the major portion of their sales are not included here (e.g. Hoechst, Dow Chemical, American Cyanamid, Bayer, Mitsubishi Chemicals).
Sources: Fortune (1982); Dow Jones-Irwin Business Almanac; Moody's Investors Fact Sheets; Moody's International Manual; Standard and Poors; corporate annual reports.

thirteen are headquartered in the US, three in Switzerland, and two in England. In addition, giant German and Japanese firms produce pharmaceuticals as part of their product line. Yet it is more and more difficult to define a true home for the transnational pharmaceuticals. Not only do US and European-based companies have hundreds of subsidiaries in other countries, but European companies are increasingly buying up US companies. By 1977, non-US companies had a 35 per cent share of the American health and drug market (*New York Times* 1978a). In the past five years, European companies have taken over US companies, for example, Germany's Bayer acquired Miles Laboratories and Switzerland's Nestlé acquired Alcon Labs. The advantages of such transnational mergers and acquisitions reveal how transnational corporations think globally, not nationally. In the words of the *New York Times,*

> Although foreigners have been rapidly expanding their share of the United States drug market, the American industry shows no signs of feeling threatened. Many American health and drug companies have found that a substantial dose of foreign investment was just what the doctor ordered.
>
> (*New York Times* 1978a)

The example of Germany's Boehringer Mannheim acquiring Bio-Dynamics, Inc. is instructive: Bio-Dynamics benefited by an influx of equity capital (of which they were short) while both companies benefited by Bio-Dynamics becoming the US marketer for the German company's products (*New York Times* 1978a).

Japanese companies, relative newcomers to the pharmaceutical field, are likewise cooperating with the Americans and Europeans in joint ventures and licensing agreements. For example, both Pfizer and Eli Lilly in the US and Hoechst in Germany are scrambling to get exclusive licenses to market new antibiotics developed in Japan (*Wall Street Journal* 1981). Clearly the important actors on this stage are transnational corporations, not nation-states.

The pharmaceutical industry and the world's periphery

In the emerging transnational organization of the pharmaceutical industry, the world's underdeveloped nations are playing an increasing role. In this paper I use the terms "core" – the locus of capital accumulation (within the transnational corporations, whose headquarters are principally located in the US, western Europe, and Japan) – vs. "periphery" – the exploited areas of the world whose resources are systematically drained to benefit the capital accumulation process in the core. Core and periphery constitute a set of opposites which provide the most fundamental designation of the world division of labor (Hopkins and Wallerstein 1977).

While research and development and the mass production of pharmaceuticals is generally concentrated in the world's core (industrialized) nations, the assembly of pills and capsules increasingly is moving to the low-wage, low-tax peripheral (underdeveloped) countries. Anyone entering San Juan, Puerto Rico, Guatemala City, or San Salvador will see one after another assembly plant of pharmaceutical transnationals. One-third of the assets of the US-based pharmaceutical industry are now located abroad (McCraine and Murray 1978). Pfizer, for example, has 63 plants in thirty-four countries. Already in 1968, U.S.-based companies had 332 manufacturing subsidiaries, 110 in Latin America, 106 in Europe, 31 in Africa and the Mideast, and 60 in Asia and other areas of the globe. These plants generally take the drug powder imported in batches from its site of manufacture and turn them into capsules or pills. Except for a small amount for domestic consumption, these countries then re-export the finished product back to the core nations or to other peripheral markets.

The benefits of this arrangement to the transnationals are enormous. Let us take the example of Puerto Rico, a tiny island which houses eighty-four pharmaceutical companies. Most of these are affiliates of US-based companies; a few are subsidiaries of German and Swiss-based companies. Many are simply assembly operations, importing raw materials, producing the capsules, then re-exporting the final product – 67 per cent – back to the US (Murray 1974). One advantage of this arrangement is cheap labor: the 1980 average hourly wage in the Puerto Rican pharmaceutical industry was two-thirds of the US wage. In nations such as Guatemala, El Salvador, and Korea, the wages are lower still.

The other major advantage is low taxes; many Puerto Rican manufacturers are 90 per cent exempt from local taxes, and can repatriate profits to the US mainland free of US federal taxes (*Journal of Commerce* 1981). In 1979, sixteen pharmaceutical corporations saved $441 million in US taxes using the Puerto Rican tax shelter (Donlan 1981). ($441 million would fund for fifteen years the entire US federal immunization program which President Reagan is cutting "for lack of funds.")

In true transnational style, the pharmaceuticals use the mechanism of transfer pricing to maximize their tax evasion. Eli Lilly, for example, supplies its Puerto Rican subsidiary with the raw materials to produce the painkiller Darvon at an artificially low price. The subsidiary then sells the finished capsules back to Eli Lilly at an artificially high price (Donlan 1981). The result? The US company books show low income from selling the raw materials and high costs from buying the capsules, that is, low profits and correspondingly low taxes. The subsidiary shows low costs for raw materials and high income from sales, that is, high profits, which are largely shielded from local Puerto Rican taxes. The subsidiary then repatriates the high profits back to the parent US-based company tax-free.

In other cases, transfer pricing works the other way around, with the parent transnational charging subsidiaries in peripheral nations huge prices for intermediate products that are converted into capsules and pills. In these cases much of the final product is sold within the peripheral nation itself, and the nation has substantial tax rates. Paying high prices to import materials, the subsidiary shows low profits and pays low taxes to the peripheral nation. This mechanism, of course, also allows the subsidiary to justify charging high prices for the final product. For example, the Colombian prices for Valium and Librium were eighty-two and sixty-five times higher, respectively, than the estimated world market price (Barnet and Mueller 1974: 158).

At times, global profit maximization schemes become rather complex. European or US-based transnationals supply materials at low prices to their subsidiaries in low-tax Panama. The Panamanian subsidiaries then export to subsidiaries in higher-tax Colombia at substantially raised prices. The Panamanian firms realize high profits at low taxation, while the Colombian firms have low profits and thus escape high taxation (Murray 1974). Naturally, the benefits of all these maneuvers accrue to the parent transnational corporation which owns all the subsidiaries.

The scale of operations of pharmaceutical companies in peripheral nations is increasing rapidly. Foreign sales made up 38 per cent of total pharmaceutical sales for US-based companies in 1974. In 1974, peripheral nations imported $2 billion in drugs; now the figure is $6 billion. The entire mortgaging of peripheral economies to transnational corporations through growing debt is shown in the pharmaceutical industry; already in 1974 peripheral nations were $1.5 billion in debt for imported drugs (Brisset 1979). The beneficiaries of this debt are generally transnational banks, which in fact are closely interlocked with the pharmaceutical industry. In many peripheral nations, 20–30 per cent (in some up to 50 per cent) of the entire health budget is spent on the purchase of drugs, compared to less than 10 per cent for most core countries (Yudkin 1980).

Interlocks and mergers

Though displaying its own particular global pharmacokinetics, the pharmaceutical industry cannot be separated from transnational capital as a whole. First and foremost, pharmaceuticals are generally chemicals; thus one view of the drug industry would place it as a subgrouping of the vast chemical industry. Lederle, for example, is the pharmaceutical division of American Cyanamid; and Dow Chemical, the US's twenty-fourth largest corporation, has a pharmaceutical division, as does Hoechst, the world's twenty-fifth largest industrial corporation. A number of drugs are manufactured from petrochemicals, but large oil companies do not generally own pharmaceutical companies. There are some interlocks between oil companies and pharmaceutical corporations; for example, Howard Kauffman, president of Exxon, is on Pfizer's board, and William Wrigley is a director of Texaco and American Home Products. But these interlocks are not extensive.

Far more significant are the interlocks between pharmaceutical companies and financial institutions. In 1976 the average large drug company had thirteen interlocks with financial institutions (McCraine and Murray 1978). Such banks as Chase Manhattan, Citibank, and Morgan Guarantee Trust have directors on the boards of such pharmaceutical companies as American Home Products, Bristol-Myers, Eli Lilly, Merck,

SmithKline, Abbott, and Searle. These interlocks assist the banks by providing investment outlets for their excess capital, and assist the drug companies in obtaining loans for foreign expansion or for pulling off mergers and acquisitions. In some cases, the relation between a bank and pharmaceutical company is close and long-lasting; for example, American Home Products had three different chairmen of its board of directors in 1961, 1966, and 1972; each of the three was also a director of Manufacturers Hanover Trust (Murray 1974).

Another way in which the pharmaceutical industry is typical of transnational corporations is the increase in mergers and acquisitions. Some companies buy up smaller companies; for example, Pfizer made sixty acquisitions between 1961 and 1973. Other large companies merge, as took place between Warner-Lambert and Parke-Davis in 1970, and between Schering and Plough in the same year.

With the increase in mergers and acquisitions, the pharmaceutical industry as a distinct entity is ceasing to exist. Abbott has entered table salt production, medical electronics, and the manufacture of golf clubs. The old-time drug makers, Eli Lilly and Upjohn, now have 30 per cent of their sales in nonpharmaceutical products. Bristol-Myers is in the movie and TV business, and Merck bought the Calgon water purification company. American Home Products, the largest pharmaceutical producer, marketing its drugs through Wyeth, Ayerst and Ives Laboratories, has 50 per cent of its sales in fields unrelated to drugs. The Swiss giants Hoffmann-La Roche, Ciba-Geigy, and Sandoz have gone into agrochemicals, medical electronics, plastics, aerospace products, and foodstuffs (*Economist* 1980). In addition, huge conglomerates have recently acquired pharmaceutical facilities; examples are Coca-Cola, Standard Oil, Liggett and Myers, Penn Central Railroad, and United Fruit Company (Murray 1974).

The process of transnationalization generally occurs through foreign acquisitions. Pharmaceutical companies begin as suppliers for the national market only. Then they begin to sell their products in other nations. After penetrating foreign markets, the next step is the acquisition of manufacturing facilities in the nation, often by purchasing smaller national companies. The final step is the planning on a global scale of the transnational's total operations, using the "foreign" plants not only to sell to their own national markets, but employing them also for re-export to the core or as a link in tax-evading transfer pricing.

For example, Brazil used to have its own national pharmaceutical industry, but with the invasion of its markets by US and European firms, the Brazilian companies were unable to compete, and either went out of business or were acquired. By 1972, 83 per cent of the Brazilian pharmaceutical industry was foreign-owned, half by European and half by American companies (McCraine and Murray 1978; Ledogar 1975: 6–24).

Surviving the economic crisis: technological innovation and patents

The two decades post-World War II constituted an era of world economic expansion, with high profits, steady growth, growing consumer demand, and relatively low unemployment. The pharmaceutical industry was no exception, with sales for US companies climbing from $1.4 billion in 1950 to over $8 billion in 1972. Profits as a percentage of stockholders' equity were consistently in the range of 17–21 per cent.

Since about 1970, however, the world economy has entered a prolonged period of overproduction and economic stagnation, caused by insufficient consumer demand and resultant inability of corporations to sell their products (Dixon 1982b). In the US, this profit crisis is worsened by heightened inter-capitalist competition, particularly from western Europe and Japan. This profit squeeze is most popularly exemplified by the well-known cases of the US auto and steel industries. The fall of the US from economic hegemony is shown by the fact that US manufacturing exports declined from 30 per cent of world exports in 1952 to 13 per cent in 1976 (*Monthly Review* 1981). It is precisely this economic crisis that explains the ascendancy of Reaganomics and the deepening cuts in social services in the US (Dixon 1982b; Frank 1982).

With some exceptions, the pharmaceutical industry thus far has come through the current crisis unscathed. Standard and Poor (1982a) Composite Industry Data for pharmaceuticals shows profit margins continuing at the astounding level of 20 per cent through the 1970s. How has the drug industry escaped the economic crisis? The two major reasons are technological innovation and monopoly patents.

Capitalism has generally resolved the recurrent crises of stagnation (overproduction) through major technological innovation (steam, railroads, electricity, the internal combustion engine) (Dixon 1982a). On a far smaller scale, technological innovation, protected by monopoly patents, has been the seedbed of continued pharmaceutical profitability. Since the 1930s one after another chemical/biological breakthrough has put one after another corporation into an economic boom: sulfa drugs, penicillin, a host of new antibiotics, high blood pressure medications, tranquilizers, ulcer remedies, and many more. Thus the productivity of the research and development programs of pharmaceutical companies, or their ability to gain exclusive rights to other people's discoveries, are fundamental to the profitability of the company (*Business Week* 1982).

A recent example is SmithKline Corporation, which in 1976 started selling a new ulcer treatment called Tagamet, now the world's most used drug (recently surpassing Valium). SmithKline's profits almost tripled from 1975 to 1979, and the price of a SmithKline share of stock went from $11 to $65 (Louis 1980). The company was not prepared for its own success, and had to farm out production of Tagamet to other chemical companies until it could expand its own facilities throughout the world. In order to break into the Japanese market, with one of the highest per capita ulcer rates in the world, SmithKline arranged a 50–50 partnership with Fujisawa Pharmaceutical Co.

Without the critical monopolistic device of the patent, pharmaceutical innovation would not sufficiently benefit the innovator. If other companies could sell innovations, competition would drive down prices and divide up markets. Thus the patent has become the key to cashing in on the research and development investment.

At first glance, the pharmaceutical industry does not appear to be highly monopolized. In coffee, cotton, copper, iron, and other basic commodities a mere fifteen companies control 90 per cent of global trade (Clairmonte and Cavanagh 1981). Yet in pharmaceuticals, it takes 136 companies to account for 95 per cent of prescription drug sales (Murray 1974). However, one cannot compare the sales of Valium with the sales of Penicillin;

they are as different as cars and vacuum cleaners. Taking each product separately, the pharmaceutical industry *is* highly monopolized. During the 17-year life of the US patent, one company is the sole producer of a drug (for example, Valium or Tagamet). Even when the patent expires, the advantage of a firm already marketing a product is enormous. In one study of pharmaceutical monopolization, it was found that of 51 chemical entities comprising two-thirds of prescription drug sales, 27 had only one producer, 8 had two producers, 10 had three, and none had more than seven (Barnhart 1972).

Because innovation and patents are the major mechanisms for growth and profitability, the pharmaceutical industry is at war with the US government on these issues. In 1962, following a series of drug disasters including Thalidomide, the US Congress stiffened the requirements for approving new drugs. Since that time, the Food and Drug Administration (FDA) approval of new drugs has been slower and more difficult to obtain (what the drug industry calls the "drug lag" (Schifrin and Tayan 1977)). The problem with the drug lag is that the FDA approval time reduces the effective life of the high-profit patent years, since the 17-year clock is ticking away during the review process (*Business Week* 1982).

According to industry spokesmen, US drug lag has given a boost to foreign competitors; in 1968 US companies produced 34 per cent of the world's pharmaceuticals; by 1981 the US share dropped to 27 per cent. Also, US pharmaceutical exports are smaller in dollar value than those of each of three countries: Switzerland, the United Kingdom, and Germany (*American Druggist* 1981). One might wonder whether this decline is actually due to drug lag, to international capitalist competition, or to transnational drug firms exporting more of their products from non-US production facilities. But whatever the true case, the pharmaceutical industry is using such figures successfully to convince the Reagan administration and Congress to "give them a break." Reagan's FDA Commissioner has already relaxed standards for approval of new drugs, and Congress is likely to approve legislation extending patents by as much as seven years (Standard and Poor 1982b).

The pharmaceutical industry and the middle class

Capitalism has never been a simple bi-polar relationship of capitalists on top and the working class on the bottom. Throughout the history of the capitalist era, there have always been intermediate strata of independent small capitalists (Dixon 1979; Dixon and Bodenheimer 1980). More recently, under monopoly capitalism, the intermediate strata (also called the middle classes) are frequently employed by capital as managers and technicians, or employed by the government, the universities, the hospitals, and other institutions as bureaucrats, academics, scientists, or other professionals. Though the middle strata have their own particular class interests (money, prestige, power), they also serve the interests of national and transnational capital and are generally rewarded (or bribed) for this service. For big capital, the middle classes are extremely useful to manage the discontent of the working class:

> Their conditions of employment are affected by the need of top management to have within its orbit buffer layers, responsive and "loyal" subordinates, transmission agents for the exercise of control and the collection of information, so that management does not confront unaided a hostile or indifferent mass.   (Braverman 1974: 406)

Thus foremen directly control factory workers, who never see their real bosses hidden in their boardrooms; the police and military perform the visible function of corporate rule by force; the media, politicians, and top government bureaucrats perform the function of corporate rule by law/consensus, and so forth. In the case of the pharmaceutical industry, the intermediate strata – particularly physicians, but also research scientists, pharmacists, university professors and administrators, government bureaucrats, and politicians – are critical to the two pillars of pharmaceutical profitability: research and marketing.

The commercialization of research

In 1978, FDA Commissioner Donald Kennedy told a US Senate Subcommittee that thirteen physicians hired by such drug companies as Hoffmann-La Roche, Bristol-Myers, and Johnson

& Johnson, had committed fraud in drug testing (*Washington Post* 1978). The physicians reported on patients who did not exist, patients who did not have the disease the drug was supposed to treat, and patients who never got the drugs they were supposed to have received. For each drug tested, the physician received up to $100,000, and it was clearly in the interest of both the physician and the company to have the most favorable result as to the drug's efficacy and safety.

While these are extreme cases, drug companies do provide research grants to universities, and in their promotional literature are constantly citing medical school experts praising their products. Science is supposed to be objective, but when money is at stake, subjectivity may certainly come to the fore.

Research done by scientists employed by drug companies is often of questionable value. The major justification by the pharmaceutical industry for its high profits is that research on new drugs in expensive, financially risky, and of great benefit to mankind. In fact, companies spend far less on research (11.7 per cent of US sales) than they do on advertising and promotion (at least 20 per cent of US sales) (McCraine and Murray 1978). More significant, most of the research is of benefit only to the corporations themselves. The US Task Force on Prescription Drugs found that only between 10 and 25 per cent of new products represented important new chemical entities; the rest are "me-too" drugs that are simple chemical manipulations or combinations of previous drugs. These "me-too" drugs are produced to obtain new patents for drugs whose patents are running out, and have little or no value to the consumer, serving mainly to keep drug costs high and to increase the confusion of physicians faced with dozens of drugs which do virtually the same thing. Finally, much of the ground-breaking pharmaceutical research was not done by the pharmaceutical industry, but by government or university scientists.

Recent developments in genetic engineering (recombinant DNA) are bringing the academy and the boardroom closer together. Scientists can now restructure bacteria to make pharmaceutically-active chemicals, whether vaccines, insulin, or the anti-virus, possibly anti-cancer, protein interferon. One company, Biogen, S.A., formed specifically to capture these frontier discoveries, includes on its board of directors several faculty members from some of the world's leading universities.

Harvard biologist Walter Gilbert was acting president of Biogen, operating the company out of his Harvard office. These developments have created strong controversy on campuses, where, according to an article in *Fortune* magazine,

> Some scientists fear that their commercially oriented colleagues will emphasize secrecy and fast payoff rather than basic research. And politicians are beginning to ask why the fruits of this basic research, originally supported by the taxpayers through grants to universities, should become private property. (Bylinsky 1980)

The companies (and some of the transnational pharmaceutical firms are heavily involved in recombinant DNA) finance the university scientists' research, and the research becomes the sole property of the company. With cutbacks in government research grants, pharmaceutical companies can easily recruit grant-less scientists. Such research is secret, and not published for the advancement of science. Formerly "publish or perish," the motto is becoming "if you publish you'll perish."

The bribing of the world's physicians

From the moment prospective doctors enter medical school, they are bribed and brainwashed to become lifelong servants (at no small reward to themselves) of the pharmaceutical industry. Incoming US medical students are greeted with free stethoscopes from Eli Lilly Co., the beginning of the $5000 per year per doctor cost of drug company promotion (Concerned Rush Students 1976). Though a number of honest medical school professors insist on teaching generic rather than brand names, there is inadequate emphasis on the serious side effects of medications, the overmedication of the world today, or non-drug models of healing. To insure that medical education is dominated by the pharmaceutical model, prominent medical educators are placed on pharmaceutical industry boards of directors; for example, Dr Paul Russell, Professor of Surgery at Harvard Medical School, on Warner-Lambert's board; and on Squibb's board sit former Harvard Medical School dean Dr Robert Ebert, Dr Helen Ranney, Chairman, Department of Medicine, University of California at San Diego, and Dr Lewis Thomas, Chancellor, Memorial Sloan-Kettering Cancer Center.

Practicing physicians are inundated with gifts, patient educational materials, and free samples, all promoting the latest brand name products. A practicing physician myself, I am actually writing this manuscript with an Eli Lilly pen, on a Pfizer scratch pad, with a SmithKline calendar reminding me of my deadline, and a Squibb paperweight perched on top of the Parke-Davis paper clip holder.

The book I read more than any other is the *Physicians' Desk Reference*, written by the drug companies, which I receive free and from which I can most conveniently obtain information I need about prescription drugs. The journals I read to keep up on medical advances are heavily paginated with multi-colored drug advertisments; in fact, the money paid by drug companies for these ads allows me to receive many of these journals free. Each day in the office I see at least one drug company detail man who gains admittance by bribing me with multiple free samples, which can be used to save money for my patients. Even as I write this manuscript about the huge cost of brand name prescribing, I catch myself prescribing brand names out of habit.

In addition to its influence over individual doctors, the drug industry has enormous power over the American Medical Association, partly through its advertising in AMA journals, which has provided the AMA with up to 26 per cent of its total yearly income. In return, the AMA has used its powerful lobby to support pharmaceutical corporate interests (Concerned Rush Students 1976).

In peripheral nations, pharmaceutical promotion to physicians is even more intense. Whereas the US has a ratio of one detail man to about ten doctors, Guatemala, Mexico, and Brazil have approximately one detail man to every three physicians (Silverman 1977). From Sao Paulo, Brazil:

There are benches on both sides of the hospital's main entrance, where more than a dozen men sit chatting and watching. They are not patients. They look healthy, and they carry large briefcases. They belong to the army of company salesmen, and the Santa Casa Hospital is their main target every morning of every day. A doctor is coming in and stops to talk to one of them. He is given a free sample of a drug and some leaflets. Soon after, he is encircled by four other salesmen. Each in his turn, with care and respect, hands the doctor drug samples and exchanges a few words. Then one of them produces a plastic bag and gives the bag to the doctor with great courtesy. More free samples and leaflets are handed over; the doctor fills up the plastic bag, exchanges a few more words with the salesmen, and leaves.

(Ledogar 1975: 22)

One Brazilian physician kept track for twenty-one days of salesmen's visits to his clinic:

He was visited on 18 of the 21 days by a total of 69 salesmen. He was given 452 free samples of drugs; he received 25 gifts including coffeepots, notebooks, plastic bags. 'It has become a plague,' said an official of Santa Casa. (Ledogar 1975: 22)

Pharmacists in the US have little to say about sales of prescription drugs, though in peripheral nations they are heavily promoted by the pharmaceutical industry because they can dispense almost all products without a doctor's order. In the US, over-the-counter drugs are promoted by pharmacists due to the simple economic fact that every bottle of aspirin or Maalox sold means money to both manufacturer and pharmacist.

The pharmaceutical industry and the health of the world's people

The untrammeled power of the transnational pharmaceutical industry has wrought untold negative effects on the health of the world's people. The potentiality of an enterprise capable of employing chemical and biological substances to intervene in sickness and to promote health represents an enormous hope for humankind. Medical science has indeed made steps toward such a goal. The great advances of such discoveries as immunization against childhood disease, antibiotics, insulin, and digitalis have brought many years of useful and fulfilling life to millions of people. Yet most of these fundamental discoveries were not made in the direct pursuit of profit. The expansion of profit-motivated capitalist enterprise into the pharmaceutical area has turned its life-giving potential into at best a mixed, at worst a negative factor for the people of the world.

Unsafe drugs

> I firmly believe that if the whole materia medica, as now
> used, could be sunk to the bottom of the sea, it would be
> better for mankind and all the worse for the fishes.
>
> (Dr Oliver Wendell Holmes 1860)

If 130,000 people die each year in the US from adverse drug
reactions (Silverman and Lee 1974: 264), and if 60 per cent of
those drugs should never have been prescribed (Burack 1970:
49), then we have 78,000 entirely needless deaths per year
caused by the profit-created overpromotion of toxic drugs by
the pharmaceutical industry and the domination by that
industry of the medical profession. In the peripheral nations of
the world, we find even greater devastation from the profit
motive gone wild. Chloramphenicol, banned due to lethal side
effects (aplastic anemia) from almost all uses in the US, is
widely sold over the counter in Latin America for multiple
minor illnesses including the common cold. As one physician
stated, "Indeed, it is agreed by all Colombian hematologists
that as soon as chloramphenicol became freely available in this
country, the expected occurred – that is, aplastic anemia
became a dreadfully common disease" (Silverman 1977).

Infant formulas aggressively promoted as a substitute for
breast-feeding by Nestlé, Abbott, Bristol-Myers, and American
Home Products are estimated to kill one million infants each
year from malnutrition, disease, or death (*Newsweek* 1981).
For more details of this almost incomprehensible corporate
brutality, readers are encouraged to look at Robert Ledogar's
Hungry for Profits (1975).

Hundreds of pages have been written on one after another
disastrous – in fact, criminal – outcome of discoveries supposedly designed to improve life. But rather than recount these
already well-researched cases, we must ask the question: are
these disasters honest mistakes from potentially positive
developments whose ill effects could not have been seen in
advance? The answer is, no. In many cases the problems were
covered up by pharmaceutical corporations whose only concern
is profit.

MER/29 was marketed by William S. Merrell Company in
1960 for lowering cholesterol. In 1962, it was withdrawn due
to at least 5,000 cases of skin damage, baldness, changes in

reproductive organs, and serious eye damage (Mintz 1967, 1976; Silverman and Lee 1974: 89). During the late 1950s, a Merrell lab technician observed that a monkey being tested with MER/29 appeared to be partially blind. The company's director of biological sciences threw out the sick monkey and instructed the lab technician to alter her records. When the FDA finally investigated, Merrell's lab notebooks revealed high death and eye injury rates among the MER/29 treated animals, data that were never reported to the FDA. In addition, independent physicians testing the drug found extremely toxic effects and had been convinced by Merrell to withhold publication of their findings. During the two years of MER/29's life, Merrell, knowing the opposite to be true, promoted the drug to thousands of doctors as non-toxic and free of side effects.

Dr Milton Silverman (1982) has co-authored an entire book documenting how pharmaceutical companies in peripheral nations promote drugs proved to be potentially unsafe without adequate warning. For example, in the US, physicians are warned of possible serious or fatal effects of oral contraceptives. Yet Searle, Wyeth, Parke-Davis, Ortho, Syntex, and Johnson & Johnson provide few if any warnings of side effects in peripheral nations, and promote the drugs for entirely unsuitable uses such as premenstrual tension (Silverman 1977).

Similar refusals to warn physicians or limit the use of dangerous drugs have been proved for products of Ciba-Geigy, Lederle, and Upjohn. The inescapable conclusion is that in general, pharmaceutical companies (not simply one or two companies) hide the facts about dangerous effects of their products in order to sell more drugs and earn higher profits.

Monopoly price fixing

When a company introduces a new drug, the drug is given two names, a generic name and a brand name. The generic name is generally long and hard to remember while the brand name is often catchy and popular. For example, Roche's tranquilizer with the well-known brand name Librium has as its generic name chlordiazepoxide/hydrochloride. When Librium's 17 years of patent protection are over, any company could make chlordiazepoxide/hydrochloride . . . Roche, of course, will continue to have a competitive advantage because doctors and patients know the name Librium.

Among the most significant components of high pharmaceutical profit is the abnormally high price of brand-name drugs. The price of brand-name drugs has virtually nothing to do with production costs and other industrial expenses, but rather is based upon the maximum the public in its medical need can be induced to pay. From among numerous examples consider prednisone: Schering's name brand, Meticorten, sells for $102.57/1000 while Wolins (a large respected wholesaler of generic drugs) sells prednisone for $4.40/1000.

(Barnhart 1972)

A 1972 study of generic vs. brand name prices showed brand name reserpine (a blood pressure-lowering drug) to cost thirty-six times as much as generic reserpine, and a number of other brand-name drugs to cost from five to eighteen times their generic equivalent. Yet almost all studies show that generic and brand name drugs are identical in quality (Silverman and Lee 1974: 162, 334).

The US federal government has been urging physicians and pharmacies to use cheaper generic drugs to reduce the costs of the Medicare and Medicaid programs, but the Pharmaceutical Manufacturers Association has lobbied and gone to court to prevent this. Use of generic drugs could save US consumers as much as $400 million a year (*Wall Street Journal* 1979).

The sexism of the pharmaceutical industry

Women are exploited by the capitalist system at a far greater rate than men. Women receive less pay for comparable work, women are concentrated in the lowest-paying jobs, women work countless hours in the home with no pay, and women assume the vast majority of the burden of contraception, reproduction, and childrearing (Dixon 1978).

The pharmaceutical industry uses this exploitation of women to exploit women more. The very real stresses facing women, particularly working-class women, under capitalism are celebrated by the drug industry as a profitable market for the sale of drugs – whether tranquilizers, antidepressants, hormones, or contraceptives. The major technique employed by the pharmaceutical industry is the constant and unrelenting publication – page after page, week after week, year after year – of advertisements in journals read by physicians. The ads stereotype women as neurotic and unhappy, needing an unending variety of pills to make life worth living. And if the women are depicted as thinking that life is not worth living, there are pills for that too. The ads are designed to play on and reinforce male physicians' sexist view that women are inferior, and to exploit the physician's busy schedule within which the writing of a prescription is far less time-consuming than serious problem-solving. Thus we find "You've talked . . . you've listened . . . but here she is again . . . Looks like a case for Stelazine (a major tranquilizer)" or "It may just be a mild depression. But she needs help . . . and needs it right now. Prescribe Ritalin" (Kiefer 1980).

These advertisements have clearly succeeded in causing or reinforcing doctors' tendency to treat women differently from men. A study by a Canadian clinic found that men complaining of depression are given physical examinations while women are more likely to simply get a prescription. In the US, physicians write more than twice as many prescriptions for women as for men. Tranquilizers account for most of this disparity (Kiefer 1980). Needless to say, these drugs are no solution whatsoever to women's exploitation; on the contrary, they cause an added burden: addiction.

The other major pharmaceutical exploitation of women involves reproductive-related drugs. Oral contraceptives have a significant risk borne completely by women. And hormones pushed hard for post-menopausal symptoms have caused countless cases of uterine cancer.

The racism of the pharmaceutical industry

The peripheral nations of the earth are overwhelmingly inhabited by people of color. Peripheral populations – as well as minority people in the core nations – have always borne a greater degree of exploitation under capitalism. The resources of peripheral nations have been drained from these nations; their land has been converted from use in feeding the population to mass export agriculture, thereby sowing widespread malnutrition in Africa and Latin America; and with the taking of their lands, formerly rural populations have been forced into the cities (or into immigration to core nations as exploited minorities), with staggering levels of unemployment and underemployment.

As it has done with women, the pharmaceutical industry has taken the special exploitation suffered by people of color and has added a burden of pharmaceutical exploitation central to the profit strategy of transnational drug firms. This pharmaceutical exploitation falls into two headings: excessive sales of unneeded drugs to peripheral nations, and the marketing to and testing of dangerous drugs on people of color.

Excessive sales to peripheral nations   By the late 1950s, markets for drug sales in the core nations were becoming saturated. Only the development of new drugs promised assured high profits. The response of the pharmaceutical industry was aggressive marketing in the poor nations of the world. And since most people in these nations are far too impoverished to buy pharmaceutical products, the target for marketing drugs became the government ministries of health, which provide free medical services through hospitals and clinics. Up to 40 per cent of the health budgets in peripheral nations are now spent on drugs, draining funds badly needed for basic health services (*New York Times* 1978b). Another effect is increased government debt to transnational banks, allowing the banks to virtually control these nations' economies (Dixon 1980).

Well-documented studies provide the details of excessive governmental purchase of drugs with constant pressure from the pharmaceutical industry, use of expensive brand name products, use of expensive injections when inexpensive pills are equally effective, and – in the case of the African nation Ghana – an incredibly plentiful supply of drugs in health clinics which are generally characterized by shortages of medical equipment, supplies, and personnel (Barnett, Creese, and Ayivor 1980; Lall and Bibile 1978; Yudkin 1980). The unrelenting promotion by detail men of government-employed physicians is one factor creating the excessive drug purchasing. But equally as significant are bribes of government officials by pharmaceutical transnationals:

> Merck admitted providing $3.5 million to employees of 36 separate foreign governments between 1968 and 1975; and

G.D. Searle admitted paying $1.3 million to foreign government employees from 1973 to 1975 alone. These payments have been characterized by the pharmaceutical firms as 'commissions' or as a means 'to obtain sales of products or services.' Johnson & Johnson admitted to payments by its subsidiaries of almost $1 million between 1971 and 1975 (94 percent of which was paid as commissions on government sales). Sterling Drug made 'payoffs' in 19 countries between 1970 and 1975, mainly to low-ranking government employees, ranging from $103,000 to $180,000 annually. The Upjohn Company made payments totalling $2.7 million to employees of 22 foreign governments 'to obtain business overseas' between 1971 and 1975 . . . American Home Products, from an 'initial inquiry' into 1973, 1974 and the first three-quarters of 1975 concluded that the amount of its foreign bribes 'wouldn't have exceeded $750,000 in any one year.'   (McCraine and Murray 1978)

The case of Afghanistan provides the results of the excess drug purchasing by peripheral nations. Dr N.D.W. Lionel, author of a World Health Organisation committee report on drugs in the Third World, concludes that in Afghanistan, ''Three-fourths of the total expenditures for drugs was for those that were inappropriate, toxic or provided only symptomatic treatment for self-limited illnesses'' (*New York Times* 1978b).

Testing and marketing of unsafe drugs   After new drugs have been screened on animals, they must undergo clinical trials on humans in order to be approved for commercial sale. Much of the initial testing on humans is carried out on people of color: US minorities who obtain medical care in urban public hospitals used for teaching, prisoners who are disproportionately minorities, and people in peripheral nations. Birth-control pills were tested in Puerto Rico, and one version of the live-virus polio vaccine was tested in the Congo (Ehrenreich 1972).

Not only are people of color the subject of drug experimentation, but they receive the least benefit of drug research. Few drugs are produced to treat diseases common in peripheral nations; for example, the total world expenditure on research in tropical diseases (which affect hundreds of millions of people) was only 2 per cent of the sum spent annually on cancer research (Yudkin 1980).

Finally, as discussed earlier in this chapter, drugs that are tightly regulated in core nations are dispensed without prescription, without warnings, and for every possible illness in peripheral nations. Currently, the injectible contraceptive Depo-Provera, banned from use in the US for serious side effects, is widely sold by Upjohn in peripheral nations. Now, the US FDA is considering its use in the US for special populations, that is, the poor and minorities. The drug apparently is being used already among American Indians. The racism involved in the marketing of this drug is highlighted by its use in South Africa: it is given widely to black women, but when a white woman asked her doctor for the shot, she was told, ''Oh, I couldn't give you that, you'd bleed like a pig'' (Talbot 1980).

The pharmaceutical industry and the state

Critics of the drug industry contend that the FDA has done little or nothing to regulate drug prices or unsafe drugs. Spokesmen of the industry complain that the FDA overregulates the industry and keeps patients from enjoying the latest fruits of scientific discoveries. Liberals who believe in the effectiveness of government regulation under capitalism point to the improved record of the FDA since the Drug Act of 1962, and argue that regulation is possible (Simmons 1974).

In fact, the only interest of the FDA appears to be the avoidance of the worst scandals of pharmaceutical abuse, scandals which undercut people's faith in ''private enterprise,'' and which can lead to extremely expensive lawsuits for drug companies. Both of the major laws regulating the pharmaceutical industry within the US came as the result of such scandals. The Food, Drug and Cosmetic Act of 1938 followed the killing of over 100 people, many children, by an untested sulfa preparation made by Massengill & Co. The Drug Act of 1962 was spurred by the Thalidomide disaster in which 10,000 babies in twenty countries – born of mothers taking the German-produced sedative during pregnancy – had seal-like flippers in place of arms and legs (Silverman and Lee 1974: 86, 94).

Yet even since the 1962 law, the US has experienced 130,000 deaths per year from drug reactions, with the majority of prescriptions written being for unneeded drugs. Not even a serious capitalist could call that regulation. In addition, the FDA has done nothing about drug prices, the costs of drug promotion, the bribes and gifts to doctors, the influence over medical education, or the unneeded research on "me-too" drugs. Thus the role of the state has been to attempt to soften the worst abuses, and to guarantee the highest possible profits.

The influence of the pharmaceutical industry over the state is accomplished by campaign contributions to political candidates, whether in Congress or in the Executive branch, thereby securing the laws the industry wants, and the proper appointments to posts such as FDA Commissioner. The only FDA Commissioner outspokenly critical of the drug industry was Dr James Goddard, who lasted only two and a half years.

FDA officials have tended to go back and forth between the government and the drug industry itself. Brad Mintener, an Assistant Health, Education and Welfare Secretary supervising the FDA under President Eisenhower, started as an executive in the food industry (also regulated by the FDA), and after leaving the government became a lawyer representing the food and drug industries (Mintz 1967: 128). Theodore Klumpp was a high official in the FDA and then became head of Winthrop Laboratories, a drug firm (Mintz 1967: 132). Dr Henry Welch, head of the FDA's Division of Antibiotics, received $287,000 from the drug industry while in the FDA (Mintz 1967: 133). FDA Commissioner Alexander Schmidt, who served during the Nixon administration, is now a director of American Cyanamid. Naturally, it goes much higher than simply the FDA. Current Vice-President George Bush was recently a director of Eli Lilly (*New York Times* 1981).

Proposals for reform

Pharmaceutical discoveries are now distorted to exploit humanity. What can we do to free up these great scientific advances to serve the world's people? We must pursue change on several levels. First are immediate reforms, without actually changing who controls the pharmaceutical industry. We must pursue these reforms as an international community. The pharmaceutical corporations are transnational so we must be transnational in opposing them. The major existing international body currently active in pharmaceutical reform is the World Health Organisation, which is a progressive and appropriate vehicle for international action.

1 The 1981 WHO resolution (which only the US voted against) calling on corporations to stop their discouragement of breastfeeding and their advertisement of infant formulas in peripheral nations, must be supported and implemented.

2 The WHO 1977 list of essential drugs should be implemented in all possible nations. This recommendation of a WHO committee would pare down available drugs to the essential drugs, and would thereby promote generic rather than brand name products, would cut out imitative products that add nothing to therapy, and would eliminate drugs with high toxicity. The acceptance of such essential drug lists by countries and physicians would enormously reduce the cost and toxicity of drugs. Needless to say, this recommendation is vigorously opposed by the transnational pharmaceutical industry (Silverman, Lee, and Lydecker 1982: 141).

3 All countries should have substitition laws whereby pharmacists can substitute cheaper generic drugs for expensive brand name drugs.

4 The use of the drug company-written *Physicians' Desk Reference* in the US and similar reference volumes in other countries should be banned, and in their place every physician in the world should have available in his or her language a WHO-written guide to the prescribing of pharmaceuticals. This guide should be uniform for all nations so that information on side effects of drugs is equally available throughout the world.

5 Pharmaceutical detail men should be banned from the face of the earth. The education of the world's physicians about pharmaceutical products must be carried out not by drug company representatives, but by required medical education courses and seminars provided by reputable educational institutions that do not receive drug company money.

6 Worldwide guidelines for research and human experimentation on new drugs should be developed and implemented through the WHO so that research truly serves the

health needs of the world's population, and experimentation is performed openly, safely, and in a fair manner without turning the world's people of color, the poor, and women into guinea pigs.

7 All payments and gifts (i.e. bribes) by pharmaceutical companies to the world's governments, physicians, pharmacists, and university scientists should be declared as conflict of interest, banned, and prosecuted.

With the immense power of the pharmaceutical industry, the likelihood of the passage of such reforms is slim. More direct and far-reaching – though no easier to obtain – is the nationalization of the pharmaceutical industry all over the world. There is no doubt that nationalization of one industry within an overall capitalist world economy, with a capitalist-controlled state, has marked limitations. In addition, nationalization in one or a few countries would simply hasten the departure of the industry from those countries, therefore further eroding whatever tax and employment base the industry does provide. But whatever the limitations of nationalization, it is a goal which we must strongly support.

The long-term solution to the pharmaceutical situation is the development of a form of socialism in the world that truly places control over the world's resources, over the great discoveries, over the channels of information and communication, and over the governmental apparatus, in the hands of a majority of the world's people, such that those who need safe, cheap, and effective pharmaceutical products can organize the production and distribution of those products. When that day arrives, justice might dictate that only one small group of people must pay monopoly brand-name prices for drugs, and must endure toxic side effects of fraudulently tested drugs prescribed by detail men-infested physicians – that small group would be the former directors of the defunct transnational pharmaceutical industry.

References

American Druggist (1981) Schweiker has Encouraging Words for Drug Producers. (May): 62.

Barnet, R. and Mueller, R. (1974) *Global Reach*. New York: Simon & Schuster.

Barnett, A., Creese, A.L., and Ayivor, E.C.K. (1980) The Economics of Pharmaceutical Policy in Ghana. *Internationl Journal of Health Services* 10(3): 479–99.

Barnhart, R. (1972) Getting Fix: The US Drug Monopoly. In T. Bodenheimer, S. Cummings, and E. Harding, *Billions for Bandaids.* San Francisco: Medical Committee for Human Rights.

Braverman, H. (1974) *Labor and Monopoly Capital.* New York: Monthly Review Press.

Brisset, C. (1979) Third World Medicines: Multinationals Rule. *Guardian*, 21 January.

Burack, R. (1970) *The New Handbook of Prescription Drugs.* New York: Ballantine Books.

Business Week (1982) Drugs: Rich Profits from New Lines. 11 January: 70–4.

Bylinsky, G. (1980) DNA Can Build Companies, Too. *Fortune*, 16 June: 144–53.

Clairmonte, F.F. and Cavanagh, J. (1981) The Corporate Stranglehold on Commodities Markets. *Monthly Review*, October: 27–39.

Concerned Rush Students (1976) MDs in the Drug Industry's Pocket. *Science for the People* (November–December): 6–21.

Console, D. (1960) U.S. Senate, Committee on the Judiciary, Subcommittee on Antitrust and Monopoly. Administered Prices in the Drug Industry. Washington: Government Printing Office.

Dixon, M. (1978) *Women in Class Struggle.* San Francisco: Synthesis Publications.

——(1979) *In Defense of the Working Class.* San Francisco: Synthesis Publications.

——(1980) The Challenge of Transnational Capital. *Our Socialism* 1: 2–5.

——(1982a) Dual Power: The Rise of the Transnational Corporation and the Nation-state: Conceptual Explanations to Meet Popular Demand. *Contemporary Marxism* 5: 129–46.

——(1982b) World Capitalist Crisis and the Rise of the Right. *Contemporary Marxism* 4: 1–10.

Dixon, M. and Bodenheimer, T. (1980) *Health Care in Crisis. Essays on Health Services Under Capitalism.* San Francisco: Synthesis Publications.

Donlan, T.G. (1981) Tax Headache Strikes. *Barron's*, 13 April.

Economist (1980) Swiss Drugs. Sweetening the Pill. 5 July.

Ehrenreich, J. (1972) Fixing the Drug Industry. In T. Bodenheimer, S. Cummings, and E. Harding, *Billions for Bandaids.* San Francisco: Medical Committee for Human Rights.

Fortune (1982) The 500 Largest Industrial Corporations. 3 May: 260–73.

Frank, A.G. (1982) After Reaganomics and Thatcherism, What? From

Keynesian Demand Management via Supply-side Economics to Corporate State Planning and 1984. *Contemporary Marxism* 4: 18–28.

Hopkins, T.K. and Wallerstein, I. (1977) Patterns of Development of the Modern World-system. *Review* 1(2): 111–45.

Journal of Commerce (1981) Puerto Rico Ships Record Quantity of Pharmaceuticals. 5 January.

Kiefer, T. (1980) The 'Neurotic Woman' Syndrome. *The Progressive*, December: 26–9.

Lall, S. and Bibile, S. (1978) The Political Economy of Controlling Transnationals: The Pharmaceutical Industry in Sri Lanka, 1972–1976. *International Journal of Health Services* 8(2): 299–328.

Ledogar, R.J. (1975) *Hungry for Profits*. New York: IDOC/North America.

Louis, A.M. (1980) SmithKline Finds Rich is Better. *Fortune*, 30 June: 63–6.

McCraine, N. and Murray, M.J. (1978) The Pharmaceutical Industry: A Further Study in Corporate Power. *International Journal of Health Services* 8(4): 573–88.

Mintz, M. (1967) *By Prescription Only*. Boston: Beacon.

——(1976) Faulty Testing of Drugs. *Washington Post*, 2 July.

Monthly Review (1981) The Deepening Crisis of US Capitalism. (October): 1–16.

Murray, M.J. (1974) The Pharmaceutical Industry: A Study in Corporate Power. *International Journal of Health Services* 4(4): 625–40.

New York Times (1978a) European Drug Companies on a US Buying Spree. 22 January.

——(1978b) The Drugs in Developing Countries Now Cause Worry. 12 March.

——(1981) The Drug Business Sees A Golden Era Ahead. 17 May.

Newsweek (1981) The Breast vs. the Bottle. 1 June: 54–5.

Schifrin, L.G. and Tayan, J.R. (1977) The Drug Lag: An Interpretive Review of the Literature. *International Journal of Health Services* 7(3): 359–81.

Silverman, M. (1977) The Epidemiology of Drug Promotion. *International Journal of Health Services* 7(2): 157–66.

Silverman, M. and Lee, P.R. (1974) *Pills, Profits and Politics*. Berkeley: University of California Press.

Silverman, M., Lee, R., and Lydecker, M. (1982) *Prescriptions for Death. The Drugging of the Third World*. Berkeley: University of California Press.

Simmons, H. E. (1974) The Drug Regulatory System of the United States Food and Drug Administration: A Defense of Current Requirements for Safety and Efficacy. *International Journal of Health Services* 4(1): 95–107.

Standard and Poor (1982a) Industry Surveys. 20 May: H31.
——(1982b) Industry Surveys. 20 May: H11–H17.
Talbot, M. (1980) Controversial Contraceptive Sold in Third-World Countries. *Daily Californian*, 25 November.
Wall Street Journal (1979) Generic-drug Use Will Be Urged By US. 10 January.
——(1981) Japan's Drug-makers try World Market, Challenging US and Europe Producers. 7 August.
Washington Post (1978) Drug Testing Abuses Laid to Doctors. 8 March.
Yudkin, J.S. (1980) The Economics of Pharmaceutical Supply in Tanzania. *International Journal of Health Services* 10(3): 455–77.

Acknowledgements

The author extends his heartfelt thanks to Marlene Dixon, Research Director of the Institute for the Study of Labor and Economic Crisis, whose wisdom and theoretical insight guided the writing of this chapter; to Kenneth Barnes and Bernie Fox who provided the research; and to all his colleagues at the Institute for the Study of Labor and Economic Crisis.

Six

Physicians and their sponsors: the new medical relations of production

Charles Derber

Introduction

The dramatic shift from solo to organizationally-based practices of physicians has been widely noted (Larson 1977; McKinlay 1982; Starr 1982). Physicians now work in a remarkable array of different organizational contexts, with a significant percentage on full or part-time salaries, or in other contractual relations with hospitals, health maintenance organizations, or other provider institutions. The question to be addressed here is whether the new arrangements reflect the proletarianization of physicians, as has been suggested recently by a number of social theorists, or, more conservatively, a process leading in that direction. The proletarianization thesis is that physicians have been drawn into new dependent relations of production with providers of capital, militating toward forms of wage-employment. It suggests this entails loss of control over the process of work, much like the loss of autonomy experienced by the crafts in the nineteenth century as they became absorbed within the factory system of capitalist production.

I shall examine here the structural relations between physicians and those who capitalize them in some of the most important types of medical settings and financing arrangements. I shall argue that the proletarianization thesis does not adequately explain the current medical relations of production, which are profoundly different from those in industry and are not easily characterized by structural concepts associated with full-time employment and industrial management. I shall suggest, however, that this does not point to continued professional sovereignty nor invulnerability to new occupational relations of dependency. Rather, physicians have been drawn into a historically unique relation to providers of capital, conceptualized here as a special mode of "sponsorship," in which their vulnerability to control has been significantly mitigated. The analysis offers a new structural perspective on physicians' traditional autonomy, but also points to emerging forms of sponsorship in medicine in which physicians are likely to experience new and greater management control.

Conceptualizing sponsorship

We must begin with a refinement of classical Marxist concepts that can account for the distinctive relation between physicians and those capitalizing their production. As suggested by proletarianization theorists, physicians, like almost all other producers of commodities or services in advanced economies, have now become dependent on external sources of capital. Yet for reasons peculiar to medicine, providers of capital are not primarily capitalist employers, and have been differentiated in a manner that significantly fragments their class-wide interests and weakens their capacity to manage physicians' work.

Historically, proletarianization has meant the emergence of a production system in which producers become wage-employees, dependent on their employer to provide capital for two fundamental purposes. The first was capitalization of the process of production itself. Because of mechanization and increased capital-intensiveness of production, producers were unable themselves to purchase necessary fixed-capital, including plant, tools, and equipment. Second, producers increasingly became dependent on external capital for mediation of the market

(Pirenne 1933; Hunt 1972). Geographical expansion as well as growing competition for local markets increased the capital required for recruitment, promotion, and distribution to the market. Moreover, through specialization and intensification of the division of labor, at least partly created by providers of capital themselves, fewer producers made goods that were directly consumable (Marglin 1974). Coordination with other components before final sale was increasingly required, a coordination undertaken initially by merchants with capital reserves and capacity to market beyond the local community, who simultaneously provided supplies to craft or cottage workers in the putting-out system (Pirenne 1933; Hunt 1972; Marglin 1974).

Historically, the two functions of capitalization of production and mediation of the market were thus assumed by a single actor, to a limited degree by the merchants and suppliers in the "putting-out" system of production and more fully by the proprietor-employer in the factory system. The loss of both functions and their concentration in a single agent produced the extreme dependency and vulnerability to control experienced by the industrial working class. The monopolization of production-capitalization and market-mediation by the purchaser of labor constituted the central preconditions for capitalist relations of production as formulated in the classical model of proletarianization, since if labor had retained its capacity to capitalize its own production it would not have been faced with the underlying imperative described by Marx for entering the employment relation, and if it had capitalized and retained a direct relation to the market by recruiting its own clientele and selling its product directly, it would have appropriated its own surplus.

While the functions of production-capitalization and market-mediation have thus been joined in the capitalist employer, it is crucial in understanding relations of production in medicine to recognize that they can be separated in two senses. First, producers who lose control over one function do not necessarily surrender control of the other; thus physicians who by the 1890s lost the capacity to capitalize a significant part of their own work, none the less maintained a direct relation to the market until the post-war period, and continue, in certain limited respects, to do so today. Capitalization and market-mediation can also be separated in the sense that even when both are lost by the producer, they are not necessarily joined in a single outside agent. Again, in the case of medicine, the two functions are not typically united in a single employer but reside separately in what I shall call *proprietary sponsors* (normally hospitals) and *market sponsors* (typically insurance companies and other third party reimbursers).

The concept of sponsorship is introduced here to identify any relation between producers and providers of capital on whom they are dependent for capitalization of production and/or mediation of the market. Employment represents a major sponsorship relation, but there are other types – of major importance in medicine as well as other occupations. Sponsors are defined as agents who provide external capital to producers for production and distribution, but not necessarily as employers nor necessarily with the aim of securing a maximum economic return on their capital. Sponsors are often members of the capitalist class in the sense that they possess and invest substantial amounts of capital in production, but a sponsor can also be the state (with its own pool of capital), or a non-profit private actor representing one or several class interests. While they do not necessarily seek maximum return on their capital, sponsors typically act to advance their own class interests, either short or long-term, or those of the fraction of the class they represent.

A *proprietary sponsor* can be defined precisely as one who capitalizes production, typically by providing fixed capital, such as physical plant, supplies, and machinery required for production, or by purchasing the services or labor-power of auxiliary producers required for integrated production. Such sponsors exercise control over producers, whether or not they employ them, by virtue of the proprietary rights associated with the capital they provide and the option to withdraw capital. In medicine, the most important proprietary sponsors have historically been hospitals, which typically have not been employers of physicians for reasons to be developed.

A *market sponsor* can be defined as an actor who provides capital to mediate the market between a producer and consumers. Market-mediation involves recruitment and retention of clientele as well as the promotion, distribution, and sale of the product or service. In a relation of fully developed market sponsorship, as in most employment relations, the market sponsor assumes all these market-mediation functions and thus obviates the requirement of the producer to capitalize or assume responsibility for any of his marketing imperatives. The various market-mediation functions can themselves be divided, however, some reserved for producers and others for one or more market sponsor, creating relations of *partial* market sponsorship. Market sponsors will differ in the amount of power they exercise over producers depending on the number of market-mediation functions they provide and the amount of capital required to carry them out. The evolution in medicine from market-mediation monopolized by physicians to a system of partial market-sponsorship organized around third party reimbursers who mediate financial exchanges between physicians and patients, underlies important changes in the forms of control physicians experience.

The structural relations of medical production are determined by the divided and partial character of the sponsorship system. Unlike proprietary sponsors in industry, hospitals, the main proprietary sponsors of physicians, have not also become market sponsors, reflecting both the continued success of physicians in keeping control of certain market-mediation of functions and the success of external third party reimbursers in gaining control of others. To the extent that physicians remain their own market sponsors, they can exercise key structural leverage against proprietary control exercised by hospitals. I shall suggest that a situation of "mutual sponsorship" between hospitals and physicians has developed, in which the dependency of physicians on the hospital is muted by a reciprocal market-dependency of the hospitals on the physicians. Mutual sponsorship will be discussed as a special form of divided sponsorship, where producers are not fully dependent on external providers of capital for market-mediation functions.

The growing importance of third party reimbursers as market sponsors to physicians is critical to the current form of divided sponsorship in medicine. The separation of third parties from hospitals creates radically distinct systems of proprietary and market sponsorship. Each subjects physicians to special relations of dependency and control that are structurally distinct from classical employment or "putting-out" forms of production. The central objective here is to suggest the utility of sponsorship as a concept for characterizing these relations and distinguishing them from industrial employment, conceived as an integrated or united mode of sponsorship.

Sponsorship systems are differentiated fundamentally by their structural capacity for control of producers. Divided and partial sponsorship generates relations of sponsor control significantly less powerful than united and fully developed sponsorship. Without the monopolization of functions enjoyed by the capitalist employer, hospitals and third party reimbursers have limited capacities to manage physicians' work. United sponsorship tends to produce very substantial loss of control by producers over their work. This loss of control to employers can be analytically divided into four areas: *ideological control* or loss of autonomy over organizational policy and objectives; *bureaucratic control* or loss of autonomy over auxiliary producers and their tasks; *productivity control* or loss of autonomy over scheduling and work-load; and *technical control* or loss of autonomy over technical skills and knowledge (Derber 1982).

The relations between producers and separate proprietary and market sponsors are less likely to produce these far-reaching forms of loss of autonomy. Our concern in what follows is first to examine the systems of separate proprietary and market sponsorship in their major contexts within medicine and, on the basis of preliminary findings from a large empirical study of these settings, indicate the type of control each generates over physicians. This will include a discussion of three types of proprietary sponsorship relations: the community hospital as sponsor to private physicians; the teaching hospital as sponsor to academic physicians; and the private group practice as a special collective sponsor of its own members. The discussion of market sponsorship will follow with a primary focus on Blue Shield as the single most important third party market sponsor of physicians. We shall then turn to a consideration of existing forms in which proprietary and market sponsorship are unified; and the tendency of such structures, including state hospitals and health maintenance organizations, to significantly increase sponsorship control over physicians. Finally, we shall consider an emerging political economy of cost-control in medicine that is likely to further break down the dual sponsorship system in medicine and further increase sponsorship control.

Proprietary sponsorship

Proprietary sponsorship in medicine emerged in the late nineteenth century with the development of a significant number of hospitals for acute care. Before 1870, most physicians capitalized themselves, working with their own tools and with patients who stayed at home (Freidson 1963; Stevens 1971). The rise of the hospital reflected the development of new capitalization requirements, associated with the increased application of science in medical care and medical technology. The rapidly escalating costs of medical capitalization reflected, as well, the intensification of the medical division of labor, rendering physicians dependent on proprietary sponsors who could not only provide for the fixed capital costs of hospitals but the variable costs associated with the labor of nurses and other hospital workers (Ehrenreich and Ehrenreich 1971; McKinlay 1982).

Hospitals are the principal proprietary sponsors of physicians, and special features of the relation between hospitals and physicians have determined the dual sponsorship pattern in medicine. Most important, hospitals while capitalizing physicians have historically not broken the direct relation between physicians and patients or "mediated" physicians' markets (Starr 1982). They thus have not joined the two functions that generated the employer role in industrial production. This reflects, first, the fact that hospitals capitalized only a portion of physicians' work, namely that which involved patients when they required hospitalization. Physicians typically capitalized that portion of their work which generated their initial relation to the patient and thus independently established and consolidated a market relation to patients (Stevens 1971; Starr 1982).

This, in turn, reflected broader considerations regarding the economic and class interests represented in hospitals and in medical production generally, that can be touched on only briefly here. A small number of basic types of hospitals historically have played a major role in the United States. The most important has been the non-profit voluntary community hospital, which as late as 1972 represented 40 per cent of all beds and 47 per cent of all hospitals (Greenfield 1975). Non-profit academic teaching hospitals and public sector Veterans

Administration (VA) and public health hospitals also historically have played an important role. Very recently, chains of
for-profit hospitals have emerged as another important proprietary sponsor in medicine (Earle 1982; Iglehart 1982a; Starr
1982).

Each type of hospital, through its board and sources of
funding, has its own distinctive economic identity and interests, and represents a particular form of proprietary class sponsorship of medicine. Two features distinguish this sponsorship
from capitalization of industrial production. First, the state
plays a much more important role. This is obviously the case in
federal or state hospitals, where government is the exclusive
proprietary sponsor. But, in the vast number of non-profits as
well, the state is an important actor, especially in the supply of
fixed capital (Greenfield 1975). The non-profits typically represent a blend of economic interests involving the state and
various sectors of private capital. In the major academic
teaching centers, nationally-based monopoly capital interests
are more heavily represented along with the state, medical, and
other professional interests (Ehrenreich and Ehrenreich 1971),
while in the community hospitals, the state, community, and
local capital are the more important proprietary actors. Private
capital is an important proprietary sponsor, as reflected in the
composition of hospital boards nationally (Alford 1975; Greenfield 1975), but the major role of government at all levels has
contributed to the ways in which relations of production in
hospitals have historically differed from those in industrial
production.

Equally important, however, is the nature of the interests
that private capital has had in assuming proprietary sponsorship. While *immediate* accumulation interests, particularly
within the construction, pharmaceutical, and medical supplies
industries, have influenced the non-profits' identity and
behavior, there is little evidence that the predominant investment or contribution of private capital to these institutions is
determined by these interests (Greenfield 1975; Starr 1982).
Whether private capital's involvement should be seen as primarily serving *long-term* accumulation interests, legitimation
interests, or purely philanthropic objectives, it is clear that
their proprietary sponsorship is not hinged primarily to short-
term profits as in industrial production. Why this has been the

case has been the subject of a number of important historical investigations (Larson 1977; Starr 1982), but the lack of capital's commitment or capacity to organize the hospital as a corporate profit-center underlies the unique relations of production in medicine and the historic autonomy of physicians.

Proprietary sponsorship, because it is not linked generally to market sponsorship, tends to produce a weak form of control of physician behavior. There are important instances where proprietary and market sponsorship are united, including VA hospitals and health maintenance organizations; in these, control over physicians is much stronger as will be discussed in a later section. Our concern here is with the predominant form, in which proprietary sponsors do not also act as major market sponsors. This takes the unusual form of "mutual sponsorship," since, while the hospital acts as a proprietary sponsor to the physician, the physician keeps control of market-mediation functions that allow him or her to act as both his or her own market sponsor *and* market sponsor to the hospital.

The relation of the solo practitioner with the community hospital reflects a classic model of mutual sponsorship. In regard to non-hospitalized patients, the solo practitioner can be said to be non-sponsored or self-sponsoring; capitalization requirements of a practice in the home have been growing but remain within the reach of today's solo practitioners (Glandon and Shapiro 1980). Since individually, however, they cannot capitalize their own hospital, they are required to enter in a relation with a proprietary sponsor for that part of their work, subjecting them to potential hospital management of their work with acute patients (Alford 1975; McKinlay 1982).

The classic relation developed with community hospitals is one of an attending physician with "privileges," often called "private staff." This represents neither full nor part-time salaried employment, although many hospitals have objective interests in such arrangements (McKinlay 1982). Physicians' success in resisting such rationalization reflects the unique reciprocal market dependency of the community hospital on the physicians. They have remained dependent on the physician both for the recruitment and retention of the patient, and bill the patient for their own services without mediating the financial exchange between physician and patient (Stevens 1971; Goldsmith 1981). Hospitals survive on their bed census, and continue to remain largely dependent on physicians to fill their beds (Starr 1982).

This anomaly of productive relations historically has rested on the unique ability of physicians to both capitalize and protect a direct relation with their patients. This has been viewed by many scholars (Freidson 1970; Larson 1977; Starr 1982) as a key source of physician power and success in resisting external control. It reflects, within our framework, an exceptional capacity of physicians to keep control over limited but key market-mediation functions, namely patient recruitment and retention, and thus to remain partial market "self-sponsors." Starr (1982) argues that this developed from the special qualities of the physician–patient relation as a market relation, historically governed by the substantial cultural authority of physicians and a sustained unusual quality of personal dependency by patients. Such unusual features contribute to the distinctive patterns of market sponsorship in medicine, increasing the importance of knowledge or other cultural resources in gaining control of market-mediation functions and contributing to physicians' capacity to keep such functions despite the superior capital resources of the hospital. Cultural, legal, and political factors fostered by physicians' organizations militated against hospitals' undermining physicians' direct relation to their market, and it was only with the rise of the third party reimbursement system that physicians began to become partially dependent on market sponsors – actors typically separate from hospitals (Juba 1977; Hsiao and Stevens 1981).

Mutual sponsorship between solo practitioner and community hospital therefore can be viewed as the coordination of two mutually dependent businesses (Goldsmith 1981). Physicians receive partial capitalization in exchange for providing a marketing function for their sponsoring hospitals. None the less, significant aspects of formal control over the physicians' work in the hospital remain with the hospital, including the right to refuse admission for uninsured or other types of patients, and schedule facilities, auxiliary personnel and tasks the physician may require. The hospital can even monitor the cumulative technical performance of a physician and apply sanctions where this does not conform with standard practice (McKinlay 1982). The sanction with clout is the denial of privileges but the community hospital is not eager to terminate its relation with physicians, so the only significant customary form of control over the physician is what I have called bureaucratic control. The physician is routinely required to accommodate to the scheduling of functions, facilities, and personnel managed by the hospital, which under certain circumstances may affect the physician's own pattern of treatment and the quality of service delivered (McKinlay 1982).

Proprietary sponsorship by community hospitals of physicians in private group practice does not differ markedly from the pattern with solo practitioners. The relation is again one of mutual sponsorship. The market dependency of the hospital on the physicians may be heightened if the group is large, however, as the physicians' sanction of shifting their collective allegiance to another hospital in the area would have more significant financial implications. Another difference is that a very large group practice is sometimes able to capitalize its own hospital. Where this occurs, with the group normally establishing a separate hospital corporation controlled by its own physicians, physicians become their own proprietary sponsors (or can be considered "unsponsored") and remove any form of external proprietary dependency.

A unique and "tighter" mutual sponsorship has emerged between physicians with teaching appointments and the major academic hospitals serving as their proprietary sponsors. Because of their size, prestige, and resources, many of the major academic medical centers are potentially capable of exercising very substantial proprietary control over physicians (Ehrenreich and Ehrenreich 1971; McKinlay 1982). The capacity for control is weakened, however, by relations of mutual sponsorship that exist in two senses. While the teaching hospitals act as major capitalizers and, to a limited degree, market sponsors of the physicians, the physicians also function as reciprocal market sponsors for the hospitals and as reciprocal proprietary sponsors to a much smaller extent.

This extraordinarily complex relation of sponsorship arises from the multiple functions of teaching, research, and clinical care that characterize academic medicine, each with different funding sources. The primary sponsor for medical teaching and research historically has been the state (Deitrick and Benson 1953; Stevens 1971). Federal research funds, alone, increased 2,500 per cent between 1941 and 1951 and, through National

Institutes of Health (NIH) have continued to grow dramatically all through the post-war period, at a level now well over $3 billion (Endicott and Allen 1953; Starr 1982). Some funds are channeled directly to the hospital for specific programs, but others, particularly research funds, are awarded directly to physicians, who then bring them to the particular institutions with which they are affiliated. To the extent that public funds for teaching and research are awarded on the basis of institutional capacities and reputation, proprietary control accrues to the hospital and academic physicians become dependent on it. To the extent, however, that grants are awarded to program directors or physician-researchers on the basis of their academic merit and reputation, hospitals become dependent on their staff for funds and the overhead they provide for the institution (Price 1973).

In this respect, the physician becomes a proprietary sponsor of the hospital, while simultaneously being in the traditional position of the "sponsee" of the hospital. This simply reflects the existence of more than one proprietary sponsor for academic physicians, a condition of "multiple sponsorship," corresponding to their multiple functions. By having direct access to state grants and funds, they are able to bring funds to the hospital that historically have been used to service other hospital costs or programs than those for which the funds were awarded (Iglehart 1982b). While the physician is now beholden to several proprietary sponsors, including the state, medical school deans, and the teaching hospital, each of which constitutes an agent of control, the control any one can exercise is limited by the leverage of the physician in playing one sponsor off another and being fully dependent on none (Stevens 1971; Starr 1982).

Unique patterns of mutual market sponsorship result from the position of the teaching hospital as a tertiary-care institution, dependent on recruiting patients from a national or international market. The most important of these hospitals can rely on their reputations alone to attract a significant number of patients. Physicians attached to these institutions will become visible in the medical community simply by virtue of the affiliation and are thus more likely to receive referrals. In this respect, the hospital can function as a market sponsor for physicians unlike any other type of hospital.

At the same time, institutions depend on the recruitment and holding of academic staff with the best talent, because affluent tertiary-care patients will tend to follow the physicians with the most outstanding reputations in whatever institution they are housed (Stevens 1971). In acute complex disease, the reputation of the physician will count more than in routine medicine, and the relation between physician and patient will be less vulnerable to hospital mediation or disruption. Even the most prestigious teaching hospitals thus remain profoundly economically beholden to their physicians (Ehrenreich and Ehrenreich 1971; Starr 1982).

These complex mutual sponsorship patterns imply considerable variability in the control teaching hospitals can exercise over their physician staff. This relation however, has been characterized historically by more extensive contractual ties and greater control over the physician than that developed by the community hospitals (Stevens 1971). A significant and unusual percentage of academic doctors have traditionally been full or part-time salaried employees of the hospital.

The principal form of control by the hospital experienced by academic physicians is bureaucratic. This relates partly to the size of the large teaching hospitals. Centralized management typically assumes responsibility for hiring and firing of all non-medical physician staff, scheduling facilities, and tasks of these personnel, and organizing records and ancillary procedures. One of the incentives of academic physicians who leave salaried positions to form autonomous physician group practices that contract for services with teaching hospitals is to gain more control in this area.

Academic physicians also suffer what I have called "ideological control" in the sense that they do not exercise control over overall organizational policy and budget. This is monopolized by chief executive officers, the medical director, and chiefs of service, as well as the boards of trustees (Duff and Hollingshead 1968; Ehrenreich and Ehrenreich 1971). That staff physicians do not express major concern about this may reflect disinterest in matters beyond their own immediate work or simple accommodation to realities of power in traditional academic hierarchies. It may also reflect a significant convergence of interests between institutional imperatives and physicians' interests, especially shared priorities of research and teaching and commitment to state-of-the-art technology and specialized procedures (Ehrenreich and Ehrenreich 1971; Starr 1982). Physicians most likely to be sensitive to lack of policy and budget control are those committed to patient care in ambulatory clinics of the teaching hospitals, which may not carry high priority with the administration and are more likely to be cut back under conditions of budget constraint.

Academic physicians are not subject to significant direct productivity or technical control. The lack of the former may simply reflect that the hospital can sensibly rely on the academic incentives and internal motivations of the physician to elicit more performance than any direct productivity norm. In regard to technical control, the esoteric and highly specialized expertise of the academic physician by itself makes this problematic for any administration. Yet it should be noted that greater collegial review and monitoring of technical performance is likely to go on in teaching hospitals than in any other settings, because the teaching function requires open sharing of cases; extensive referrals of complex cases are also routine in the hospital and require frequent consultation (Freidson 1970).

Proprietary self-sponsorship

A qualitatively different form of proprietary sponsorship is that exercised by private group practices over their members. Such groups, consisting of partnerships or professional corporations of two to thirty or more physicians, are growing rapidly and are becoming an extremely pervasive form of practice (Roemer, Mera, and Shonick 1974; Henderson 1982). In 1980, they represented one-quarter of all physicians, up from 1.2 per cent in 1940 and 12.8 per cent in 1969 (Starr 1982). Groups deserve attention as a special form of proprietary sponsor because the physicians, while collectively in control, individually are subject to the control of the collectivity. Proprietary sponsorship by the group is obviously radically different from that by the hospital, since the physicians are capitalizing themselves and are not dependent on external providers. The group is thus "unsponsored" or "self-sponsoring." Yet it exercises important forms of control over physician work not confronted by the solo practitioner.

The control is weakened, however, by a form of mutual sponsorship existing between each individual physician and the group. This is based on the partial separation of production-capitalization and market-mediation functions. While individual physicians are largely dependent on the group as a proprietary sponsor, they remain in some measure responsible for the recruitment and retention of their own patients. Except for sub-specialists, dependent on the group for referrals, the group tends to function minimally as a market sponsor (except for large, well-established groups with high visibility and outstanding reputations in the community). As Starr (1982) has pointed out, this historically has weakened the control or hold of the group over the physician and, in earlier periods, has permitted younger associates of the practice to achieve the autonomy they seek or leave the group.

None the less, the group can exercise considerable control over members, particularly in the face of the mounting obstacles to the option of solo practice. The group can be defined as a "guild-organization," an organizational form highly resonant with the interests of professions, with its own distinctive system of control. Guild-organizations differ from other corporations because equity or ultimate authority is legally reserved to those credentialed by the profession, normally professionals working within the organization itself. This assures that substantial proprietary sponsorship and control remain with the professionals themselves. In most medical partnerships, governance is formally democratic, each partner having one vote (Henderson 1982). Unlike most law firms, another major guild form, members become full or vested partners within a year or two and thus quickly share in the full governance of the firm.

While proprietary control exercised by the guild over its members does not represent proletarianization since it is collectively self-imposed, none the less it can lead to loss of individual autonomy and a substantial degree of centralized management. This is most likely to happen in groups organized as health maintenance organizations, and will be considered separately as a manifestation of market sponsorship and control. Most private group practices are organized on a fee-for-service basis, however, and permit greater individual autonomy (Roemer, Mera, and Shonick 1974; Henderson 1982).

The organizational controls that frequently emerge in

"guilds" vary with historical development, size, and financial and administrative systems (Henderson 1982). In some groups, senior founders autocratically dominate overall organizational policy and management, even where governance is formally democratic. A *de facto* form of "ideological control" exists in such groups, not inconsistent with the hierarchy and authority of guild cultures, particularly in medicine. Such control is often accepted by members on the basis of historical commitment and service by the founder or special managerial or medical expertise.

Increased size of groups is associated with increased bureaucratic control. Scheduling of patients and facilities in large groups tends to be removed from the purview of individual physicians and centralized and routinized. Physicians often do not participate in hiring or firing of nurses or other non-physician staff. Such bureaucratic guild control is less profound than in a hospital, where the physicians do not have ultimate authority to intervene, but physicians in private groups may experience it as a serious day-to-day constraint.

Perhaps the major issue of policy or administrative control arising in groups emerges in multi-specialty groups, where medical or surgical specialists earning high fees for procedures have different structural interests regarding systems for compensation and contribution to overhead, than general internists or others less well compensated by third parties (Freidson 1970). While groups often agree to compensation formulae based on individual billing, permitting specialists to maintain their higher market earnings, they may also insist on every physician paying the same percentage of his gross billing to overhead, requiring specialists to pay in absolute terms substantially more than others for the same administrative facilities or services (Henderson 1982). Any arrangement, given the competing interests among specialties, will rankle certain groups, normally surgeons, and may be experienced as a very significant form of policy control exercised by the organization.

Market sponsorship

Market sponsorship developed far later than proprietary sponsorship, reflecting physicians' fierce resistance and success in preventing any intermediary coming between themselves and their patients. We have seen that the hospitals, the logical intermediaries given their capitalization function, did not assume this role. While a series of other actors tried to do so, none was successful prior to the Great Depression and the onset of health insurance and third party reimbursement in the 1930s. Even then, the American Medical Association (AMA) strenuously resisted the inclusion of physicians within the first hospital insurance plans developed by Blue Cross (Law 1974). Many physicians resisted as well the development of the Blue Shield plan in the late 1930s, the first third party reimbursement system to encompass physicians' services and fees. The profession accommodated shortly thereafter only when it became clear, first, that the alternative was compulsory insurance or lay-controlled prepayment systems and, second, that physicians themselves were developing a position of control over Blue Shield policy (Hirschfield 1970; Starr 1982).

With the rapid expansion of health insurance and other forms of third party reimbursement in the post-war period, however, and with the increase in the share of total health expenditures paid by third parties from 45 per cent in 1960 to 67 per cent in 1975 (Juba 1977), almost all physicians are now required to accommodate to relationships with powerful market sponsors. These include the large commercial insurance companies, one of the largest and most important institutional sectors of private capital, and the state, which, with the rise of Medicare and Medicaid, has developed profoundly greater economic involvement with the health care system. Increased market mediation by these actors has great significance, since market sponsorship has historically been associated with the rise of employment and proletarianization of labor. None the less until the current decade, market sponsors have not imposed a profound system of control on physicians, and this is closely related to the character of third party reimbursers as *partial* and unique types of market sponsors.

Since they are not physicians' employers the commercial insurers and Blue Cross and Blue Shield carry out only a limited range of market-mediating functions, leaving to the physicians some of the most important, especially the recruitment of patients and generation of more visits from each. The third parties, in fact, have a direct interest in discouraging the latter, since each additional visit increases their outflows without increasing their revenues. On the other hand, all third party systems serve a major market function for physicians as a whole by substantially increasing the aggregate demand for physicians' services and rendering that demand relatively insensitive or inelastic to price increases (Feldstein 1971). The aggregate demand is fueled because the third party system socializes or collectivizes costs of care to all those enrolled in the plan, while maintaining benefits as private or individual. Price increases tend not to dampen demand because they are absorbed by all subscribers.

Distinguishing between "collective" and "individual" market sponsorship clarifies the unique role of third parties as market sponsors. All third parties serve as "collective" market sponsors in the sense that they carry out a critical market function for physicians *as a collectivity* by vastly expanding aggregate market demand for the profession's services. Their sponsorship of individual physicians, however, varies substantially by the type of third party system (Hsiao and Stevens 1981; Starr 1982). In the traditional insurance or "indemnity" model of the commercial insurers, the third parties act as only minimal "individual" market sponsors, since they develop no direct relation to individual physicians and do not carry out for them any of the meaningful market-mediating functions involving billing, fee-setting, specification of services, or recruitment of patients. In the "prepayment" model, however, characterized most fully by health maintenance organizations (HMOs), a fully developed model of "individual" market sponsorship emerges, with the HMO plan serving not only as a "third party payer" but also as a direct provider of physician services, responsible to all participating physicians for recruitment of patients as well as billing and fee setting, and regulating most aspects of the actual delivery of care. A third and historically predominant third party system has been Blue Cross and Blue Shield, lying somewhere between the insurance and prepayment model. Partial "individual" market sponsorship develops, with the third party assuming responsibility for the billing and fee setting of individual physicians, but leaving individual physicians responsible for recruitment of their own patients (Hsiao and Stevens 1981; Starr 1982).

These different types of third parties have different structural interests and, as market sponsors, different capacities to control physicians. The "indemnity" or insurance model created minimal market sponsorship and control because the commercial insurers conceived the third party system as a traditional insurance business with no responsibility for providing medical services, but only for protecting clients against the financial "losses" of illness (Hsiao and Stevens 1981). They thus developed a traditional financial relation to clients (patients), collecting premiums and paying for costs associated with "losses," but established no relation to or financial exchange with the individual physician. The insurer controlled risks and costs not by exercising constraint over individual physicians but rather by influencing clients, largely by offering plans in which certain services were not reimbursed and a substantial deductible or "co-insurance" served as a disincentive for overutilization by patients (Juba 1977; Hsiao and Stevens 1981).

Market sponsorship and control in the "prepayment" model is much more fully developed because the pioneers in prepayment plans saw themselves as offering comprehensive preventive health care services rather than simply "health insurance" (Starr 1982). Unlike commercial insurers, they saw themselves in the business of capitalizing, promoting, and marketing specific types of individual physicians who practiced preventive medicine. They also, correspondingly, sought to influence physicians, both to promote progressive care and to control costs. To achieve such control, sponsors of early prepayment plans, including companies, community cooperatives, unions, and innovative physicians, developed radical organizational forms, characterized by unified market and proprietary sponsorship and employment of physicians (Falkson 1980; Starr 1982).

Yet neither the early prepayment nor the traditional "indemnity" models emerged as the prevailing form of market sponsorship in medicine. On the one hand, the prepayment plans were effectively resisted and undermined by local and national physicians' organizations, largely by boycotts and stringent sanctions against physicians who cooperated. At the same time, the classical "indemnity"or insurance model has been modified through the effects of competition with Blue Cross and Blue Shield, which historically represented a blend of the insurance and prepayment models (Starr 1982). The hybrid system developed by the "blues" has emerged as the prevailing reimbursement model. Historically linked to the physicians themselves, Blue Shield, the physicians' single most powerful market sponsor, has carved out a limited but important set of market-mediating functions. A more partial sponsorship than the prepayment model, it none the less offers the potential for significant types of ideological and technical control over physician behavior (Hsiao and Stevens 1981).

Blue Shield functions like all third parties to increase aggregate demand for physicians' collective services, but acts as an "individual" market sponsor primarily by mediating the financial exchange between physician and patient. Since Blue Shield does not recruit patients for individual physicians, it creates far less market dependency of the physician than in the comprehensive prepayment model and less vulnerability to control. Its primary capacity to control physicians lies in its regulation of fees. This is an enormously important form of market sponsor control, although it historically has not been used in a manner unfriendly to physicians' collective interests because of the cozy relation between Blue Shield and physicians themselves. Traditionally most Blue Shield plans regulated fees through a fixed-fee schedule, determined primarily by panels of physicians, establishing invariant fees for all physicians for each service. A new arrangement has emerged since 1975, used increasingly by Blue Shield plans and commercials, known as "UCR" – "usual, customary, and reasonable" reimbursement. This is a modification in which individual physicians are paid according to individual schedules, based on a "profile" of their own "usual" charges and those "customarily" charged by other physicians in the area. The maximum reimbursable is typically either a figure set at 90 per cent of the prevailing local customary rate or the physician's own "usual" rate, whichever is lower (Juba 1977). Profiles for the physician and area are updated on a regular basis, thus permitting constantly increasing charges. The system has an extraordinary capacity for escalation of charges, since physicians have every incentive to keep upping their profile by submitting higher new "usual" or "reasonable" charges each year.

The system none the less permits Blue Shield a certain form of control over physician incomes, measurably increased to the extent that its market-share in the area rises (Hsiao and Stevens 1981). The system is, in general, a kind of "piece-rate" compensation, with traditional market determination of the piece-rate supplanted by Blue Shield mediation. Blue Shield constrains physicians' incomes generally by enforcing "participation agreements" where physicians contractually agree to accept Blue Shield reimbursement as full payment; such agreement can be enforced to the extent Blue Shield functions as a "monopoly" market sponsor and can jeopardize the business of physicians who do not contract with them. It can also constrain the incomes of certain physician groups based on its control over the geographical "screen" or area defined as relevant to the establishment of the community profile and the length between "updates" of profiles. Certain physicians of given areas or ages have been fixed at a comparatively low level compared to others, because of decisions regarding both specific "screens" and periods between "updates" (Hsiao and Stevens 1981).

Much more important, the income of certain specialties is dramatically enhanced at the expense of others (Blumberg 1979). Surgeons and certain medical sub-specialists, such as cardiologists, are reimbursed at rates much higher than general internists, family practitioners, and certain medical specialties such as infectious disease (Roe 1981). The reason lies in the principle underlying the traditional fee schedules, that reimbursement should be tied primarily to tangible "hands-on" procedures rather than diagnosis of symptoms (Blumberg 1979). Procedures such as cardiac catheterizations or surgical interventions are "quantitative," discrete, and measurable skills compared to the more diffuse and intangible mental skills involved in general medical consultations and visits. They also are presumed to carry more risk and involve extended years of specialized training. The linking of reimbursement to manual rather than mental skill is a peculiar principle for a profession presumed to be organized around theoretical knowledge, but reflects the historical ascendancy of surgeons within Blue Shield (Law 1974). The result is a very profound income stratification among specialties, with those whose work typically does not involve procedures, experiencing relative material deprivation. The huge differential in piece-rates constitutes a real form of productivity control for the general internists, requiring them to work many more hours than procedure-oriented specialists without prospect of ever achieving their average income (Blumberg 1979; Delbanco, Meyers, and Segal 1979).

A more profound form of physician control, which I have earlier called "ideological" control, is exercised through this particular system of fee regulation. Any sponsor who regulates fees exercises potential financial leverage both over general approaches to medical practice and specific technical behavior by physicians. The general approach fostered by procedure-oriented reimbursement is, first, to discourage preventive health care by providing financial rewards only for procedures required in the treatment of illness and, second, to encourage unnecessary acute procedures. It is thus a structural basis of what Illich (1976) and others have called iatrogenic medicine. Preventive care carries strong financial disincentives since it requires few reimbursable procedures. While reflecting an approach to medicine by most physicians that predates the rise of the third party sponsorship system, Blue Shield's fee system has frozen in place a policy that makes it difficult for even those physicians ideologically predisposed toward preventive care to develop a practice consistent with their principles.

The disincentive to preventive care is paralleled by incentives for iatrogenic or illness-producing care. First, the fee system encourages utilization of procedures even when their need or value is problematic since it handsomely rewards the physician. This carries health risks for the patient (Illich 1976). Second, since the fee system tends to reward care in the hospital rather than in the office, usually by reimbursing at a higher rate for the same procedure in the hospital (Blumberg 1979), it encourages unnecessary hospitalization, also a health risk for the patient (Illich 1976).

This ideological control is closely linked with what I have called technical control. Blue Shield, as a market sponsor, indirectly exercises such control in two ways. First, it will reimburse only those services defined as "medically necessary," thus discouraging practices not so defined. Blue Shield's definition, while drawn from recommendations of panels of physicians, may or may not correspond to the judgment of individual practitioners, but will none the less influence their behavior (Hsiao and Stevens 1981). Second, the differential in rates for different technical interventions will encourage those rewarded more highly. While the discretion remains with the physician, the financial incentives constitute a powerful indirect control system.

Despite these indirect controls, market sponsorship in medicine, as exemplified by Blue Shield, has not *fundamentally* altered traditional patterns of physician behavior, nor served as a system of *direct* control of physician behavior for several structural reasons. The first involves the dual sponsorship system. Unlike the market sponsors of the industrial craft workers, the market sponsors of physicians did not directly capitalize physicians' work and become their employers. Market sponsorship divided from proprietary sponsorship can ony produce "control at a distance." This constraint is much like that classically faced by the "putter-outer" to the cottage crafts. Since physicians are working in institutions not owned or capitalized by the market sponsor, they cannot be directly managed or supervised (Marglin 1974). Labor control is necessarily indirect, taking the form maximally of control through contractual arrangement, primarily in relation to fee determination. Direct bureaucratic, productivity, or technical control is not feasible under these structural arrangements.

A second structural consideration is the partial and collective character of the dominant form of market sponsorship. Blue Shield assumes only a limited number of market-mediating functions for the individual physician. The physician recruits his or her own patients and is, in this fundamental sense, "self-sponsoring." Market dependency on the sponsor is thus reduced and the potential for control correspondingly weakened.

A third consideration is the lack of structural forces impelling the dominant market sponsors to exercise direct control. This is intimately related to the financial arrangements by which third parties have been able to pass costs through to consumers (Juba 1977; Starr 1982). As long as such "pass throughs" are possible, third parties have no direct economic interest in controlling costs or physician behavior. Until very recently, costs have been passed through easily because of the lack of any organized consumer capacity to resist hikes in premiums. Profound change in the nature of the market sponsorship system is likely to emerge in this decade precisely because of changes in this area.

Unified sponsorship: towards proletarianization

While dual sponsorship has prevailed in medicine, there are important historical instances of unified sponsorship where proprietary and market sponsorship have been vested in a single actor. As in the industrial sector, this form of sponsorship has tended to proletarianize physicians in two senses: first, the sponsor is much more likely to employ the physician and second, tends to exercise much more substantial direct control of physician work. For this reason, physicians have forcefully resisted these forms of medical organization and have insured that they have not gained predominance. None the less, because they are likely to gain more prominence in the coming decade and suggest both the limitations of control within separate sponsorship and the forms of proletarianization that may emerge in new medical systems, they deserve brief consideration.

The two principal types of unified sponsorship are government hospitals, such as VAs and public health hospitals, where the state acts as both proprietary and market sponsors, and comprehensive prepayment plans, especially health maintenance organizations, in which the owners or boards of directors of the plans, whether they be companies, unions, communities, or physicians themselves, act as both proprietary and market sponsors. Both in government hospitals and in HMOs, the sponsor tends to monopolize most of the major proprietary and market-mediating functions, capitalizing all aspects of the physicians' work and carrying out the full range of market functions, including promotion and recruitment of patients, billing, specification of services, and comprehensive mediation and regulation of service delivery. This produces a very substantial production and market-dependency, and significant vulnerability of physicians to control within the context of employment relations. The sponsor's direct control of physicians' work is primarily in the management of policy and bureaucratic decisions, however, and historically has been associated with substantial relative autonomy of physicians, who typically play a major role as medical managers within the organization and remain relatively free of direct technical control.

Both in state hospitals and comprehensive prepayment plans, the key to the emergence of unified sponsorship has been the sponsor's commitment and capacity to finance a particular type of medical market and service and, in so doing, to undermine the most important function historically monopolized by physicians: recruiting and retaining their own patients. The traditional privileged and personal relation between physicians and patients created a critical market leverage for physicians that prevented either the private hospitals which capitalized them or the third parties which carried out other market-mediating functions for them from consolidating full control. Only in unified sponsorship is this key market function assumed by the sponsor because of special market interests.

In the case of the state hospitals, the distinctive feature is the commitment of the state to provide medical care for specific populations who otherwise would not receive it. In public health hospitals, these are the uninsured working poor, indigent, or special populations such as prisoners with no capacity to pay. In the VAs, it is veterans who won the right to care as a political entitlement; those who use the hospitals are, in the main, the poorest who can not afford care elsewhere (Starr 1974).

This creates a fundamental difference from the classical pattern of market sponsorship in the hospitals. We have seen that in community and other private hospitals, patients are brought to the hospital via the physicians, who thus serve as market sponsors for the hospital. In state hospitals, patients come not because of any connection to the physicians, but because they are the only hospitals which serve them (Greenfield 1975). The state hospitals become, in this instance, their own market sponsor as well as that of their physicians.

This creates a radically different relation of physicians to the hospitals. The hospital, as agent of the state, serves both as proprietary and market sponsor to the physician. The market-dependency of the physician on the hospital, combined with classic dependency for capitalization, creates conditions and power relations appropriate to employment. The physician becomes a salaried employee of the state, subject to management control like other employees. The unattractiveness of this arrangement to physicians creates special problems of recruitment for the state. It is forced to compensate physicians on special salary scales well above those of other government employees, although below incomes of those in private practice. It also resorts to hiring foreign physicians. A third mechanism is to create links with medical schools and attract academic physicians with special research funding and attractive clinical research settings (Starr 1974). Poor patients with plenty of acute and serious illness represent "interesting" and pliant cases for teaching and clinical research purposes.

The state hospital as a special unified sponsor exercises significantly greater direct control over physicians than other hospitals. Overall policy direction of the hospital is ultimately determined by the VA administration and Congress, or by state departments of public health and state legislatures. All critical budget decisions are made in these political arenas far removed from physicians in the hospital, although the hospital administrator retains important discretion within overall figures (Greenfield 1975). Physicians also experience substantial bureaucratic control, since rules governing hiring and firing of all personnel, and levels of salary are codified in state authorizations, and authority over medical support staff is, in large measure, administered by non-physician hospital managers. In addition, scheduling and the work load of physicians are also largely subject to state regulation, with standard hours of work and, for many physicians, essentially fixed patient quotas.

Even within this context, physicians none the less retain substantial autonomy. Most important, unlike industrial workers, they are not subject to extensive technical control. High relative autonomy in treatment choices is protected by tradition, knowledge not shared by non-physician management, and legal rights and responsibilities, enshrined in state licensing and enabling acts, that accrue to the physician alone. The medical organization of the state hospital, moreover, has many of the characteristics of what I have called a "guild-organization." The medical director of state hospitals is a physician and the chiefs of all services, who constitute middle management of the hospital, are also all physicians (Greenfield 1975). Physicians, while subject to important forms of management, are managers themselves, almost all having some measure of authority over some medical support staff. Even as employees, then, physicians experience "proletarianization" of their labor process only in the sense of losing control over important but limited kinds of decisions; they are no more likely in this than in other settings to experience the "de-skilling" typically associated with industrial proletarianization, and they continue to function as managers, even as workers (Derber 1982a; Larson 1980).

The HMO is, perhaps, the more significant form of unified sponsorship because of its rapidly increasing prevalence (Iglehart 1971; Falkson 1980). The HMO is the contemporary manifestation of the comprehensive prepayment plan discussed earlier. An enormous variety of HMOs have developed since the early 1970s, when they became attractive politically as a means of controlling health costs (Iglehart 1971; Starr 1982). HMOs include for-profits and non-profits and have been established and operated by corporations for their employees, unions for their members, groups of entrepreneurs, including physician groups, and a wide range of non-profit and community groups, including Blue Cross itself. Many plans employ physicians in a "staff" HMO model, but some contract for services with autonomous physician groups in a "group" model (Luft 1981).

All these forms share a unified proprietary and market sponsorship in which the plan's administration markets the plan to corporations and individuals and simultaneously capitalizes and manages the delivery of medical services. While physicians opposed the early prepayment plans, many have accommodated to the HMO concept in the last decade, primarily as a cost-effective alternative to national health insurance (Ellwood 1971), which they could potentially control organizationally by becoming owners of particular HMOs. None the less, it is an organizational form in which the HMO administration can exercise very substantial control over its physicians, not only because it integrates proprietary and market sponsorship, but because its appropriation of market functions is far more profound than that of other third parties. Consolidation of control is linked to the undermining of the physician–patient link and the historic responsibility of physicians for recruiting their own patients. The consumers of the plan, whether corporations acting for their employees or individuals, typically join the HMO not through a pre-established relation with its physicians but rather because of the financial and/or ideological appeal of a low-cost preventive health plan (Falkson 1980). Patients are thus recruited through the success of the plan's marketing schemes rather than through the traditional aegis and sponsorship of physicians. The erosion of this key market function of physicians is highlighted by the special characteristic of the HMO to which its physician and consumer opponents both point: the loss of patients' "free choice" of physicians (Christianson 1980). Unlike other reimbursement systems, patients are not free to select any physician, but only those on the plan's staff. "Free choice" is the other side of a traditional system in which physicians recruit their own patients; by appropriating this market role HMOs thereby remove one of physicians' historic bases of power in relation to those that capitalize them.

HMOs not only are characterized by a structural capacity to control physicians but a strong economic incentive to actually exercise that capacity (Luft 1981). Because of their freedom to pass through costs to consumers, traditional third party systems had little incentive to control costs or physician behavior. HMOs do not have this "pass through" luxury. The edge of HMOs in competitive marketing with other third parties comes only from offering lower costs for more comprehensive services, since patients sacrifice "free choice" of physician in the HMO plan (Christianson 1980). An HMO that passed through costs by raising subscribers' fees would lose members not only to commercial insurers and the "blues," but to competing HMOs (Starr 1982).

Direct control of physician behavior is required not only as part of the imperative to control costs, but to assure the type of care that attracts subscribers. Offering comprehensive high quality preventive care while holding costs low requires efficient management of physician behavior, as well as socialization of the physician to the plan's medical philosophy and objectives. Incentives exist for the HMO to exercise all types of the control – ideological, bureaucratic, productivity, and technical – that characterize industrial management (Christianson 1980).

These structural imperatives manifest themselves in unusual ways in HMOs owned and administered by the physicians themselves. These are often private group practices, which have moved to incorporate an HMO plan because of its market potential. Such groups, traditionally characterized by great individual autonomy, are required by the economic logic of the HMO to impose new and significant control over their own behavior. While this represents a form of professional self-management rather than orthodox proletarianization, it can create significant stress within the group. Physicians accustomed to setting their own schedules may now find it necessary to submit to centralized schedules and to unexpected chastisement from colleagues when they miss appointments. Such behavior adds to overhead costs and wastes support staff time in ways that may no longer be affordable. General bureaucratic control is also likely to be significantly increased, since the organization requires the most efficient use of both physician and medical support staff time. Since physicians have not been trained in management techniques, they are often confronted with the dilemma of hiring administrators trained in medical management, who can rationalize the organizational structure but may, in so doing, infringe on their employers' authority and autonomy. Most important, physicians may find it necessary to impose collectively significant policy and technical constraints on themselves to reduce costs. These are most likely to take the form of controls over use of outside costly laboratory tests or procedures and especially hospitalizations for which the plan must pay.

In HMOs owned or governed by groups other than the physicians, such controls, since they are not self-imposed, are more likely to create conflict between the administration and physicians who become employees of the plan. This is especially true of technical decisions which physicians regard as their exclusive preserve. Decisions regarding hospitalization are critical because these are a central component of HMO costs; this may become an arena of major conflict (Christianson 1980; Luft 1981). HMO management seeks to maximize savings elsewhere as well, primarily through bureaucratic and productivity control. Administrative control over medical support staff may be shifted, in considerable measure, from physicians to a separate administrative hierarchy, requiring physicians to accommodate to personnel decisions and organization of job functions among nurses and other staff which may conflict with their own preferences (Luft 1981). Productivity control over physicians may also be substantial, with standard hours and patient quotas established by plan administration. Fiscal pressures endemic to HMOs may also lead to pressure on physicians' salaries, often contested in heated bargaining between physicians and administration at annual salary negotiations.

ntrols physicians experience as employees some-
:hem to opt for another relation to the HMO, where
an autonomous private physicians' group and con-
:rvices. In this "group" model, in which physicians
do not uᴗᴗome staff employees, they may be better able to protect themselves from bureaucratic and productivity control.
This is particularly true if the contractual arrangements call for
the physicians group to assume responsibility for providing
total medical services, including nursing and other support
staff services, since physicians then manage the entire medical
care delivery. The "group" model also generally gives physicians more freedom to regulate their own schedules and patient
loads (Christianson 1980; Starr 1982).

Physicians, none the less, do not always opt for the group
model. It requires certain capitalization and risk, as well as a
range of administrative responsibilities, which they do not
necessarily want to assume. Similarly, HMO administration is
not always eager to salary the physicians, since the "group"
model absolves them of certain fixed financial obligations to
the physicians and also places the incentives directly on the
physicians themselves to achieve efficiency in the use of their
own and support staff's time.

In both "group" and "staff" model, market sponsorship and
primary proprietary sponsorship lie primarily with the owners
or board of directors of the HMO. The key market function of
patient recruitment is always primarily exercised by the plan,
as well as capitalization of the physical facilities. Both models
thus represent "unified" sponsorship and a significant control
relationship, whether in employment relations or contractual arrangements resembling the "putting-out" system of
production.

Future prospects

A new political economy of medicine is arising, with powerful
class forces developing a new and direct interest in control of
medical costs. This will profoundly affect all sectors of medicine, including physicians. The new political economy will
lead to major changes in the prevailing patterns of sponsorship.
Sponsorship systems with greater capacity to control costs and

physician behavior are already in the process of develo these should fail, a system of political control may with direct regulation of prices and costs by the state.

New sponsorship arrangements are arising from fund: change in the organization of the medical market. It is becoming a predominantly institutional market in which individual patient demand is channeled through two central consumers: corporations and the state. This has three consequences that will profoundly affect sponsorship relations. First, powerful class actors now have a direct interest in limiting medical costs. The "pass through" of costs by the traditional third party reimbursers creates direct new costs for corporations and the state, putting pressure on their budgets rather than those of thousands of individuals (Earle 1982; Iglehart 1982a).

Second, the capacity of corporations and the state to absorb these "passthroughs" has disappeared because of major changes in the national and international economy. Previously, these institutions responded to the "passthrough" costs by passing them on, in turn, to the population at large; monopoly-sector corporations simply raised prices and the state raised taxes (Iglehart 1982a). These arrangements are undermined by the current economic crisis. Corporations that raise prices will be undercut by international competition, while the "tax revolt" precludes tax increases for social programs (O'Connor 1973). Moreover, neither corporations nor the state can absorb increased medical costs by increased debt, because of their already serious indebtedness and budget deficit crises (Iglehart 1982a).

Third, corporations and the state not only have an interest now in controlling medical costs, but the resources and capacity to exercise such control. As the most powerful institutional forces in society, they fundamentally shift the balance of market power in medicine. Thousands of individual consumers lacked the organization and resources to affect the providers; powerful institutional consumers can apply coordinated massive economic and political pressure to change the behavior of providers and third parties (Earle 1982). Corporate and state interests will increasingly seek to develop contractual care arrangements with the lowest-cost provider organizations, changing sponsorship patterns in two fundamental directions.

First, it will increase the prevalence of unified sponsorship models, such as HMOs, which are cost effective and capable of exercising strong control over physician behavior. The proliferation of HMOs in some parts of the country has been fueled by the increase in the market provided by industrial and company plans. This will be regarded as a threat by some physicians, but a growth opportunity by others who, within group practices, already have or are developing HMOs (Starr 1982).

Divided sponsorship patterns will continue to be prevalent, but the traditional market and proprietary sponsors will be under greater pressure from corporations and the state to control costs (Earle 1982; Iglehart 1982a). This has already begun to affect the behavior of major market sponsors such as the "blues" which, in the case of Blue Cross, is shifting from traditional cost-based and "cost-plus" reimbursement to complex new "prospective" formulas which tend to cap annual outflows to hospitals based on below-inflation extrapolations of previous years' allotment (Greenfield 1975; Goldsmith 1981). Blue Shield is likely to move toward an identity and posture more independent of the physicians and to impose more constraining fee policies designed to provide disincentives for dubious costly procedures or hospitalizations.

The main way in which physicians are being affected by changes in third party policy, however, is through its effects on their proprietary sponsors, the hospitals. The emerging Blue Cross policy will force hospitals to develop a more rationalized management (Greenfield 1975; Goldsmith 1981). The shift from blanket reimbursement of costs to contractual "caps" and direct incentives for cost containment and efficiencies changes the logic of hospital economics toward classic corporate logic. Traditional cost reimbursement gave no incentive for efficiency and was consistent with a non-profit sector, since hospitals could retain no surplus beyond their costs. The new system gives a competitive edge to more efficient hospitals and no longer allows hospitals to expect reimbursement for costs incurred above the negotiated "cap."

The new hospital economics is not only leading non-profits to function more like for-profits, with many even incorporating for-profit clinics and laboratories to suplement their income, but it is also bringing more for-profit hospitals into the hospital business (Starr 1982). While these represented only 6 per cent of hospital beds in 1972, they have expanded to over 12 per cent of beds in 1980 and are growing rapidly (Starr 1982). The most rapidly growing are for-profit chains such as Hospital Corporation of America and Humana, Inc., which bring highly centralized and rationalized accounting and management techniques to the operation of their hospitals. While they vary in their tendency to salary physicians, they provide their affiliated physicians with far less opportunity to influence policy (which is made in corporate headquarters) or to control support staff which are governed by non-medical administrative hierarchies within the corporation.

The exact shape of the relation between hospitals and physicians in the coming decade is unclear, but as a system of proprietary sponsorship, it will almost certainly subject physicians to greater control. Not only will both non-profits and for-profits have greater economic incentives to control physician behavior, but a greater structural capacity to do so because of the slowly dwindling role of the physician as the principal market sponsor of the hospital. This role, the physician's traditional power base in relation to the hospital, is decreased because of the increased percentage of patients which comes through HMOs and other provider institutions rather than individual physicians. The relations of control will tend to emerge out of negotiations between institutional providers like HMOs and the hospitals, where both may have an interest in limiting the discretion of the physicians in order to control costs (Goldsmith 1981).

Another major factor weakening physicians' position is their newly adverse market situation. While the dramatic increase in the supply of physicians who will enter practice in this decade has been documented elsewhere (Juba 1977; Starr 1982), it is highly significant. Within any system of sponsorship relations, the actual power of the sponsor to enforce structural capacities for control will significantly depend on market leverage. Should a real oversupply of physicians develop, employers, such as HMOs as well as hospitals, whether or not they employ physicians directly will be able to extract concessions from physicians competing for scarce jobs or admitting privileges. A "reserve army of physicians" will aggravate internal strife within the profession and reduce its historic capacity for highly organized guild behavior (Larson 1977, 1980).

While sponsors, particularly HMOs and other "unified sponsors," will exercise more control over physicians than in the past, it is problematic whether the new sponsorship patterns will produce proletarianization in the classic sense of pervasive wage-employment and thoroughgoing control of the work-process. Industrial employers, as "unified sponsors," consolidated sponsorship functions primarily for purposes of direct accumulation. This has been neither the dominant historical trend nor the current imperative underlying the changing sponsorship system in medicine. The new system is emerging primarily in response to interests of corporations and the state acting not as sponsors of medical production but as consumers of it. As institutional consumers, their interests lie not in generation of profits from medicine but control of costs. The class interests underlying the changing sponsorship relations in medicine are thus radically different than those in industrial production and are likely to produce very different relations of control.

One of the indirect effects of the dominant imperative of cost control, however, may be the rise of new class sponsors with direct accumulation imperatives. The corporations and the state have transformed economic incentives in medicine so that, for the first time, sponsorship fundamentally geared toward accumulation may achieve a substantial footing (Starr 1982). Should the for-profit hospital chains continue to expand at their current rate, the parallels between industry and medicine will increase, as will their systems of labor sponsorship and control.

In a sponsorship system that has been fueled historically primarily by sponsorship interests other than direct accumulation, however, fundamental control may emerge primarily through the agency of the state rather than the sponsors themselves. The traditional proprietary and market sponsors have not been the principal initiators of the changing system, but have been reactive, changing their sponsorship roles to accommodate the interests of the powerful institutional consumers. Control fueled by consumer rather than sponsor interests may ultimately be achieved only through the state. Political control is a viable alternative to sponsor control as a vehicle to control costs. Its most likely mechanisms are state control of wages and prices, and stringent regulation and/or administration of delivery of medical services.

The latter is unlikely in the United States because of the historic aversion to socialized health care, where the state itself becomes a "unified sponsor," acting as capitalizer and market-mediator of medical services (Hirschfield 1970; Falkson 1980). More probable is the development of state regulation of prices. This is already visible in the emergence of public rate setting commissions in many states, which take over the determination of reimbursements from the traditional third parties. Some interaction of such political control with heightened sponsorship control is likely to become predominant in medicine, greatly reducing physicians' historic control, but within the context of a sponsorship system quite unlike the one dominant in industry.

References

Alford, R. (1975) *Health Care Politics: Ideological and Interest Group Barriers to Reform.* Chicago: University of Chicago Press.

Angel, M. (1982) Professionals and Unionization. *Minnesota Law Review* 66: 383–457.

Bell, D. (1973) *The Coming of Post-Industrial Society.* New York: Basic Books.

Blumberg, M. (1979) Physicians' Fees as Incentives. In *Changing the Behavior of the Physician: A Management Perspective.* Chicago: University of Chicago Press.

Braverman, H. (1974) *Labor and Monopoly Capital.* New York: Monthly Review Press.

Christianson, J.B. (1980) The Impact of HMOs: Evidence and Research Issues. *Journal of Health Politics, Policy and Law* (Summer): 5: 354–357.

Deitrick, J. E. and Benson, R.C. (1953) *Medical Schools in the United States at MidCentury.* New York: McGraw-Hill.

Delbanco, T., Meyers, K.C., and Segal, E.A. (1979) Paying the Physician's Fee: Blue Shield and the Reasonable Charge. *New England Journal of Medicine* 301: 1314–320.

Derber, C. (1982a) *Professionals as Workers.* Boston: G.K. Hall.

——(1982b) Managing Professionals: Ideological Proletarianization and Mental Labor. *Theory and Society* (forthcoming).

——(1983) *The Future of the New Class: Work, Knowledge and Power in Post-Industrial Capitalism.* New York: Oxford University Press (in preparation).

Dobb, M. (1963) *Studies in the Development of Capitalism.* New York: International Publishers.

Duff, S. and Hollingshead, A.B. (1968) *Sickness and Society.* New York: Harper & Row.

Earle, P.W. (1982) Business Coalitions – A New Approach to Health Care Cost Containment. *American Medical Association* (January).

Edwards, R. (1979) *Contested Terrain.* New York: Basic Books.

Ehrenreich, J. and Ehrenreich, B. (1971) *The American Health Empire.* New York: Vintage.

——(1977) The Professional-Managerial Class. *Radical America* II (2): 7–31.

Eilers, R.D. (1963) *Regulation of Blue Cross and Blue Shield Plans.* Homewood: Richard D. Irwin.

Ellwood, P.M. (1971) The Health Maintenance Strategy. *Medical Care* 9: 291–98.

Endicott, K.M. and Allen, F.M. (1953) The Growth of Medical Research 1941–1953 and the Role of the Public Health Service Research Grants. *Science* 118: 337.

Falkson, J. (1980) *HMOs and the Politics of Health System Reform.* Chicago: American Hospital Association.

Feldstein, M.S. (1971) Hospital Cost Inflation: A Study of Nonprofit Price Dynamics. *American Economic Review* 61: 853–72.

Freidson, E. (ed.) (1963) *The Hospital in Modern Society.* New York: Free Press.

——(1970) *Profession of Medicine.* New York: Dodd, Mead.

Garbarino, J. (1960) *Health Plans and Collective Bargaining.* Berkeley: University of California Press.

Glandon, G.L. and Shapiro, R.J. (1980) *Profile of Medical Practice 1980.* Chicago: American Medical Association.

Goldsmith, J.C. (1981) *Can Hospitals Survive? The New Competitive Health Care Market.* Homewood: Dow Jones-Irwin.

Gouldner, A. (1979) *The Future of Intellectuals and the Rise of the New Class.* New York: Oxford University Press.

Greenfield, H. (1975) *Accountability in Health Facilities.* New York: Praeger.

Health Policy Advisory Center (1976) *Prognosis Negative.* New York: Vintage.

Henderson, S.R. (1982) *Medical Groups in the US, 1980.* Chicago: American Medical Association.

Hirschfield, D. (1970) *The Lost Reform: The Campaign for Compulsory Health Insurance in the United States 1932–43.* Cambridge: Harvard University Press.

Hsiao, C.L. and Stevens, B. (1981) Cooptation Versus Isolation: Health Insurance Organizations and Their Relations with Physicians. Harvard University School of Public Health.

Hunt, E.K. (1972) *Property and Prophets*. New York: Harper & Row.

Iglehart, J. K. (1971) Prepaid Group Medical Practice Emerges as Likely Federal Approach to Health Care. *National Journal* 3: 1444.

——(1982a) Health Care and American Business. *New England Journal of Medicine* 306: 120–24.

——(1982b) Moment of Truth for the Teaching Hospitals. *New England Journal of Medicine* 307: 132–36.

Illich, I. (1976) *Medical Nemesis*. New York: Vintage.

Johnson, T. J. (1972) *Professions and Power*. London: Macmillan.

Juba, D. A. (1977) Price Setting in the Market for Physicians' Services: A Review of the Literature. Report of Health Care Financing Administration.

Kass, D.I. and Pautler, P.A. (1980) Physician and Medical Society Influence on Blue Shield Plans. Paper presented at Conference on Health Care, American Enterprise Institute.

Larson, M. (1977) *The Rise of Professionalism*. Berkeley: University of California Press.

——(1980) Proletarianization and Educated Labor. *Theory and Society* 9(1): 131–75.

Law, S.A. (1974) *Blue Cross: What Went Wrong?* New Haven: Yale University Press.

Luft, H.S. (1981) *Health Maintenance Organizations: Dimensions of Performance*. New York: Wiley.

Marglin, S. (1974) What Do Bosses Do? The Origins and Functions of Hierarchy in Capitalist Production. *Review of Radical Political Economics* 6:33–60.

McKinlay, J. (1982) Towards the Proletarianization of the Physician. In C. Derber *Professionals as Workers*. Boston: G.K. Hall.

Mills, C. Wright (1951) *White Collar*. New York: Oxford University Press.

Montgomery, D. (1979) *Workers' Control in America*. Cambridge: Cambridge University Press.

Munts, R. (1960) *Bargaining for Health*. Madison: University of Wisconsin Press.

Navarro, V. (1976) *Medicine Under Capitalism*. New York: Prodist.

O'Connor, J. (1973) *The Fiscal Crisis of the State*. New York: St James Press.

Oppenheimer, M. (1975) The Proletarianization of the Professional. *Sociological Review* 20: 213–27.

Pirenne, H. (1933) *Economic and Social History of Medieval Europe*. New York: Harvest.

Price, D. D. (1973) A Political Hypochondriac Looks at the Future of Medicine. National Academy of Sciences, Washington DC, 9 May.

Roe, B. R. (1981) The UCR Boondoggle: A Death Knell for Private Practice? *New England Journal of Medicine* 305: 41–5.

Roemer, M.I., Mera, J.A. and Shonick, W. (1974) The Ecology of Group Medical Practice in the United States. *Medical Care* 12:627–37.

Rothstein, W. (1972) *American Physicians in the 19th Century.* Baltimore: Johns Hopkins University Press.

Sloan, F. A., Cromwell, J., and Mitchell, J.B. (1978) *Private Physicians and Public Programs.* Lexington: D.C. Heath.

Somers, H. M. and Anne, R. (1961) *Doctors, Patients and Health Insurance.* Washington DC: The Brookings Institute.

Starr, P. (1974) *The Discarded Army: Veterans After Vietnam.* New York: Charterhouse.

——(1982) *The Struggle for Medical Care.* New York: Basic Books.

Stevens, R. (1971) *American Medicine and the Public Interest.* New Haven: Yale University Press.

Turner, T.B. (1967) The Medical Schools Twenty Years Afterwards: Impact of the Extramural Research Support of the National Institutes of Health. *Journal of Medical Education* (February) 42: 109–18.

Walker, P. (1979) *Between Labor and Capital.* Boston: South End Press.

Wright, E.O. (1978) *Class, Crisis, and the State.* London: New Left Books.

Acknowledgements

I want to express gratitude to Bill Schwartz and Steven Brint, who played a major role in stimulating and critiquing this analysis. Both read the manuscript in various drafts and provided many extremely helpful suggestions and insights.

This paper was written with the support of funding from the National Institute of Mental Health, Grant No. 1 RO1 MH 35893–01, a three-year research project entitled "Professionals as Workers."

Part Four

The penetration of the developing world by the transnational medical industrial complex

Seven

The political economy
of western medicine in
Third World countries
Debabar Banerji

Introduction

Many serious flaws in the health services systems of affluent countries have been identified by such scholars as Lalonde (1974), Illich (1977), McKnight (1978), and Sterkey (1978). Others (e.g. Navarro 1976, Brown 1979), have made a critical analysis of health services systems in these countries in terms of their political economy. It is, however, significant that despite all the flaws and influence of certain political forces in these countries, health services have evolved as an organic component of a given social structure. Perhaps the most distinctive feature of the growth of health services in Third World countries is that these services have been profoundly influenced by affluent countries. In this process such influence has severely inhibited the growth of health services in Third World countries as organic components of their respective social structures. It is interesting to note that even for an indication of the gross interference of affluent countries in the shaping of health services in Third World countries, one has to fall back on the works of western scholars like Cleaver (1976), Demerath Sr (1976), Donaldson (1979), and Gunnarsson (1980).

Conforming to this trend, during the colonial period Third World countries were "given" health services based on concepts developed in schools of so-called tropical medicine in London, Amsterdam, Paris, or Brussels. After independence, an attempt was made by the new leaderships to cover this abject dependence on the western model by recognizing the necessity of adapting western medicine to suit local conditions. Following this, the World Health Organisation (WHO) became an agency to promote what came to be known as vertical programmes against individual diseases that were considered to be amenable to a military command style, technocentric approach (WHO 1975). Bryant (1969), Morley (1973), Taylor (1976) and King (1978) represent another group of scholars from western countries who have worked with missionary zeal to give a new direction to the practice of medicine in the tropics. Again, it was the WHO-backed institution, Appropriate Health Resources and Technologies Action Group (1979), based in London, which voluntarily took upon itself the (white man's?) burden of developing appropriate health technologies for Third World countries. Werner's *Where There is No Doctor* (1977) represents a further development in the same direction. WHO's labors in this field are represented by two of its contributions: *Health By the People* (Newell 1975) and *Alternative Approaches to Meeting Basic Health Needs in Developing Countries* (Djukanovic and Mach 1975).

It is important to note that even in the best of the works referred to above, adequate recognition is not given to the fact that the introduction of western medicine in Third World countries set in motion very complex interactions within each country. By its nature western medicine includes the body of knowledge, different agencies for providing services of various kinds, institutions for education, training, and research, and practitioners; these are all major factors that influence these interactions. The introduction of western medicine also causes complex interactions between it, on one hand and the preexisting health culture of the population, on the other. Health culture is taken to include cultural perceptions, the cultural meaning of health problems encountered by the community, and health behaviour in terms of various cultural devices available and accessible to the community (Banerji 1982: 2). The concept is used here to underline the need for understanding community health behaviour, availability and accessibility of health institutions, and cultural meanings and cultural perceptions of health problems as an integral whole.

The far-reaching political, social, cultural, and economic consequences of colonialism and imperialism, which have been associated with the introduction of western medicine in most Third World countries form another major category of factors that also influenced the process of interactions leading to the formation of health services in these countries in the colonial and post-colonial eras.

This trend has been reinforced by the increasing commercialization of western medicine, which is often followed with increasing sophistication and super-specialization, with a corresponding increase in the dependence of the ruling classes of most Third World countries on "experts" from other industrialized countries, particularly those that earlier had colonized them.

The nature of western medicine

The Industrial Revolution in western countries brought about a very extensive and far-reaching disruption in the lives of people, which affected their social, economic, and political relations as well as health culture. Technology became a potent force in the hands of the exploiting classes (Rosen 1958: 131). Much of the labour force employed in factories in the early phases of the Industrial Revolution had to endure poverty, hunger, long working hours under trying conditions, inadequate clothing, overcrowding, poor housing, and filthy environmental conditions. This in turn caused widespread suffering from such health problems as undernutrition, malnutrition, diseases of childbirth, childhood disorders, and a high incidence of smallpox, typhus, cholera, dysentery, tuberculosis, typhoid, worm infestation, and other communicable diseases (Rosen 1958: 141–43).

It is significant that when such widespread suffering created a political and social counter-reaction and when it was realized that health problems were threatening industrial production and profits, the very same technological forces that earlier had caused this depredation were deployed by the captains of industry (who also had the political power) to develop the western system of medicine (Rosen 1958: 233–58). Economists, who had hitherto regarded medical expenditure as a mere consumption item, came to realize that allocation to health care can also be an investment – an investment for increasing the productivity of labour (Winslow 1951). Concurrently, the welfare state movement made rapid gains in western countries. These two considerations, that is, increased productivity through health services and the welfare state movement, acted synergistically to increase several-fold the trickling down of health care services to segments of the population hitherto unserved or underserved (Rosen 1958: 344–48).

This brief analysis of the evolution of health problems in industrialized countries and the development of medical and public health services to deal with them, can also explain why the very same technological forces which allegedly enabled these countries to "conquer" their earlier health problems, were instrumental in creating conditions actively promoting a "second generation" of health problems. For example, automobile accidents, proliferation of mental health problems, problems of the elderly, alcoholism, and drug addiction (McKnight 1978).

Yet another motive force for the growth of the health care system in industrial countries was the business world's recognition of the fact that a health services system is itself an "industry". The health industry is now regarded as a thriving social service-based industry with virtually endless potential for swelling the GNP (Lalonde 1974; Sterkey 1978). As a result of the concerted efforts of these business interests through the classical style of sales promotion, people have been made to increase their dependence on the health industry to enable it to maintain a rapid rate of growth. An entirely new set of folklores has been created to reinforce this dependency (Illich, 1977: 39–48; Borremans 1978). The medical establishment not only generates new health needs, it also determines how these needs are to be met. Its growth has taken place at such a fast pace that the dependence elements of the health care system have far outstripped the suffering-alleviation elements. Worse still, this monstrous growth of dependence elements has actually started to cause suffering among its own consumers by actively creating diseases – the iatrogenic diseases (Illich 1977: 41–6; Borremans 1978).

Health services development under colonialism and imperialism

Before World War II, most Third World countries had what can be called a colonial pattern of health services systems. Colonial powers had brought with them the western system of medicine.

The launching of the health services in these countries was subservient to the overall imperial policy of the colonial powers. Unlike the industrial European countries, the colonial countries were plunged directly from a pre-industrial health culture to a complex, alien pattern of colonial-based health culture. Colonialization created conditions that led to the decay and degeneration of pre-existing health cultures, some of which had attained an astonishingly high level of development of self-sufficiency in alleviation of suffering (as in the case of Ayurveda in India; see Chattopadhyaya 1977).

As the people rapidly became pauperized, they were unable to maintain the health services that they had developed earlier as a component of their overall way of life. This vacuum was filled by faithhealers, sorcerers, magicians, and other quack medical practitioners, who exploited the suffering of people for their own gains. In addition, unlike in European countries, colonial rulers were not overly concerned about public opinion because the population was subjugated by the sheer brute force of the colonial government. They could also get away with a much more ruthless oppression of the working classes. For the same reasons, they could sustain this oppression for a much longer period (National Planning Committee 1948). Also, there was no welfare state lobby.

Health services, which were shaped on the western model, were made available only to the ruling classes – namely, the army, civil services, the European trading community, and to the native gentry auxiliary to the ruling classes (Jeffery 1978; ICSSR-ICMR 1981: 8–9). These constituted a very small fraction of the native population. Christian missionaries enjoyed state patronage in the distribution of health services as a vehicle to preach the gospel – and, often, to glorify colonial rule (Banerji 1975; Cleaver 1976).

By ensuring that they had access to available health services, the exploiting classes could acquire additional strength to further exploit the masses. On the other hand, the oppressed masses became weaker and more vulnerable to exploitation because they had no access to health services and because colonialism brought with it the destruction and decay of their pre-existing health practices. Western medicine was thus used as a weapon for exploitation of the people (National Planning Committee 1948: 190; Banerji 1975).

During the colonial period the health services were dominated by curative activities, with preventive aspects being confined to providing environmental sanitation, water supplies, and immunization coverage to particular areas, such as cantonments, civil lines, and localities inhabited by affluent sections. For the rest of the people, anti-epidemic measures were adopted only when there were outbreaks of serious epidemics and pandemics (National Planning Committee 1948: 20; Banerji 1975).

Colonialism also promoted the abject dependence of these countries on the colonial powers for health manpower, supplies of drugs and equipment, and research and development. Health professionals from the armed forces of the colonial powers were seconded to occupy key positions in civilian health administrations. This had far-reaching implications for the development of health services in the Third World. The medical corps of colonial armies certainly does not attract the cream of the medical profession and this set of professionals held complete sway over the health services of Third World countries during colonial rule.

Health services development in the post-colonial era

After the overthrow of colonial powers during the post-war period, a native ruling elite took power. Conforming to the "soft-state," these new rulers made "lofty" egalitarian pronouncements while using essentially the same machinery bequeathed to them by former colonial rulers. This ensured that the fruits of independence benefited them most and perpetuated their hold on the government (Myrdal 1972).

In the field of health, the new rulers promised to take active steps to make benefits available to the masses, particularly to the weaker sections. In fact they continued to follow the old colonial tradition and the urban health services systems continued to receive much greater attention in the development of both the curative and the preventive aspects in contrast to the rural health services system (Banerji 1977; ICSSR-ICMR 1981: 8-9). Community resources were made available to establish a number of hospitals, many with the latest sophisticated equipment for intensive care, open heart surgery, brain surgery, and cancer therapy services, on the model of the industrialized countries. The western industrialized countries also provided a reference frame for institutions of education, training, and research. Personnel from these sophisticated urban-based institutions have remained heavily dependent on their counterparts in the industrialized countries who have actively encouraged such dependence by providing technical "assistance" in the form of education and training, consultation, and "cheap" textbooks (Government of India 1975).

This arrangement proved convenient to both the colonialists and the privileged few among the natives. It ensured the native physicians power, prestige, status, and money at home, while their mentors from foreign countries were assured of considerable influence on them because the top leadership of the medical profession in Third World countries remained heavily dependent on them.

Due to the increasing commercialization and professionalization of health services in affluent countries, which were actively promoting the dependence of people on health professionals (Illich 1977: 41-8), the elite-oriented services in Third World countries also acquired these elements. In this process they swallowed more and more scarce resources. The excessive preoccupation of the leadership at political, bureaucratic, and technocratic levels with urban health services systems led to the neglect of rural health services (Government of India 1977; ICSSR-ICMR 1981: 8-9). Not only were they starved of resources, but perhaps more importantly, the technical content of services and the "culture" and value system that governed personnel of the rural system, were often inimical to the needs of the rural population (Banerji 1975). Because of these factors, this system could provide coverage to just a small fraction of the rural population. Even for the population that had access to services, the services were "handed down", and educators and motivators were employed to make people accept what was handed down to them (Government of India 1977).

However, as shown by the findings of a nine-year study of nineteen villages in India (Banerji 1982: 83-6), because of the generation of internal tension in the ruling classes and because of some awakening among the masses, political leadership in the Third World is now realizing that it is no longer possible to perpetuate the present social order without making some "concessions" to the masses (Banerji 1978c; Banerji 1982: 97-99). Imposition of a State of Emergency in India in June, 1977 showed that a major crisis had developed within the prevailing social and political system. The study of nineteen villages has revealed that this crisis had not only created major divisions within the ruling classes, but forcible sterilization of large numbers of people had made the masses politically more aware (Banerji 1982: 144-60). The study also revealed that the many elections held at various levels during the nine-year period also contributed to the increased political consciousness of people (Banerji 1982: 162-72).

The area of health services has been singled out for making concessions on the presumption that, unlike such sensitive areas as land reforms, minimum wages, and democratization, it will not pose much of a threat to the social system. In India, for example, the leaders who took over political power in March, 1977 by taking advantage of the deep-seated resentment and revulsion of the people to family planning excesses in previous months (Banerji 1982: 151-60), redeemed their election pledge and initiated a new programme based on village level community health workers, entrusting "People's Health in People's Hands" (Government of India, 1978). This is a remarkable development, though it is obvious that the existing social structure and prevailing "culture" of the elite-oriented professionalized health system of the country are grossly incompatible with such a philosophy. In fact, this philosophy has been greatly distorted by these forces (Banerji 1978a; Bose 1978; National Institute of Health and Family Welfare 1978, 1979; Ghoshal and Bhandari 1979). Nevertheless, the commitment to bypass the medical establishment and go directly to the people created a very favourable setting to challenge the basic scientific, sociological, and economic premises of the earlier approach to development of health services in India and for formulating an alternative approach (Banerji 1977b; ICSSR-ICMR 1981).

Political subversion of knowledge

The political leadership and health administrators in Third World countries sought an aura of social legitimacy for their lopsided health services development by getting ill-defined or often not very relevant social, cultural, and psychological issues raised by social scientists and health educators (Banerji 1975). Social scientists dutifully raised such value-loaded issues as "modernization", as against traditionalism and urban culture, as against rural folk culture. These could be used to justify the urban and privileged class orientation of health services in these countries on grounds that backward, superstition-ridden, uneducated villagers first have to be educated by a corps of "well-trained" health educators from the cities on the virtues of "modern" health services (which carry with them all the trappings of dependency promotion and profit orientation) (Banerji 1978b).

An extreme but also very alarming facet of such political subversion of medical knowledge can be found in the creation of the idea that severe undernutrition in early life causes permanent mental retardation due to brain damage (National Academy of Sciences 1973). From an objective scientific standpoint, there has never been any convincing evidence to support this idea (Banerji 1979). Yet presumably because of its political potential, in the late 1960s, some eminent nutritionists from the affluent countries, with full backing from their Third World camp followers, managed to generate intense pressure on a global scale (Banerji 1979). The then Secretary-General of the United Nations was moved to appeal to member states for immediate action to fill what was then termed the "Protein-Gap" and to avert the impending disaster of permanent brain damage to millions of undernourished children in the Third World (United Nations 1968).

If these premonitions are true, there ought to have been millions of mental cripples among various age groups, scattered all over the affluent world – those who were exposed to severe early childhood undernutrition, say, during World War I or the Russian Revolution, during the recession of the 1930s and in the concentration camps and elsewhere during World War II. The proponents of the mental retardation theory have not been able to produce any convincing evidence that this is actually so. Perhaps the most deplorable aspect of these so-called scientific studies is that it is presumed that intelligence tests really measure intelligence, particularly that of children socialized in the Third World. All these indicate the extent of ethnocentric bias among some scientists in western countries.

The global food and drug industry has also mobilized scientists to promote sales by raising the bogey of the "Protein-Gap", overemphasizing the need of so-called first-class proteins, essential amino-acids, vitamins and tonics, and of bio-availability. It is only recently that these scientists have veered reluctantly and slowly towards the now well-established view that the primary nutritional problem in most Third World countries is calorie deficiency (Gopalan and Narsingarao 1971; Sukhatme 1978); that diversion of particularly meagre resources of the poor to pay for nutritional products of multinational drug firms often exacerbates the condition of under-nutrition (Banerji 1979). This subversion of knowledge forms one of the many political issues related to health and health services (Banerji 1978c).

Political issues in health and health services

Health services are only one of the many factors that influence the health status of a population. It is also influenced, sometimes even more significantly, by such social and economic factors as nutrition, water supply, waste disposal, housing, education, income and its distribution, employment, communication and transport, and the social structure. Second, just as other factors influence health status, so the health services of a community are usually a function of its political system (Banerji 1978c; Mahler 1979). Political forces play a dominant role in the shaping of the health services of a community. For instance, decisions on resource allocation, manpower policy, choice of technology, and the degree to which health services are to be available and accessible to the population, are taken at the political level.

These political dimensions of health services are brought into sharp focus by cases described in the World Health Organisation's publication, *Health by the People* (Newell 1975). In countries exemplifed by China and Cuba, very positive efforts have been made to involve the entire population in the process of decision-making as part of a nationwide political movement for bringing about radical social change. An alternative perspective for rural development and, as one of its components, an alternative health services system, developed as a logical corollary to this. In these countries, the very process of bringing about democratization of the political system had led to serious questioning of the technological, social, and economic bases of the health services system prevailing earlier.

In the case of Tanzania, where serious attempts are being made to promote democratization at a grassroots level, the earlier health services system, inherited from colonial rulers, is being subjected to close scrutiny. This scrutiny has led to a shift in allocation of resources from the urban to the rural, from the curative to the preventive, and from the privileged class orientation of services to those that are oriented to the underprivileged.

In these three instances, all sections of the community, particularly the weaker sections, have been actively involved in shaping an alternative primary health care service and in its implementation.

Significantly, in countries where the process of democratization has not made deeper inroads, there is considerable hesitation and often confusion in the formulation of alternative health services systems. The WHO publication describes two types of cases. One is exemplified by two oil rich countries. In both these countries, the political system has not allowed any change in the highly sophisticated, state subsidized curative services in urban areas which are accessible mainly to the privileged classes. However, both these countries happened to have very dedicated leaders in the persons of C.L. Gonzales (in Venezuela) and Majid Rehnama (in Iran). Even within stifling political constraints, they were able to make significant innovations in the rural health services of their countries. Subsequent political changes in Iran which led to the overthrow of the Shah, have demonstrated the tenuous nature of health services that are developed without a mass base.

The other category is exemplified by Guatemala, Indonesia, and India. In all three countries, the process of democratization has not reached the underprivileged and deprived sections of the population to any extent. There has also been a conspicuous lack of leadership in the field of health care. This might explain why WHO sought inspiration for alternatives from the experiences of Christian missionary organizations. These experiences were derived from programmes that had available to them disproportionately large amounts of resources (when compared to the very small population served by them). They had workers with a missionary zeal. These conditions are certainly not reproducible, neither can they be considered alternative health care systems for rural populations of these countries (George 1976; Ram 1976).

The formation of alternatives is thus essentially a political question. A crucial determinant of the nature of an alternative is whether the political system encourages oligarchical rule or actively promotes a change in the social system that enables the masses, particularly the underprivileged and the underserved, to actively participate in the affairs of their country (Banerji 1977b).

Development of super-specialties to provide services mainly to the privileged classes can be cited as an instance of an alternative health care system within a political framework which perpetuates an oligarchy. In poor countries, the establishment of Rotary Club supported cancer hospitals, the setting up of units for cardiothoracic surgery and neurosurgery and other such super-specialties, and the opening of elaborate intensive care units, form the medical components of alternatives under such political systems. Campaigns for cancer control, development of genetic counselling services, and control of noise pollution are examples of the preventive components. Imposition of compulsory sterilization on weaker sections of the population, without making available the most elementary health services and economic security to them is another facet of an alternative within this political framework.

In a political system where there is a commitment to extend the process of democratization and involve the entire population in decision-making, the circumstances for formulating an alternative health services system are basically different. In the first place, there is considerable enthusiasm among people to actively participate in the shaping of their health services system and in running it. Second, the very process of democratization ensures that those working at technological levels are impelled to evolve an alternative technological framework more meaningful to the entire population, particularly to the weaker sections.

No doubt more often than not, this commitment to democratization is used as a mere facade to perpetuate old unjust social relations. It is also very likely that under such political conditions formulation of an alternative system, however scientific and relevant, becomes at best an academic exercise. None the less, even an academic exercise can become a useful instrument for bringing pressure to bear for desired political change by offering concrete, well-thought out alternatives. It can in any case, serve as a blueprint for action when political changes finally take place (Banerji 1978a).

Political economy of primary health care

Changes in the approaches of the World Health Organisation to the health services development of member states during the past three and a half decades provide very interesting data on the consequences of the social tensions, conflicts, and confrontations on health services development within Third World countries. Policies of WHO are governed by its member states through its World Health Assembly and its Executive Board. Countries of the Third World form an overwhelming majority of the member states. Even otherwise, as the need for assistance is most acute in these countries, they form the principal focus of activities of the WHO. Characteristically, WHO began with considerable enthusiasm for what have been referred to as vertical programmes. These programmes were in the form of mass campaigns against individual health problems like malaria (WHO 1950a), smallpox (Basu, Jezek, and Ward 1979), tuberculosis (WHO 1950b), filariasis (WHO 1954), leprosy (WHO 1953a), trachoma (WHO 1952), schistosomiasis (WHO 1950c; 1953b), and yellow fever (WHO 1950d). These campaigns were designed according to a model consisting of a preparatory phase, an attack phase, a consolidation phase, and a maintenance phase. It involved an "above–down" approach, with an expectation that technological interventions with weapons like DDT spraying or the administration of pencillin, hetrazan, and dapsone would lead to the conquest of such dreaded diseases in "underdeveloped countries". It was assumed that these countries needed merely an effective "technological fix" for their individual health problems. When, after a decade and a half, it was realized that such simple solutions did not work, WHO turned in favour of the integration of mass campaigns against individual diseases with the general health services (Gonzalez 1965). This basic shift in favour of developing integrated health services led to an emphasis on development of what was then termed the "basic health service" (WHO, SEARO 1978: 69). Yet another major shift in the approach, in 1969, led to promotion of health planning (WHO 1967; Hilleboe, Barkhuss, and Thomas 1972). First it was health planning based on a more centralized concept. Later the emphasis shifted to looking at health planning against the background of actual conditions prevailing in specific countries. The approach of "Programme Systems Analysis" (Bainbridge and Sapirie 1974; WHO 1976; WHO, SEARO 1978: 58) was followed with "Country Health Programming" (WHO 1975); WHO SEARO 1978: 58–66; Mahler 1979), which in turn, was succeeded by "Country Health Planning".

The linking of the entire health services system with the social and economic development of a country marked yet another phase (Abel Smith and Leiserson 1978). Universal acceptance of the philosophy of primary health care at Alma Ata (WHO 1978) by countries of the world can be considered the climax of WHO's efforts at health services development: a major watershed, if not the most important in the history of medicine. Primary health care seeks to virtually overturn the entire health services system of all countries to ensure that medical technology serves the community and that distortions brought about by powerful market forces, undue professional dominance, iatrogenesis, and obsession with technological fixation stand corrected. It also advocates an intersectoral approach, integration of health services, and restructuring of the support structure to strengthen health work at the community level.

Considering the political power structure of WHO at the initial phase, it is not surprising that it should have embarked on a crusade against individual diseases in the form of military style mass campaigns. But then, why did member states go along with, if not actively promote, the various shifts that culminated in the acceptance of the primary health care approach at Alma Ata? It is possible to identify three factors contributing to this. First, and perhaps the most important, is the gradual increase of forces of democratization among the masses of people in Third World countries. This pressure within some member states impelled WHO to bring about shifts in its approach. Second, headed by the Director-General himself (Mahler 1975), some thoughtful workers within WHO Secretariat realized the need for change and used the forums of the organisation to persuade member countries to accept the proposed changes. Finally, as a result of the momentum generated jointly by some member states and the WHO Secretariat, other member states were swept into the mainstream and were identified with the new perspective proposed by WHO at Alma Ata.

As a corollary to this analysis of the political economy of primary health care it follows that the extent of implementation of this approach in different countries is different. It depends on the extent of democratization among the masses and the readiness of the respective political leaderships to respond to these democratic aspirations.

Health services development as a political activity

The concept of primary health care, with its emphasis on people-oriented technology and intersectoral approach to development can thrive only under political conditions where the people have acquired power to take care of their needs and interests at various levels of the decision-making machinery. Obviously, by the very definition, Third World countries do not have political systems that allow such a degree of democratization. It has not been possible for the people to acquire adequate political power to ensure a health services system that involves their participation and is capable of delivering services to them. This is a particularly difficult task under conditions where resources in terms of manpower, funds, and equipment are severely limited. Also, the pattern of health problems, actual disease load in the population, settlement pattern, and social and economic conditions in Third World countries are basically different from that prevailing in western countries. Provision of primary health care also requires that the entire population of a country enjoys adequate levels of nutrition, environmental sanitation, water supplies, housing, education, employment, and social justice. Primary health care thus calls for health services development as a component of a strategy for integrated social and economic development. As developments along such a wide spectrum require far-reaching changes in the distribution of power, the struggle for raising the health status of a population becomes essentially a struggle for democratization of the political system (Mahler 1979). Thus, struggle for health would mean the mobilization of people to wrest more political power from the ruling classes. Essentially, the motive force for such mobilization will emerge from within the masses themselves. They cannot be "taught" how to mobilize by people brought from outside. At most, people from outside can gain acceptance by local people as one of them. People from outside can also make available to local people, when asked to do so, the wherewithal to increase their organizational strength in their struggle for democratic rights.

One of the cardinal postulates of the approach of primary health care is to entrust "people's health in people's hands". This offers opportunities for strengthening organization of the masses by promoting self-reliance, by enabling them to cope with their own problems. The process of choosing their own representative as a community health worker also has the potential for strengthening the forces for democratization among them. Furthermore, if community health workers also happen to be politically sensitive community organizers, their roles provide them with a valuable platform for strengthening community organization by rallying the community on health issues. As they are community representatives and part-time workers, they also are free to change platforms and rally the community around other issues which contribute to promotion of democratization among the masses – for instance, elections to representative bodies, adult education, and cooperative activities. Providing the masses access to curative services thus offers one of the many entry points to local community activists to carry on many-faceted activities, which all contribute to democratization. Democratization, in turn, would lead to improvement in the health status of the people through the development of health services as an integral part of social and economic development (as visualized in the Alma Ata Declaration).

Tasks before community health physicians

Once the political potential of a concession is properly understood, the next logical step is to mobilize the technological resources needed to transform the facade into a reality. How to ensure under existing constraints that health services become more accessible to the masses of people so that their use as a weapon of oppression of the masses is minimized? This then, is the challenge before socially conscious community health physicians of Third World countries. Recognition of the potential of health services development for promoting democratization and preparation of suitable conditions for developing an alternative people-oriented technology, requires political workers and socially conscious community health physicians to work as a well-orchestrated team to make use of the commitment of the ruling classes to health services development as a tool to promote democratization amongst the masses.

Formulation and implementation of an alternative health services system that is specifically designed to alleviate the suffering from health problems, thus acquires considerable significance. It is to be noted that formulation of such an alternative not only requires removal of dependence on commercial elements that have infiltrated so heavily and extensively in the so-called modern system of medicine, but also considerable innovative talents to devise alternative technologies and health care delivery agencies which are in consonance with available resources, the epidemiological characteristics of the problems, and the cultural and social setting of the population to be served.

Western medicine has been grafted onto Third World countries, and an important challenge before community health physicians therefore, is to separate the central scientific core of medicine from the rather thick socio-cultural layers of western countries and surround this central scientific core with layers that harmonize better with conditions prevailing in individual Third World countries (Banerji 1966).

Subordination of medical technology to the needs of the most needy, as envisaged in the approach of primary health care, is yet another challenge for developing a people-oriented health services system. The task will be to select or develop technologies which ensure that available resources are effectively used for alleviation of suffering of the maximum number of people, particularly those who hitherto have been denied access to services.

The top priority in such a framework for an alternative system is to meet those felt needs of the people that also happen to be epidemiologically assessed needs. People should not be "educated" to discard the measures they have been adopting, unless a convincing case to do so is made out. This should show that, taking into account their own perspective of the problems and under the existing conditions of resource constraints, it is possible to have an alternative technology that will yield significantly greater benefits to people in terms of alleviation of suffering from health problems. For this it is necessary to recognize that delivery of health care to a community is a very complex and extensive field for research and requires a qualitatively different approach from other research work. This is much more than field research, clinical research, and laboratory research combined; it requires a framework in which data from different conventional research approaches are brought together for the purpose of examining health care delivery in its entire complexity and formulating alternatives by bringing about changes in some of the key components of that complexity. A system for the delivery of health care to a community involves consideration of at least five major factors:

1   epidemiological factors;
2   availability of resources;
3   technology to be delivered;
4   agency for delivering the technology; and
5   the community (or the consumer of the technology and resources).

The challenge of research on delivery of health care is to devise a mechanism for identifying the weak links in the system and to strengthen the links thus identified either through findings of specifically designed research studies or through a shift of resources to these weak links from the relatively stronger links. By this process of strengthening the weakest links in the chain, it is possible to strengthen the entire health care delivery system. A shift from liquid to freeze-dried smallpox vaccine, a changeover from a streptomycin injection regime to one of oral thiacetazone in tuberculosis programmes, and the replacement of the conventional BCG vaccination of only the tuberculin negatives with BCG to all, are instances where the weak links in the chain of the health care delivery have been specifically identified on the basis of a holistic analysis of the entire system (Chakraborty 1979; Barua 1981). Here specific research data concerning these weak links have been used to strengthen these links, thus making critical contributions to the strengthening of the entire delivery system.

Techniques such as operational research, systems analysis, and linear programming are very relevant for studying such complex systems (Luck *et al.* 1971; Banerji 1972; Feldstein, Pilot, and Sundaresan 1973; WHO 1974, 1976; White *et al.* 1977). By the use of such techniques, data concerning the different components of the systems, which are derived from concepts and methods of a variety of disciplines, are processed and synthesized with a view to formulating an alternative system which is more effective; these techniques are employed in an attempt to "optimize" the use of available resources. They also provide a framework for identifying the direction of research to be carried out in the laboratories, hospital wards, and in the community at large in order to make the system as a whole more effective.

Suggestions for immediate action

This, however, does not imply that action will have to wait till findings from complex and often time-consuming researches are made available. In fact, following the basic premises for development of an alternative health services system outlined above, it is possible to work out some specific alternative approaches by making use of all available data and, where required, supplementing them with carefully formulated hunches. A built-in feedback system and ongoing research on alternatives will ensure that the suggested alternative for immediate action is constantly monitored and its performance improved.

Taking India as an example, the following are suggestions for immediate action in the major components of the health services:

Medical care

Community members may be encouraged to make maximum use of self-care procedures through continued use of various home remedial measures. These should be supplemented by the services of locally available practitioners of various systems of medicine. Another supplementary community resource can be created by providing training to primary health workers selected by the community and specifically drawn from among the weaker sections. They can make available home remedies and remedies from the indigenous and western systems of medicine for meeting medical care needs. Such workers will also have available to them the services of full-time health auxiliaries and health professionals to tackle more complicated cases and those which need more specialized care.

Maternal and child health services

Here also the key workers are those who already have been providing services to the community – the family members who assist in childbirth and child-rearing and the traditional birth attendants. A birth attendant or any other community-selected member can be trained as a primary health worker to work with members of the community, improve work that is already being carried out, and provide assistance when called for. They, in turn, are supported by full-time auxiliary health workers, the primary health managerial physician, and other personnel in the referral chain of services.

Control of communicable diseases

Even with existing strategies which were developed mainly to deal with many communicable diseases as "vertical" programmes, primary health care workers and other community level personnel can take over many of the duties presently being carried out by specialized unipurpose health workers. Surveillance of malaria, diagnosis and treatment of tuberculosis cases, leprosy, filaria and trachoma, spraying of houses with insecticides, and water management, including vector control, are some of the duties that can be taken over by a community.

Fertility regulation programme

The primary health care approach, particularly when it is a component of a rural development programme, is likely to have a profound influence on fertility regulation measures. The education of women, opening up of employment opportunities for them, their participation in community activities, greater social justice, and a fall in maternal and child mortality and morbidity in particular, and mortality rates of the total population in general, are likely to materially change the level of motivation for a small family norm in the community. This will also stimulate a rise in the age at marriage of men and women which is expected to have a direct demographic impact (Agarwal 1967). Even within the limited framework of primary health care, methods such as use of condoms and other "conventional" contraceptives, the rhythm method, and the contraceptive pill may acquire much greater significance with the people. Community health workers will be the most appropriate people to support such community activities by providing the needed contraceptives. They can also be a vital link between the community and the health centre for other methods to be used, such as male and female sterilization, induced abortion, and IUD insertion.

Environmental sanitation programme

Thus far progress in this field has been very sluggish due to the heavy cost and lack of community participation. However, community involvement in environmental sanitation programmes through efforts of community health workers, and interdisciplinary research efforts to develop technologies that are appropriate to both the felt needs of the people and the specific conditions in different rural communities, will contribute significantly in increasing the cost-effectiveness of the programme.

Summary and conclusion

It is obvious that the inroads made by the colonial approach associated with western medicine continue to influence health services systems in Third World countries to this day. While half-hearted efforts have been made to overcome the adverse effects of such influence, these have not proved very successful. This is so largely because of the nature of the political systems and social structures prevailing in many Third World countries, which have placed at the helm of affairs a political leadership not capable of severing its links with western conceptualization, development, and delivery of health care services systems.

However, due to various factors (most important being the rising political consciousness among people) the iniquitous sociopolitical system has been superseded by a people-oriented health services system. The degree of political commitment to this goal will determine the level of success it is able to achieve. The degree of political commitment depends on the degree of mobilization of people. The struggle for health thus becomes a struggle for democratization. In this struggle for democratization, alleviation of suffering due to health problems becomes a political device for community mobilization. Once this is understood, it is the task of those involved in democratization to mobilize community health physicians to devise community-oriented health services.

References

Abel Smith, B. and Leiserson, A. (1978) Poverty, Development and Health Policy. Public Health Papers no. 69. Geneva: WHO.

Agarwal, S.N. (1967) *Population*. Delhi: National Book Trust.

Appropriate Health Resources and Technologies Action Group (1979) Annual Report. London: AHRTAG.

Bainbridge, J. and Sapirie, S. (1974) Health Project Management: A Manual of Procedures for Formulating and Implementing Health Projects. Offset Publication no. 12. Geneva: WHO.

Banerji, D. (1966) Social Change and Scientific Advance: Their Relation to Medical Education. *Journal of Indian Medical Association* 47: 429–33.

Banerji, D. (1972) Operational Research in the Field of Community Health. *Opsearch* 9: 135–42.

——(1975) Social and Cultural Foundations of Health Services Systems of India. *Inquiry* 12: 70–85.

——(1977a) Public Health and Population Control. In S.C. Dube (ed.) *India Since Independence: Social Report on India 1947– 1972.* New Delhi: Vikas.

——(1977b) Formulating an Alternative Health Care Strategy for Rural Population in India. In J.P. Naik. *An Alternative System of Health Care Services in India. Some Proposals.* Bombay: Allied Publishers.

——(1978a) Facade of the Rural Health Care Scheme of India as an Opportunity. *Yojana* 22: 23–6.

——(1978b) Health as a Lever for Another Development. *Development Dialogue* 1: 19–25.

——(1978c) Political Issues in Health, Population and Nutrition. *Social Scientist* 7: 159–68.

——(1979) Epidemiological Issues in Nutrition. *Indian Journal of Nutrition and Dietetics* 16: 189–94.

——(1982) *Poverty, Class and Health Culture in India.* New Delhi: Prachi Prakashan.

Barua, B.N.M. (1981) BCG Vaccination. In K.N. Rao (ed.) *Textbook of Tuberculosis.* New Delhi: Vikas.

Basu, R.N., Jezek, Z., and Ward, N.A. (1979) The Eradication of Smallpox from India. Regional Publications Series no. 5. South-East Asia. Geneva: WHO.

Borremans, V. (1978) Inverse of Managed Health. *Development Dialogue* 1: 26–34.

Bose, A. (1978) *Assessment of the New Rural Health Scheme and Suggestions for Improvements.* New Delhi: Institute of Economic Growth.

Brown, E.R. (1979) *Rockefeller Medicine Men: Medicine and Capitalism in America.* Berkeley: University of California Press.

Bryant, J. (1969) *Health and the Developing World.* London: Cornell University Press.

Chakraborty, A.K. (1979) Twentieth Anniversary of NTI – What Has the NTI Achieved? *NTI Newsletter.* 16(4): 104–10.

Chattopadhyaya, D. (1977) *Science and Society in Ancient India.* Calcutta: Research India Publications.

Cleaver. H. (1976) Political Economy of Malaria Decontrol. *Economic and Political Weekly.* 11(36): 1463–473.

Demerath, N.J. (1976) *Birth Control and Foreign Policy: The Alternatives to Family Planning.* New York: Harper & Row.

Djukanovic, V. and Mach, E.P. (eds) (1975) *Alternative Approaches to Meeting Basic Health Needs in Developing Countries*. A Joint UNICEF/WHO Study. Geneva: WHO.

Donaldson, P.J. (1979) Foreign Intervention in Medical Education: A Case Study of the Rockefeller Foundation Involvement in a Thai Medical School. In V. Navorro (ed.) *Imperialism, Health and Medicine*. New York: Baywood.

Feldstein, M.S., Pilot, M.A., and Sundaresan, T.K. (1973) Resource Allocation Model for Public Health Planning: A Case Study of Tuberculosis Control. *WHO Bulletin* 48 (Supplement): 110.

George, M.V. (1976) A Community Approach to Health Care Services by Popularising Co-operative Rural Dispensaries. In *Alternative Approaches to Health Care: Report of a Symposium*. New Delhi: Indian Council of Medical Research and Indian Council of Social Science Research.

Ghoshal, B.C. and Bhandari, V. (1979) Community Health Workers Scheme: A Study. New Delhi: Directorate General of Health Services.

Gonzalez, C.L. (1965) Mass Campaigns and General Health Services. Public Health Papers no. 29. Geneva: WHO.

Gopalan, C. and Narsingarao, B.S. (1971) Nutritional Constraints on Growth and Development in Current Indian Dietaries. *Indian Journal of Medical Research*. 59(6): 111.

Government of India, Group on Medical Education and Support Manpower (1975) Health Services and Medical Education: A Programme for Immediate Action. Report. New Delhi: Ministry of Health and Family Planning.

Government of India (1977) Health Care Services in Rural Areas, Draft Plan. New Delhi: Ministry of Health and Family Welfare.

——(1978) Annual Report 1977–78. New Delhi: Ministry of Health and Family Welfare.

Gunnarsson, B. (1980) Japan's Abortion Laws and Birth Control Ambitions in the Underdeveloped Countries in Asia. In L. Bondestam and S. Bergstrom (eds) *Poverty and Population Control*. London: Academic Press.

Hilleboe, H.E., Barkhuss, A., and Thomas, W.C. (1972) Approaches to National Health Planning. Public Health Papers no. 46. Geneva: WHO.

Illich, I. (1977) *Limits to Medicine*. Bombay: Rupa.

Indian Council of Social Science Research and Indian Council of Medical Research (1981) *Health for All: An Alternative Strategy*. Report of a Study Group set up jointly by ICSSR and ICMR. Pune: Indian Institute of Education.

Jeffery, R. (1978) Medical Policy-Making in India in the 1970s: Out of Dependency? Sixth European Conference on Modern South Asian

Studies, 8–13 July. Paris: Editions du Centre National de la Recherche Scientifique.

King, M. (1978) *Primary Child Care*. London: Oxford University Press.

Lalonde, M. (1974) *A New Perspective on the Health of Canadians: A Working Document*. Ottawa: Govt of Canada.

Luck, G.M., Luckman, J., Smith, B.W., and Stringer, J. (1971) *Patients, Hospitals and Operational Research*. London: Tavistock Publications.

Mahler, H. (1975) Health for All by the Year 2000. *WHO Chronicle* 29: 457–61.

——(1978) Country Health Programming: Time Now for Practical Testing of Concepts and Approaches. *WHO Chronicle* 32(9): 358.

——(1979) 32nd World Health Assembly. *WHO Chronicle* 33(7–8): 245.

McKnight, J.L. (1978) A Cancerous Health Development: The Case of American Medicine. *Development Dialogue* 1: 14–18.

Morley, D. (1973) *Paediatric Priorities in the Developing World*. London: Butterworths.

Myrdal, G. (1972) *Asian Drama: An Inquiry into the Poverty of Nations*. Harmondsworth: Penguin.

National Academy of Sciences (1973) *Relationship of Nutrition to Brain Development and Behavior*. Washington DC: National Academy of Sciences.

National Institute of Health and Family Welfare (1978) *Evaluation of Community Health Workers Scheme: A Collaborative Study*. New Delhi: NIHFW.

——(1979) *Repeat Evaluation of Community Health Volunteers Scheme: A Collaborative Study* (3 vols). New Delhi: NIHFW.

National Planning Committee, Sub-Committee on National Health (1948) Report (Sokhey Committee Report). Bombay: Vora.

Navarro, V. (1976) *Medicine Under Capitalism*. London: Croom Helm.

Newell, K.W. (ed.) (1975) *Health By the People*. Geneva: WHO.

Ram, E.R. (1976) Integrated Health Services Project, Miraj. In *Alternative Approaches to Health Care: Report of a Symposium*. New Delhi: Indian Council of Medical Research and Indian Council of Social Science Research.

Rosen, G. (1958) *History of Public Health*. New York: MD Publications.

Sterkey, G. (1978) Towards Another Development in Health. *Development Dialogue* 1: 4–13.

Sukhatme, P.V. (1978) Assessment of Adequacy of Diets at Different Income Levels. *Economic and Political Weekly* 12 (31–3): 1373–384.

Taylor, C.E. (1976) *The Functional Analysis of Health Needs and Services.* Bombay: Asia Publishing.

United Nations (1968) *International Action to Avert the Impending Protein Crisis.* New York: United Nations.

Werner, D. (1977) *Where There is No Doctor.* California: Hesperian Foundation.

White, K.L., Anderson, D.O., Kalimo, E., Klezkowski, B.M., Purola, T., and Vukmanovic, C. (1977) Health Services: Concepts and Information for National Planning and Management. Public Health Papers no. 67. Geneva: WHO.

Winslow, C.E.A. (1951) The Cost of Sickness and Price of Health. Monograph Series no. 7. Geneva: WHO.

World Health Organisation (1950a) Malaria: Report on the Third Session of the Expert Committee. Technical Report Series no. 8. Geneva: WHO.

——(1950b) Tuberculosis: Report on the Fourth Session of the Expert Committee. Technical Report Series no. 7. Geneva: WHO.

——(1950c) Bilharziasis in Africa. Report on the First Session of the Joint OIHP/WHO Study Group. Technical Report Series no. 17. Geneva: WHO.

——(1950d) Yellow fever: Report on the First Session of the Yellow Fever Panel. Technical Report Series no. 19. Geneva: WHO.

——(1952) Trachoma: First Report of the Expert Committee. Technical Report Series no. 59. Geneva: WHO.

——(1953a) Leprosy: First Report of the Expert Committee. Technical Report Series no. 71. Geneva: WHO.

——(1953b) Bilharziasis: First Report of the Expert Committee. Technical Report Series no. 65. Geneva: WHO.

——(1954) Onchocerciasis: First Report of the Expert Committee. Technical Report Series no. 87. Geneva: WHO.

——(1967) National Health Planning in Developing Countries: Report of a WHO Expert Committee. Technical Report Series no. 350. Geneva: WHO.

——(1974) Modern Management Methods and the Organization of Health Services. Public Health Papers no. 55. Geneva: WHO.

——(1975) Official Records no. 221 (pp. VII-VIII). Geneva: WHO.

——(1976) Application of Systems Analysis to Health Management. Report of a WHO Expert Committee. Technical Report Series no. 596. Geneva: WHO.

——(1978) Primary Health Care: Report of the International Conference on Primary Health care, Alma-Ata, USSR, 6–12 September, 1978. Geneva: WHO.

World Health Organisation, South-East Asia Regional Office (1978) A Decade of Development in South-East Asia, 1968–77. New Delhi: SEARO.

Name index

Subject index